Portfolio Management

Portfolio Management

How to Innovate and Invest in Successful Projects

Dr Shan Rajegopal
United Kingdom

First published 2013 by
PALGRAVE MACMILLAN

Palgrave Macmillan in the UK is an imprint of Macmillan Publishers Limited,
registered in England, company number 785998, of Houndmills, Basingstoke,
Hampshire RG21 6XS.

Palgrave Macmillan in the US is a division of St Martin's Press LLC,
175 Fifth Avenue, New York, NY 10010.

Palgrave Macmillan is the global academic imprint of the above companies
and has companies and representatives throughout the world.

Palgrave® and Macmillan® are registered trademarks in the United States,
the United Kingdom, Europe and other countries.

ISBN 978-1-349-43815-0   ISBN 978-1-137-02334-6 (eBook)
DOI 10.1057/9781137023346

This book is printed on paper suitable for recycling and made from fully
managed and sustained forest sources. Logging, pulping and manufacturing
processes are expected to conform to the environmental regulations of the
country of origin.

A catalogue record for this book is available from the British Library.

A catalog record for this book is available from the Library of Congress.

10   9   8   7   6   5   4   3   2   1
22 21 20 19 18 17 16 15 14 13

The actions of today become the destiny of tomorrow. A company can change its destiny not by wishing for it, but by working for it – through its leaders' decisions and actions

.

CONTENTS

LIST OF FIGURES

LIST OF TABLES

FOREWORD: WHY READ THIS BOOK?

As business leaders we have to deliver results for our customers, shareholders, and colleagues.. Our challenge is that expectations of all these stakeholders are going on increasing and increasing rapidly. At the same time technology is accelerating the speed of change in the marketplace; it is harder to predict the future as volatility grows and competition becomes ever fiercer.

This means we have to become more "agile"; we have to be able to align our teams and embrace change more quickly and successfully. We have to get new ideas to market faster and more effectively than our competitors.

At Pcubed we work with many of the Fortune 500 companies and see many approaches to innovation, to making investment decisions, and to managing change. We see pockets of great practice. But we see huge inefficiency as well, where good ideas get rushed to production and miss their potential, where good ideas get diluted through poor delivery or simply fall by the wayside, crowded out because the key resources are prioritized to other less valuable initiatives or decisions aren't made quickly or consistently enough.

The difference you see in agile businesses is their ability to get the right ideas bubbling to the top and then to align the organization behind these key ideas to drive rapid consistent decision-making and ruthless execution.

What makes the difference? Businesses that are good at managing change have thought through their end-to-end approach to managing innovation, investment, and implementation. They have thought about how they establish a culture of innovation, how they align innovation and investment decision-making, how they prioritize resources to the right areas, and how they align the myriad of decision-making processes to manage implementation and measure results to drive continuous improvement.

In this book, Shan sets out in a clear simple style the key factors you need to address to ensure that the good innovative ideas bubble to the top, so that you make better investment decisions and can manage implementation with less wasted resources and time. Aligning innovation, investment, and implementation provides huge payback.

Martin Hodgson
Global CEO Pcubed

PREFACE

Innovation management is a subject that endlessly fascinates business leaders: All of us want to know how to instil innovation as a practice into our organization. The author not only believes but confidently predicts that over the next five years companies will increasingly turn to innovation process to capture new ideas to strategize better ways of doing business, use the project portfolio management process to decide their *investment* choices and use structured execution framework to *implement* their strategies so as to gain a competitive advantage or strategic leverage in the market.

Every success in a company comes from the mind of the human soul. As Napoleon Hill (2004) in his well-articulated book stated: "There are more gold mined from the mind of the humans than from this earth." In this then a question arises: "Are we tapping all the ideas and innovative thinking from our organization?" *Innovation* is a management discipline that transforms knowledge and creative ideas into market successes. It can involve a business model, a unique strategy, a process, technology, or services among others.

Innovation will not realize any value for your business unless you have a decision framework in place to prioritize your ideas. Generally, it is widely accepted that portfolio management framework is the management of a collection of innovative ideas in the form of projects and programs in which an organization *invests*. These projects and programs, also called initiatives, are meant to realize the organization's strategy in order to maximize business benefits, and each is undertaken with a certain level of risk and constraints. Business started to realize the relationship between strategy and execution, how we can align the strategy to business execution. The essence was then are we investing in the right innovative initiatives which can create the success we are seeking? Is our portfolio *investment* rightly prioritized and is it giving us the maximum value for the investment. Is my prioritized investment giving me the market success that we desire?

Finally, a brilliant strategy, or a blockbuster product, or a breakthrough technology can put you on the competitive map, but only solid execution can keep you there. Execution is how you *implement* on your intent. No company can deliver on its commitments or adapt well to change unless all leaders practice the discipline of implementation at all levels. Few businesses need to spend more than a tenth of their time on strategy;

disciplined implementation is all – and never more so than in today's post-recessionary world, where the ability to do more with less depends on engaged and enabled employees.

Disciplined implementation has to be part of a company's strategy and its goals. It is the missing link between aspirations and results. As such it is a major – indeed, the major – job of a business leader. The ability for a company to invest and implement its innovative strategies into actions and deliver to its customers provides a significant advantage for its organizations. If you don't know how to implement, the whole of your impact as a leader will always be less than the sum of its parts.

Many authors have covered these three areas individually, but there is no one yet who wrote a book that links and integrates these three disciplines as a holistic end to end process, and I believe that this book is attempting to do so.

How this book is structured?

Adaptability is vital in today's constantly shifting business environment. However, true learning will only happen if we take decisions first to help us unlearn. It starts with recognition of what I call "the seven sins of business". Once those are acknowledged, you're free to develop an action plan to minimize their impact. A full understanding of the seven sins can help the organization make pragmatic decisions as it puts into action the three disciplines that make up this book: innovation, investment, and implementation.

Because this book focuses on these three key disciplines needed in an organization to be successful, I've structured it into three parts as shown in Figure 1 below:

Part I discusses about *Innovation Decision as a Discipline for Business Success*. The most important parameter in this discipline is removing the fear of failure. Everyone knows that Edison had 1000 failures before his biggest discovery. What's important in business is not capital or experience, but ideas. If you have ideas you have the main asset you need, and there isn't any limit to what you can do with your business and your life. In this set of chapters, I lay out what innovation is, where it comes from, how to create a culture that supports it, how to launch an innovation process, and how to embed innovation habits into daily work. The outlines of the five chapters are as follows:

- *Chapter 1: What is Innovation and Where Does it Come From?* In this chapter, we will explore what are creativities, ideas, and innovation.

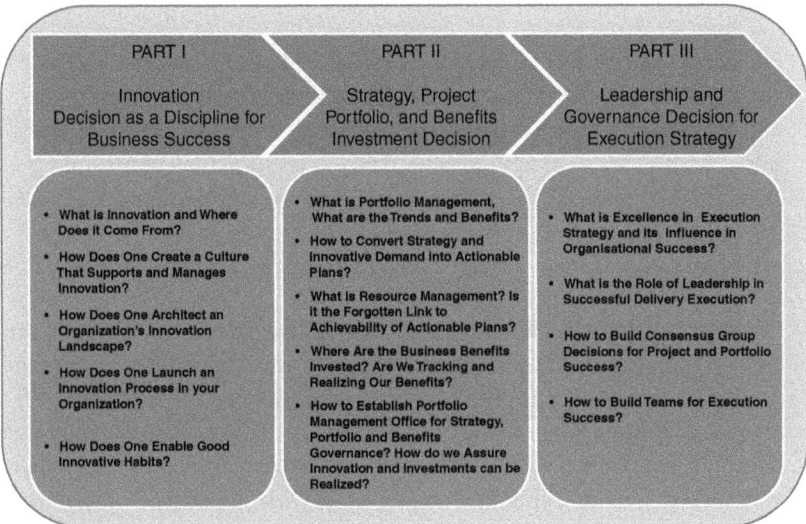

Figure 1 Structure of the book

We will also discuss the key innovative challenges that a management faces. This is followed by some examples of the different sources of innovation.

- *Chapter 2: How Does One Create a Culture That Supports and Manages Innovation?* In this chapter,we evaluate how and what it takes organizations to support an innovative culture and the process of executing an innovation strategy. In this chapter, we also examine the organizational hierarchy and executive innovation intent. Typically we look at the executives from a top–down approach where they have organizational authority and have access to budget, how they can encourage and support innovative thinking. We also evaluate the second part, that is, the bottom–up approach, whereby individual workers or project members who have limited formal power are empowered to leverage opportunity to change the culture of an enterprise from the inside.

- *Chapter 3: How Does One Architect an Organisation's Innovation Landscape?* In this chapter, we review how innovators see things and how do we architect an innovation landscape? We will discuss the necessity to design an innovation landscape in a structured and logical manner. The approach will examine in detail how companies engage, evolve, evaluate, execute, and empower innovation within their organization. We will also look at the role of a chief innovation officer and examine that innovators don't see different things but rather they see things differently.

- *Chapter 4: How Does One Launch an Innovation Process in your Organisation?* In this chapter, we discuss the organizational awareness and their innovation intent that can be used in identifying ideas, selecting the ideas, and converting them into actions. As Drucker (1984) said, "Creativity does not automatically lead to actual innovation", as such creativity or ideas generated without an investment case, business plan, and an organizational structure to administer the plan (i.e., action-oriented follow-through) are meaningless. At best, creative ideas remain good intentions if not implemented.

- *Chapter 5: How Does One Enable Good Innovative Habits?* In this chapter, we examine how to enable good innovative habits. A key essential is the change required in oneself to uncover his/her potential. This understanding of oneself is important and there are behaviors and practices that highlight this trait. We also discuss how in organizations there are "talkers". They think of themselves as "idea" people". They complain about the stand-pat senility or massive inertia of the organization. They complain about management's refusal to implement their ideas. They complain, complain, and complain. In short, they take no responsibility for implementation. There is no shortage of creativity or of creative people. That's the reason why we propose the ideation capturing process, so that people do not have the particular notion that their jobs are finished when they suggested the idea, but that if they want their ideas to be accepted they need to work out the details, implement the proposal, and finish what they suggested.

Part II of this book addresses *Strategy and Portfolio Investment Decisions.* Investment decisions will have to be fueled by the firm's strategy and tuned by experienced leadership to ensure better mileage of returns and performance from projects generated by innovative thinking and ideas. This part of the book addresses the disciplined approach to overseeing the collection of projects and programs in which an organization invests. This part comprises of five chapters as described briefly below:

- *Chapter 6: What Is Portfolio Management, What Are the Trends and Benefits?* In this chapter, we will explain what portfolio management is and why it is relevant. Why projects fail, the root causes for this failure, and what remedies portfolio management provides. We will also give a short introduction into the history and evolution of the discipline, explain portfolio in relation to established program and project management, share some examples of success stories in the corporate world, and introduce the portfolio themes and process and how these interact and are best applied.

- *Chapter 7: How to Convert Strategy and Innovative Demand into Actionable Plans?* In this chapter, we will investigate processes of converting strategies into actions. Portfolios of projects are created to deliver change. Before these are launched an organization must hence understand what it is seeking to become, what are its goals how does it want to create future value, and and how it will measure success. This chapter introduces business drivers as the currency to use to launch, steer, and measure projects. It introduces how to make the drivers tangible. Portfolio management provides guidance on how to define drivers, define their impact, and prioritize them. We also elaborate on other techniques, especially categorization, as a means to structure and manage projects and portfolios.
- *Chapter 8: What Is Resource Management? Is It the Forgotten Link to Achievability of Actionable Plans?* In this chapter, we will explore the key areas of resource management and investigate how they can be conducive to making plans achievable. Resource management's associations with portfolio management are explored. The resource manager's role is examined as the forgotten link to portfolio management. This is achieved by assessing whether we have the right people with the right skills to execute a project that goes in as a prioritized part of the project portfolio. We then throw more light on resource planning to emphasize its role in successful portfolio execution.
- *Chapter 9: Where Are the Business Benefits Invested? Are We Tracking and Realizing Our Benefits?* In this chapter,we take a good drive through the tunnels of benefit management. Starting from defining and understanding benefits, we further investigate why benefits and their measurements are needed. To understand this, we explore different indicators to measure benefits, such as net present value (NPV), return on investment (ROI). and break-even period. We also look at what is needed as breakdown for ultimate investment decision.
- *Chapter 10: How to Establish Portfolio Management Office for Strategy, Portfolio, and Benefits Governance? How Do We Assure Innovation and Investments Are Realized?* In this chapter we focus largely on the assurance and realization of benefits through a portfolio management office (PfMO). PfMO involves assuring stakeholders of the overall health of programs and projects in portfolios. This chapter talks about the various elements involved in the set-up, implementation, and running of a PfMO, including roles and responsibilities in the PfMO team, PfMO reporting, and other challenges that involve organizational and behavioral change during the transformation of a PfMO. The key factors to ensure success of a PfMO are discussed.

Part III of the book investigates the relationship between *Leadership and Governance Decision for Execution Strategy.* Here, I identify execution strategy as a discipline and delivery mechanism which involves both art and science to ensure that stated benefits in the business case for an initiative are realized to improve the business's competitive advantage. For an execution strategy to be excellent in its delivery requires clear leadership style and governance from senior executives. Excellent leaders who can convert the "right" strategy into desired business results (operations) through effective execution (implementation) of projects have a definitive personal style, attitude, and personality that make their strategy execution successful. This part of the book is divided into four chapters as follows:

- *Chapter 11: What Is Excellence in Execution Strategy and Its Influence in Organizational Success?* In this chapter, we explain a framework and perspective to establish the link between increasing shareholder value and successful implementation of projects through a delivery capability vehicle (the program management office or PMO) enhanced by a culture of execution excellence. Regardless of the size, shape, style, or organizational authority, the ultimate measure of a PMO is the degree of influence on and contribution to improving shareholder value.
- *Chapter 12: What Is the Role of Leadership in Successful Delivery Execution?* In this chapter, we discuss how leadership is an increasingly challenging role for executives, but it is not impossible or intangible nor given only to a select few "born" leaders. Our emphasis is that successful leaders select their goals, define the route to them, and equip and motivate their teams to achieve them. They are affected by external shocks, but not slaves to them. Their development and learning, and that of the people who work with them, are simultaneous and mutually supporting. They blend rational analysis with sophisticated array of behavioral abilities that they have honed in tune with their natural strengths and personalities. Successful leaders ensure that decision-making mechanisms are in place and decision-making authority and accountability are adequately assigned as part of their Governance structure.
- *Chapter 13: How to Build Consensus Group Decisions for Project and Portfolio Success?* In this chapter, we investigate the ability to make decisions as a core leadership skill. Some decisions can be made quickly by one person, while others require the whole project team to convene. Sometimes decision-makers have the luxury of time to carefully analyze all the issues involved, while some decisions must be

made with lightning speed, lest the business forfeit a market advantage or allow a deal to slip away.

- *Chapter 14: How to Build Teams for Execution Success?* The road to project success is often littered with conflict resulting from disagreement among stakeholders. Program leaders must function with incomplete or inaccurate information. And there is often ambiguity or a lack of a clear definition of success in key program elements. Some teams and team leaders appear to thrive under those conditions of conflict, uncertainty, and ambiguity, while others seem paralyzed by indecision. So building a team for project execution success is as much art as science. Many team-building efforts fail because teamwork essentials aren't fully understood. In this chapter, I examine the nature of building teams specifically in program and project initiatives and also propose a leadership model useful in managing project team dynamics.

ACKNOWLEDGMENTS

This book has been an unexpected project, brought to fruition through the efforts of several people in Pcubed. Firstly, I am deeply grateful to Pcubed senior management team, specifically Adrian Balfour (Chairman and Founder), Paul Driver (Co-Founder), Martin Hodgson (Global CEO), Dermot Brannock (GM North America), Richard Siddle (GM EMEA), and Carl Dalby (Global Sales and Marketing) whose continued enthusiasm, encouragement, and energy have motivated me and transformed my vision of this book into reality.

Secondly, I am indebted to Microsoft, specifically Simon Floyd (WW Director, Innovation & Product Lifecycle Management Solutions) for his visionary work in innovation and giving permission to publish some of the work done. Pcubed is the premier partner with Microsoft Enterprise. I also like to acknowledge PTC, partner of Microsoft and Pcubed who have worked closely with us and contributed to this book.

Thirdly, special thanks to Peter Heinrich Chairman and CEO of Portfolio DecisionWare who is not only a close friend but also one who has devoted his lifetime investigating resource management within the context of portfolio management. His experience and knowledge have been invaluable to me.

Fourthly, a great thank you to Himanshu Gupta from BP, who provided insightful comments on the draft and to Diederik Vos, COO of SQS with whom I spend enriching time during an engagement.

Fifthly, I extend my heartfelt thanks to Eleanor Davey-Corrigan and Hannah Fox, from Palgrave Macmillan, who consistently reminded me of the dateline for the draft and kept me tightly connected.

Sixthly, special acknowledgment and sincere appreciations to:

- Eric Foss and Jonathan Fryza who helped develop Chapter 10;
- Jonathan Carr whose work with our client motivated him to write up Chapter 9;
- Sharath Kumar who helped to put the tedious task of arranging the figures and tables;
- the contributions from the global innovation and portfolio team members, specifically David Wells, Richard Greenall, and David Winters from Australia, Peter Wilson, Peter Bachsleitner, Ky Nicol, John Allen, John Sheffield, Duncan Griffin, Timothy Brett, Jean-Marc Simon,

Frederic Cordonnier, Ishai Perelman, Ian Barnard, Jenny Hughes, and Ian Radcliff from EMEA and Paddy Oates, Bert Velasco, Rich Weller, Sean O'Brien, Colin Brown, Biron Crusenberry, Dan Ling, and Garbutt Byron from North America and Canada,

- to all Pcubers who have contributed ideas and shared their experiences and thoughts in one form or another in support of this project.

Finally, and most importantly, my heartfelt thanks to my wife, best friend, and soul mate Lalitha, my Princess Shauna and my philosophical son Shaun who all believed in me and were the lights that showed me the way.

ABOUT THE AUTHOR

DR SHAN RAJEGOPAL – Global Head of Innovation and Portfolio Management Practice Pcubed Ltd.

Shan is a trusted business advisor and one of the leading authorities in innovation and project portfolio management who believes that "There is more gold mined from the mind of the humans than from this earth". He provides advice and support in innovation, portfolio investments, and delivery management with value realization for companies looking to radically improve their performance. Shan doesn't like to be called a consultant or an academic, but rather a practitioner enabling companies to build better internal systems for successful performance. He is also a much sought after international speaker, inviting his audience to embark on a journey of discovery to uncover the most successful practices and the best ideas from leading global players. He sits on the Board of Aberystwyth University (Wales) and is the author of *Project Portfolio Management: Leading the Corporate Vision* and *Sun Tzu and the Project Battleground: Creating Project Strategy from the Art of War*.

Who is Pcubed?

Pcubed is a leading management consulting firm specializing in delivering critical and complex innovative initiatives, portfolio and programs for global organizations, governments, and agencies across all industry sectors.

Pcubed's innovation, portfolio, and program management expertise and approach deliver a consulting partnership that improves the structure of organizational portfolios, shapes, and drives key program initiatives, and develops underlying project management capability. Pcubed's thought leadership and execution capability helps to ensure that the outcomes of the programs and projects deliver the desired results and benefits to the company.

THE SEVEN SINS OF BUSINESS TODAY AND THE ART OF ACTION BY LEADERS

The actions of today become the destiny of tomorrow. A company can change its destiny not by wishing for it, but by working for it – through its leaders' decisions and actions

Dr Shan Rajegopal

As I look at the work and business going on around us, I have found that most of it is grounded in sin. The worse point is that these activities can slowly and painfully debilitate the organizations, making it woefully inadequate to face whatever the future might bring. In this section, I want to look at what are these sins and the salvation I believe to be at hand, and organizations will still have time to rescue their operation. What companies need to do is make decisive actions to apply the tenets of innovative thinking, decide the investments for the portfolio of projects, and deploy a disciplined execution strategy as part of their best practice approach to gain competitive advantage or strategic leverage in the market. One of the greatest lessons I have learnt in my life is to pay as much attention to the means of work as to its end ... I have been always learning great lessons from this one principle, and it appears to be that all the secret of success is there: to pay as much attention to the means as to the end. I refer to these means as "action guides", which need to be adopted by business leaders. One of our great defects as leaders or individuals in life is that we are drawn more to the vision – the goal is so much more enchanting, so much more alluring, so much bigger in our mental horizon that we lose sight of the details of actions altogether.

Whenever failure comes, if we analyze it critically, in 99 per cent of cases we shall find that it was because we did not pay attention to action details. Proper attention to a disciplined finishing and strengthening of actions can lead to success with the confidence that if the actions are right the end must come. As there are seven sins, there are also seven action guides. Let's examine each sin and then discuss how its action guide can help an organization to turn over a new leaf and even strengthen it for whatever the future holds.

Sin 1: lack of visibility

Would you drive your car using only your rear view mirror? No. Because it won't let you see what's headed your way from ahead. So why drive your business that way? I'm guessing that you've recently been part of planning sessions for the coming year in which a large portion of time has been spent reviewing historic information. After all that's how businesses tend to make strategic decisions. Yet, that information is typically out of date, just plain inaccurate, repositioned, or taken out of context for the target audience, or it's just copied from some master spreadsheet.

Action guide 1: gain visibility

Just as a lack of visibility is a sin, gaining visibility – looking ahead – is a top action guide – perhaps the most important one, since it powers the other action guides. "Real-time" data can provide visibility of the business demands, early detection of issues, and the maximization of available options. Project and portfolio management (PPM) as a discipline and set of tools can help managers make decisions based on accurate, "real-time" information that comes from a single source of data. That single source can provide unique views of the same data, based on a given person's role in the operation. Ready access to key performance indicators allows for proactive, not reactive, behavior.

Sin 2: lack of clarity on demand and capability

Do you have a complete picture of the demands being made by the business? What does that look like? Do projects appear from nowhere? When they do – and they will! – are you able to understand the effects and impacts? Can you quickly tell if you have enough capability, resources, or budget to undertake these new endeavors? Are you able to quickly re-prioritize? Can you quickly sort out how best to deliver these demands with your finite capabilities? Or do you work in an environment characterized by the classic adage, "He who shouts loudest gets what's needed"?

Action guide 2: understand and maximize your capability

A lack of clarity on demand and capability can be countered by gaining visibility of all work and turning the corporate planning activity into "business as usual". The use of a PPM system can extend the planning horizon to provide early visibility of upcoming work, portfolio balancing among projects, and early warning indicators. Those who must manage the workload can do so based on fact, not hearsay, can build scenarios to understand the full impact of additional projects, and can maximize benefits and minimize overspend by prioritizing workload based on current needs and resource availability.

Sin 3: lack of optimal use of resources

Resources – people – are typically the biggest single cost in any endeavor. So why are they managed so poorly? Do you know what your resources are doing right now or what they're supposed to be doing? Are they underutilized? How well are you able to manage your resources to keep them happy, satisfied, and motivated and working on activities that really matter to the business?

Action guide 3: optimize resource utilization

Optimizing the use of resources can only be achieved when you currently understand where and how your resources are deployed, what skill sets you have access to, and whether the resources are working on the right projects. A PPM system can help you balance the project portfolio to maximize delivery and reduce the time it takes to allocate employees best suited for a given project. The result is that your organization will be able to put more people on chargeable or business critical work and have fewer spending time "on the bench". That increased utilization and faster redeployment equates to greater value creation.

Sin 4: lack of financial control on projects

So, you have a budget for the coming year. What's your ultimate goal – to keep plodding ahead on that project until someone tells you you've run out of cash? And once that happens, do you work under the belief that you can always ask for more? Do you really have a picture of what a project should cost for resources and the use of that capital you're spending? Do you have any visibility into key metrics that keep you informed about the true status of your project? If a change is proposed to the project, do you have a way to measure what impact that would have on the budget? Do you really only know whether you met the budget or had a budget overrun once the work is done?

Action guide 4: maximize financial control

In an operation with visibility into activities, budgeting and financial reporting turns into a business-as-usual activity, not something done once a year or at the start of a new project. Financial control delivers real-time metrics such as actual-to-date and estimates-to-completion. Areas of overspend will be more readily identified and understood. The portfolio can be adjusted to maximize delivery within the budgetary constraints of the business. With time and sufficient trusted historic data, the true costs of a planned endeavor will be better understood up front.

Sin 5: lack of efficient management reporting

I'd venture that your organization uses one or another common tool for managing projects: Microsoft Excel or Word. After all, both of these applications provide for easy repositioning, the existence of multiple versions to spread the data, and the ability to give users control. Yet Excel and Word also come with problems: they tend to be used as single-user applications, the files generated frequently show a lack of consistency from one department or manager to the next, the information can be out of date (with no evidence to show it), people can use whatever version of the information will make the best impression, and a user can even hide information when status looks bad. By the time the project data has been collated, repositioned, and presented in five different formats, the information is days or weeks out of date. That's akin to reading last week's newspaper to stay up on what's current. Also, every time a report needs to be made, it requires a new round of data massaging and aligning of columns. Surely that time would be better spent reacting to the information than collating it.

Action guide 5: consistent management reporting

The right kind of tool can play a big part in supporting the decision-making process. Rather than relying on Excel or Word, a PPM system that pulls from a single repository of project details can offer relevant, accurate, and timely information. It reduces the reporting effort by allowing the user to set up a template for reporting that's populated with the latest data, unfettered and unmassaged. In fact, reports can become a by-product of the day-to-day activities, and forecast reports can be used to cement strategic objectives. Because the data can be made available to multiple people, not just the person doing the reporting, "repositioning" isn't an option, questions about validity are taken off the table, and senior and operational managers get the bald-faced facts.

Sin 6: lack of strategic alignment for delivery optimization

Strategy is set by senior management, right? Once set, it results in execution of a number of projects at the operational level of the business. But do you really know which projects are strategically aligned? Do you have visibility of all projects? Do you understand how each project is supposed to help execute the strategy? Can the details of all of this be quantified and true benefit realized? Or do you work in an organization where, if the project sounds like a good idea and the budget exists, it is just executed?

Action guide 6: align strategy with delivery optimization

Aligning strategy with delivery means that there will be far less wasted effort. People will work on those activities that help to drive the business, not simply "pet projects". The strategy execution can be measured for the first time in terms of cost and delivery of benefits. Access to the business' strategic drivers and how the projects play into those help the entire organization to achieve a common understanding of the direction it's headed. PPM can support the decision-making process by helping the company kill off those projects not tied to strategy, leaving more time, budget, and resources for the ones that are.

Sin 7: lack of benefits realization tracking

Surely, your organization believes in the value of a solid business case that answers the four Ws: why, who, what, and when. But once the business case is approved, what happens to it? Is it filed, never to be seen again? Does progress or budget tracking take place? Is the project achieving the milestones? Is it on course to achieve the benefits promised by the project in the first place?

Action guide 7: track benefits realization

Projects should deliver benefit – the rewards promised by undertaking the project in the first place. Those benefits might consist of head count reduction, cost savings, an increase in revenue and profit, and intangible components such as a boost in reputation. But frequently benefits, while defined and quantified, are rarely tracked. That means the organization never really knows if the benefits of a given project have been realized. A total PPM solution ensures that benefits and other deliverables have visibility and can be tracked. It also ensures that those involved are accountable for their delivery. Over time the project delivery structure can be refined and governance strengthened.

So you have a decision to make: Will you allow your organization to continue wallowing in its sinful practices, or will you choose a different path? It is in your hands to progress on a different path. I believe that the three disciplines discussed in this book can help deliver the visibility required to shift the inertia in your organization in a right direction to help reach the goals that are set for your organization's sustainable future.

Innovation Decision as a Discipline for Business Success

Amazon currently lists 8000 hardcover books that cover the topic of innovation management. Dozens of conferences include the term "innovation" in their titles. New applications and technology-based platforms surface regularly that promise to capture the innovations that surface in the course of our operations. This is a subject that endlessly fascinates business leaders: all of us want to know how to instill innovation – the effort of altering products, technologies, services, processes, or business models – as a practice into our organizations.

In this book we do not want to cover innovation in detail, but what we want to do is to identify that innovation is not the classical thinking of someone working isolated in the research and development (R&D) department and coming up with a breakthrough product.

Innovation in the most generic sense is the conversion of knowledge and ideas into new or improved products, processes, and services to gain a competitive advantage or strategic leverage in the market. Milind Lele (1992) claims that companies need to have a thorough understanding of strategic leverage if they need to survive – let alone prosper – in a competitive environment.

How can companies be innovative in their thinking on the kind of strategy and tactic that can help to attain their objectives? How can the companies deploy their "competencies" (resources and skills) and how can they creatively disrupt an industry for benefits? These are some examples of innovative thinking that provide the competitive advantage companies are seeking.

From a portfolio perspective what we are interested in is how a company can capture "innovative demand" or "ideas" and convert that into actions. Interestingly, both Peter Drucker (1985) and Theodore Levitt (HBR 2002) note that creativity is only one part of successful innovation. They provide a treasure trove of practical insights into the notions of creativity, ideation, and innovation. It's normally said: "People often confuse good management with a good idea that makes management look good".

However, a good idea must be put into action. This requires hard work, processes, procedures, and a structure to make it all happen. Unfortunately, there are a lot of "idea people" but a scarcity of "innovators". Organizations need people who can take a good idea and convert it into operating reality. This will require the establishment of a disciplined "innovation process" to make the right decisions to help us ensure that the right ideas are moved at the right time to gain maximum competitive advantage for us. By the end of Part I you will have a grasp on the innovation process that needs to be embedded in your organization.

Part I of this book will examine the following:

- *Chapter 1: What Is Innovation and Where Does It Come From?* – We will explore what creativities, ideas, and innovation are. We will also discuss the key innovative challenges that the management faces. This is followed by some examples of the different sources of innovation.
- *Chapter 2: How Does One Create a Culture That Supports and Manages Innovation?* – We evaluate how organizations support and what it takes them to support an innovative culture and the process of executing an innovation strategy. In this chapter, we also examine the organizational hierarchy and executive innovation intent. Typically we look at the executives from a top–down approach where they have organizational authority and access to the budget, and at how they can encourage and support innovative thinking. We also evaluate the second part, that is, the bottom–up approach, whereby an individual worker or project member who has limited formal power is empowered to leverage opportunity to change the culture of an enterprise from the inside.
- *Chapter 3: How Does One Architect an Organization's Innovation Landscape?* – Here we review how innovators see things and how do we architect an innovation landscape? We will discuss the necessity for designing an innovation landscape in a structured and logical manner. The approach will examine in detail how companies engage, evolve, evaluate, execute, and empower innovation within their organization. We will also look at the role of a chief innovation officer and examine why innovators don't see different things but rather see things differently.
- *Chapter 4: How Does One Launch an Innovation Process in Your Organization?* – We discuss the organizational awareness and innovation intent that can be used in identifying ideas, selecting ideas, and converting them into actions. As Drucker said, "Creativity does not automatically lead to actual innovation", as such creativity or ideas

generated without an investment case, business plan, and organizational structure to administer the plan (i.e., action-oriented follow-through) is meaningless. At best, creative ideas remain good intentions if not implemented.

- *Chapter 5: How Does One Enable Good Innovative Habits?* – Here we examine how to enable good innovative habits. A key essential is the change required in oneself to uncover one's potential. This understanding of oneself is important and there are behaviours and practices that highlight this trait. We also discuss how in organizations there are "talkers". They think of themselves as "idea people". They complain about the stand-pat senility or massive inertia of the organization. They complain about management's refusal to implement their ideas. They complain, complain, and complain. In short, they take no responsibility for implementation. There is no shortage of creativity or of creative people. That's the reason why we propose the ideation-capturing process so that people do not have the particular notion that their jobs are finished when they suggest the idea, but that if they want their ideas to be accepted they need to work out the details, implement the proposal, and finish what they suggested.

CHAPTER 1

What Is Innovation and Where Does It Come from?

Over the last decade, there has been an increased focus on innovation in many businesses. Several factors have contributed to this increased attention:

- The increased rate of change in competition, especially the growing capabilities of India and China.
- The fall of information costs as the web becomes more fully adopted, and consumers are demanding more.
- Greater focus on cost-cutting with a spike in outsources/near source/far source. Most of the things that could be cut, trimmed, or outsourced have been done. Many businesses are relatively lean and need to return to growth and differentiation.

All of these factors contribute to the need for innovation. However, there are ongoing trends that will continue to increase innovation focus now and in the future. These can include, for example, focus on global warming, reduction in carbon footprints, and poverty eradication – all of these mean new technologies are required to reduce emissions and genetically modify the food supply, among others. Another example is in the United Kingdom, where health care reform will mean new demands on an antiquated health care system. The banking sector is already undergoing change and disruption. All of these factors act as a catalyst for change in the government and in major businesses.

So it is not surprising that there are thousands of books that cover the topic of innovation management, with dozens of conferences including the term "innovation" in their titles. In the past we have found that managers of technology-driven businesses have traditionally had one major innovation cycle to worry about – the product innovation cycle. Several principles drive success: anticipate the next technology wave or new product opportunity, get to the market first, achieve relative market-share leadership in order to lower production costs, "cross the chasm" from early adopters to mainstream customers, and profit will follow. While this is much easier said than done, the rules of the game are relatively clear.

What has changed over the last two decades and has made management significantly more complex is the emergence of a second parallel innovation cycle – the business model innovation cycle. Many companies that formerly accepted their business model as a "given" now consider it to be a conscious choice and a competitive weapon. They are using creative business models to enter new markets, attack incumbents, and renew their own leadership positions.

The management systems for business model innovation are not as mature as those for product innovation. Yet it is easier to trace large shifts in the market value of major technology companies by the business model decisions that they have made (both good and bad) than by unique product inventions.

Allen Booz Hamilton (2010) and IBM (2006) global innovation surveys had indicated that innovation is being recognized as offering a competitive advantage, perhaps one of the few sustainable advantages, for CEOs. The Gartner Annual CIO survey (2007) showed that "improved competitive advantage, increased revenue growth, and faster innovation are among the top 10 issues for CIOs". All the surveys point out that the majority of senior executives said innovation was critical to the success of their firms as they prepared for the market and economy to improve. An interesting theme that appeared in the surveys was that executives perceive that "the recession was a catalyst for increased innovation".

What we can deduce from these surveys is that senior executives of companies are willing to invest in innovation during the economic downturn and the reasons can include the following:

- Innovation is becoming a core component of overall corporate strategy.
- There is recognition that product development cycles are longer than recessionary periods.
- Many see the recession as an opportunity to build advantages over their competitors.

We were at the Frost and Sullivan 2011 Innovation conference in San Diego, and during the CEO Forum what came out as very clear was that CEOs are willing to invest in innovations that can give quicker returns to help overcome economic recession.

One of the biggest impediments to innovation continues to be the "constraints of the product development lifecycle". The product development life cycle in many industries is simply too long and too cumbersome, and any opportunity to shorten the development life cycle could mean real rewards. Conversely, any slacking off could mean falling behind the competition.

Charles Fine (1998) very eloquently argues that in businesses today all advantages are temporary. In order to survive, let alone thrive, companies must be able to anticipate and adapt to change or face rapid and brutal extinction. His inspiration to use lessons from "fruit flies" for industries was revolutionary. The overall emphasis was that innovation and creative thinking must move away from being an occasionally interesting sideshow that is not focused and not strategic to becoming a key focus of senior executives to ensure that their firms continually grow and differentiate.

Innovative thinking is rapidly becoming a capability or enabler that strengthens and focuses the corporate strategies and must over time become a key enabler of many corporate goals and strategies. Once more firms create a continuous capability for innovation and modify their cultures to embrace innovation, we'll see the real transition occur. It is heartening to see that more and more firms are placing more emphasis on innovation at a strategic level. Companies must think of innovation in its broadest sense and our definition is:

> Innovation is the conversion of knowledge and ideas into new or improved products, business models, processes, and services to gain a competitive advantage or strategic leverage in the market.

We believe that to do any good, innovation must be linked with Project and Portfolio Management (PPM). As you proceed you will realize that the book will underpin the argument that companies need to turn to PPM processes to help them select, invest, and execute their innovation strategies in order to be successful.

The innovation of bird spit

Innovation broadly shows up in two flavors: incremental or dramatic and game-changing. The incremental change side is where you'll find tweaks and improvements to address shifting customer needs. Most mobile phone launches – but not all – fall into this category. An automated teller machine that allows you to insert your bank deposit check by check, automatically reads the amounts, and supplies you with an image of the checks on your receipt is an incremental improvement over the previous generation. A license plate-recognition video camera that can be hooked up to an access control system for raising and lowering a gate or garage door without human intervention is another instance.

On the game-changing side are these familiar examples: Netflix eliminating late fees, the Amazon Kindle turning reading into a paperless activity, or Nissan's plug-in car that can handle commuters' driving needs. It took an artist-turned-engineer to design a fan that you can put your hand through without injury; James Dyson, head of a company by the same name, not only comes up with amazing ways to use technology but has also managed almost single-handedly to turn the concept of appliances such as vacuums and fans into objects of desire for men.

Or how about this example? On a recent trip to Malaysia my wife and I stopped by a shop to buy some specialty items. We heard a huge, frightening sound of numerous birds – like something out of a Hitchcock movie. When, with panic in our voices, we inquired about the source of the noise, we were informed of a new kind of farming that was taking place in the floors above our head.

During the Asian economic crisis that struck a decade ago, a lot of small and medium companies closed down. One clever guy came up with the idea of using that abandoned space to do Swiftlet farming.

Swiftlets, specific to this part of the world, use saliva to build their nests. Many people consider the composition of those nests to have medicinal and health benefits.

This particular innovator created a sound that attracts the birds to particular localities and converted those factory spaces into nesting grounds with platforms. Every three months the business is able to collect the used nests and process them. A kilogram of unprocessed white edible bird's nest is worth about £1000–£1500. A processed kilogram is worth about £4000–£5000. Over the last ten years this innovation has grown into a three to five billion-pound industry in Hong Kong, China, Taiwan, and Macau. That's dramatic.

Out of the lab and into company cubicles

In the examples I've cited, the innovators surely reap monetary benefits. But we don't know what processes the individuals or their organizations followed in order to achieve their success. I would say that imposing management discipline on the very act of innovation will help a company transform its knowledge and creative ideas into market successes. A structured approach to creativity increases the likelihood that the business will be able to instill innovation in its operational DNA and make it the norm rather than the miracle.

The classical approach to innovation has a number of characteristics. The old-fashioned notion of innovation is that it:

1. is an individual process
2. is hidden in the R&D laboratory
3. is ungovernable and uncontrollable
4. is more or less accidental
5. is something that's been going on for ages
6. has no correlation with trending or consumer/customer demand and insight
7. has no correlation with corporate strategy or execution capabilities.

We believe that as a management discipline, innovation can be:

- a multi-disciplinary group process
- supported top–down and driven bottom–up
- guided, facilitated, and controllable
- more than just incremental improvements to products
- a process by jumps and starts
- surrounded by a risk-management envelope
- effectively governed
- effectively measured
- on the leading edge of portfolio management methodology.

Although each type of innovation – incremental and radical – tends to co-exist along a spectrum within a company for reasons having to do with the organization's level of innovation maturity and capacity for risk-taking, each also calls for a different corporate skill set.

New business innovations require capabilities in these areas: setting business priorities and growth strategy, performing market/technology disruption identification, doing build vs. buy analysis, doing customer-driven concept validation, developing business plans, and being open to customer innovation. Existing business innovation calls for expertise in doing new production development acceleration, perfecting lifecycle management, performing resource management, identifying customer needs, mastering portfolio management, and achieving phase gate modeling.

The great uncertainty

Along that spectrum is also a continuum of uncertainty. Incremental innovations greatly reduce that level of uncertainty. Historic performance can tell an organization what to expect when it updates a major product.

Breakthrough innovations, on the other hand, tend to have much greater uncertainty tied to them. The company pursuing a market shift will neither always know ahead of time what resource constraints it will have nor what its appetite is for cultural transformation. Likewise, it may overestimate its technical capabilities as well as market demand and expectation. There's far less certainty about the outcomes when the product is totally new to the market, because it may require new customers, new applications, and frequently unknown business areas. Because the innovation hasn't been done before, the process to bring it to fruition tends to be "discovery-driven". Plans must change and adapt as new information is uncovered. And unlike incremental innovations that can be fast-tracked by an existing division or business unit, radical innovations take a certain level of incubation and constant interface management to keep the work moving forward amid daily operations.

Given the great unknowns, it's remarkable that existing organizations take on breakthrough innovations at all. But we have seen it happen over and over. Some key innovation management challenges are:

- *Recognizing opportunities*: Is the senior leadership team able to identify the sources of innovation and capture the ideas that surface?
- *Living with chaos*: Managed innovation also means managed change, and continuous change can be unsettling in an organization. How prepared is the company for that kind of environment?
- *Engaging in market learning*: Does the sales force or support staff have the ability to understand customer needs and feed those insights back into the organization in the form of ideas?
- *Developing new business models*: Can management visualize what will be needed to implement an innovation fully and work with the company restructuring that may be required?
- *Acquiring essential resources*: Does the company have the right people to translate concepts into prototypes or execute new ideas?
- *Transitioning projects*: Does the company culture enable project participants to adapt or change direction of those projects as newer, better ideas surface?
- *Valuing individual initiative*: Does the company recognize that good and great ideas come from all directions and that those ideas with true value need to be captured, acknowledged, and rewarded?

Unorthodox sources of innovation

Investigating the best sources of innovations, Drucker (1985) had found that there was considerable danger from what he called "the bright idea". This was his term for an innovation that was vague and elusive and accepted for development without much real analysis. He did not disagree that one could "hit a home run" with a bright idea and he was willing to recite examples of bright ideas which had gone on to make millions of dollars for their originators, including the zipper, the ballpoint pen, the aerosol spray can, and more. But he said that these were exceptions and should be ignored when regarding how the task of innovation in an organization should be approached.

"The problem is", Drucker said, "that bright ideas are the riskiest and least successful source of innovative opportunities." He estimated that probably only one in 500 made any money above their investment costs and suggested that relying on the bright idea for innovation was akin to gambling in Las Vegas and almost certain to lead to similar undesirable results for the manager of innovation. The solution, he maintained, was a systematic analysis and approach to sources of innovative ideas. This, he declared, was purposeful innovation, the kind that all of us must pursue regardless of our specialty, discipline, or functional area.

Steve Tobak (2010) identifies ten characteristics and methodologies that help to define innovative people and how these influence innovation thinking:

1. *Standing on the shoulders of giants*: Contrary to popular belief, innovation is often far more evolutionary than revolution, and more practical and crafty than breakthrough invention. Most of the time you're redefining the use of somebody else's idea. For example, Steve Jobs didn't invent the graphical user interface (GUI) or the computer mouse, but when he saw them demonstrated, his mind was probably racing with practical applications.
2. *Left brain–right brain balance*: The whole left brain–right brain thing is a myth, but metaphorically speaking, innovation often springs from a combination of inspirational thought (right brain) and practical need (left brain). They say necessity is the mother of invention; this is probably truer of innovation.
3. *Belief that you're special*: Many, if not most, innovative people have this sort of childish belief that they're special, destined for great things. The thought of doing something new and different – changing the world, as it were – can be daunting. Unless you truly believe it's your destiny, you'll probably be too scared to even try. Bill Gates didn't invent the PC operating system and he certainly didn't come up with the idea of licensing technology, but his business model – combining the two – made Microsoft one of the most valuable and powerful companies in the world.

4. *Questioning conventional wisdom, or the status quo*: If you even mention how things are done or should be done to a true-blue entrepreneur or innovator, it's like nails screeching on a chalkboard.
5. *Vision*: Oftentimes, people just have a vision of how they think something should be. It's really that simple. But they're also driven to see it through, as in the next bullet.
6. *Driven by the need to prove something*: Innovative people are definitely on a mission to prove something to somebody and half the time we don't even think they know who. Howard Schultz didn't invent coffee, espresso, or cappuccino, but he has certainly been an innovator in bringing all that to the masses through Starbucks.
7. *Problem-solving*: If you're not a problem-solver, you're probably not going to come up with anything that anybody will find useful. Control freaks are natural problem-solvers – they can barely walk down the street without seeing all sorts of things that can be done better.
8. *Passion*: Without passion and genuinely loving and caring about what you do, you simply won't have the resilience and stick-with-it to see innovation of any magnitude through. It's never just an idea – you have to actually do stuff with it.
9. *Focused brainpower*: Athletes will tell you success is all about focus – you can't hit a 100 mph fastball or catch a 30-yard pass with defenders all up in your face without it. It's the same with innovation. Ironically, people who appear to be all over the map with Attention, Deficit Disorder (ADD) like symptoms can have rare moments of clarity when it all comes together.
10. *Work stamina*: There's loads of talk these days about working smarter, not harder, taking more breaks, and so on. While we are big believers that you should not kill yourself with work, if you don't enjoy working and work stamina isn't in your blood, you're not likely to innovate a thing.

Other sources of innovation are best discussed by Drucker (1985) in his classic book, where he identifies seven "wells" of areas where innovation and ideas can come. These are:

1. The unexpected – An unexpected success, an unexpected failure, or an unexpected outside event can be a symptom of a unique opportunity.
2. The incongruities – A discrepancy between reality and what everyone assumes it to be, or between what is and what ought to be, can create an innovative opportunity.

3. Innovation based on process need – When a weak link is evident in a particular process but people work around it instead of doing something about it, an opportunity is present to the person or company willing to supply the "missing link".
4. Changes in industry and market structures – The opportunity for an innovative product, service, or business approach occurs when the underlying foundation of the industry or market shifts.
5. Demographics – Changes in the population's size, age structure, composition, employment, level of education, and income can create innovative opportunities.
6. Changes in perception, mood, and meaning – Innovative opportunities can develop when a society's general assumptions, attitudes, and beliefs change.
7. New knowledge – Advances in scientific and non-scientific knowledge can create new products and new markets.

Drucker told us that we must innovate. However, he did not leave it there: he told us how we should approach innovation to build and maintain the success of our organizations with the best sources of new ideas.

Innovation is both conceptual and perceptual. The imperative is to go out to look, to ask, to listen. Successful innovators use both the left and right sides of their brains. They look at figures and they look at people.

To be successful, Drucker wrote that an innovation has to be simple and it has to be focused. It should only do one thing or it confuses people and won't work. All effective innovations are breathtakingly simple. They should focus on a specific need that is satisfied and on a specific end result that they produce. This makes innovation seem pretty straightforward, doesn't it?

Drucker indicated that effective innovations start small and that they should not try to be clever. Innovations try to do one specific thing. Starting small allows for adjustments. To start small, keep the requirements for people and money fairly modest. Innovations must be handled by ordinary human beings if they are to achieve any size and importance at all.

Another key factor was to not try to innovate for the future, but to innovate for the present. The innovation may have long-term impact, but if you can't get it adopted now there won't be any future.

According to Drucker, there are three conditions that must be met for an innovation to be successful, including:

1. Innovation is work. It requires knowledge, ingenuity, creativity, and so on. Plus, innovators rarely work in more than one area, be it

finance, healthcare, retail, or whatever. Their work requires diligence, perseverance, and commitment.

2. To succeed, innovators must build on their own strengths. They must look at opportunities over a wide range, and then ask which of the opportunities fits them, fits this company. There must be a temperamental fit with the practitioner and a link to business strategy.

3. Innovation is an effect in economy and society, a change in the behavior of customers, of teachers, of farmers, of doctors, of people in general. Or it is a change in a process, in how people work and produce something. Innovation must always be close to the market, focused on the market, and market-driven.

Innovation, by its nature, is risky, as is all economic activity. But defending what was done yesterday is far more risky than making tomorrow. Innovators define risks and seek to minimize them. Innovations are successful to the extent that they systematically analyze the sources of opportunity, pinpoint the opportunity, and then exploit it, whether an opportunity has small and definable risk or larger but still definable risk. Successful innovators are conservative; they are not risk-focused, but rather are opportunity-focused.

The next chapter will discuss that innovation isn't a supernatural event, or a preordained occurrence that only happens to certain people. Great innovators don't go from zero-to-great in a heartbeat. It involves creating an innovative culture and managing the innovation process in a purposeful and systemic way with analysis of opportunities. The process must be organized and conducted on a regular basis. We must avoid getting hung up on "the fuzzy front end" or any other views that make innovation seem really obscure.

CHAPTER 2

How Does One Create a Culture That Supports and Manages Innovation?

While many new companies – especially well-funded start-ups – believe they own the market on innovative thinking, mature organizations also bring multiple advantages to the field. Top among them is the ability to build a systematic approach to manage innovation. While fresh start-ups are still assembling their teams, building markets, and putting infrastructure in place, the mature company can focus on instilling innovation discipline in operations.

Let's look at some examples of mature operations continuing to push the edge in new and innovative ways:

- Seventy-four-year-old cologne maker Old Spice has found a younger audience not with a new formula but with a dramatically different approach to marketing through social channels.
- Eighty-four-year-old BBC has recently begun testing Music Showcase, which brings together all the music featured on BBC along with video clips and allows visitors to browse them in collections created by BBC presenters, guests, and staff.
- German automaker Audi, 101 years old, has used psychologists to figure out how far down buttons have to be pushed in order to have that "quality" feel that characterizes Audi vehicles. The precise distance was apparently four to six millimeters. If it's not as deep as that, the button feels ticky-tacky and cheap.

Leadership skin in the game

Innovation discipline – whether radical or incremental – calls for a holistic approach composed of equal parts of corporate commitment and effective execution. Let's examine the components.

On the commitment side are sponsorship and cultural change; funding and risk taking; and rewards and recognition. Executive commitment

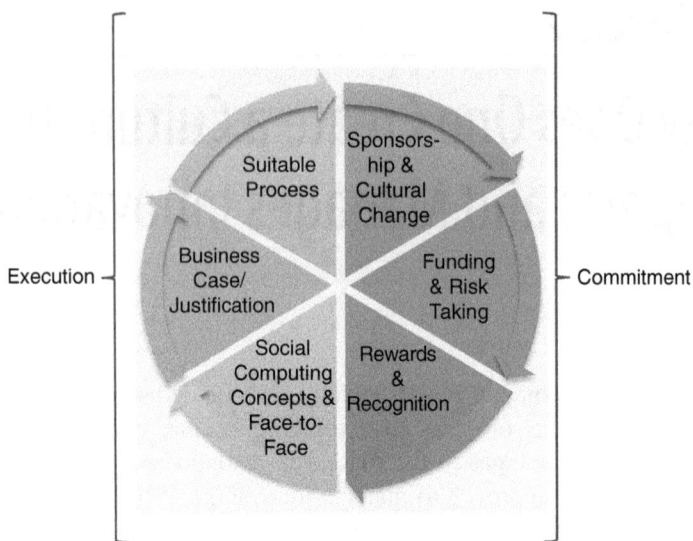

Figure 2.1 Innovation requires a disciplined, holistic, systematic approach (*with the permission of Microsoft*)

is vital for the necessary corporate changes, finding appropriate funding, facing down potential risks, and executing the vision. Without senior leader support any effort to build a structure and systems to manage innovation will fail. Figure 2.1 above shows how executive commitments and execution excellence leverage innovation culture.

Likewise, leaders need to set up and publicize a rewards and recognition program that will have impact. The best ones make a firm's innovation culture; the anemic ones blunder through and never see success.

As Jim Goodnight, Chief Executive Officer (CEO) and Founder of SAS, wrote in the July 2005 *Harvard Business Review* that companies prosper when they make best use of their "creative capital" – that is, creative thinkers whose ideas generate valuable products and services. He mentioned that "innovation is the key to success in this business, and creativity fuels innovation". He further emphasized that:

> Creativity is especially important to SAS because software is a product of the mind. As such, 95 percent of my assets drive out the gate every evening. It's my job to maintain a work environment that keeps those people coming back every morning. The creativity they bring to SAS is a competitive advantage for us.

In the past, businesses tended to believe that only the top minds could make meaningful contributions to innovation and that the concept of ideation provides a strategy for innovation. However, in today's practices:

- Ideas are potential investments;
- Ideas need to be managed;
- Everyone has a voice;
- Innovation is a process.

As such organizations need to create and leverage a culture that supports innovation in a holistic manner. The fundamental question for companies is "How can you diagnose and actively shape organizational cultures:

- To implement today's strategies and tasks?
- To create the capabilities to innovate?
- For tomorrow's competitive demands?"

Firstly, "organizational culture" is an elusive, yet powerful management tool. The word culture is used a great deal by management and organizational development practitioners to describe the climate and practices that organizations develop around their handling of people. A great deal of work has been done on corporate culture and its relationship to innovation and business performance.

For our purpose, we will use Stan Davis's 1984 definition of culture to describe how an organization shapes its culture to foster an innovative environment:

> Culture is a pattern of beliefs and expectations shared by the organization's members. These beliefs and expectations produce norms that (can) powerfully shape the behaviors of individuals and groups.
>
> (Stan Davis 1984)

Edgar Schein (1992) argues that we must explore the more complex aspects of culture, if we are to enhance the quality of organizational life.

Schein believes that the roles of leaders are primarily to create, shape, manage, and sometimes destroy cultures. Managers or administrators, alternatively, live within cultures. For Schein, culture and leadership are two sides of the same coin. Leaders first create cultures when they create groups and organizations. Once a culture comes into existence, it determines the criteria for leadership and therefore, who will or will not become leaders. And it is leaders who are uniquely placed to appreciate if a culture is no longer helpful and take steps to change it so that the organization or group can survive in a changing environment.

A good example is the Tata Group, the 117-year-old Indian power-house responsible for that nation's first steel mill, power plant, and airline, among other achievements. But when India's long-protected economy was opened in 1991, Chairman Ratan Tata decided that for his companies to survive and thrive in a global economy he had to make innovation a priority – and build it into the DNA of the Tata group so that every employee at every company might think and act like an innovator (Scanlon 2009).

Today those companies have produced such innovative products as the $2000 Tata Nano car and include firms such as Jaguar Land Rover and Tata Consultancy Services. Cultural transformation is impossible without the leadership of top executives, so Tata created the Tata Group Innovation Forum (TGIF), a 12-member panel of senior Tata Group executives and some CEOs of the independently run companies. Key lessons learned from TATA in building a culture of innovation include the following:

- *Leadership Lays the Foundation*: The CEO is the cornerstone of any effort to build a culture of innovation. He or she needs to communicate the importance of innovation directly to managers and to celebrate innovative efforts, including those that failed but were valiant attempts. The paradox of leadership is that the best leaders may not lead but set the context so:
  - people know what to do;
  - people can generalize from one situation to another;
  - people have feelings of autonomy, control, and responsibility.

The real job of a leader is to set the culture so that people know what tradeoffs and judgment calls to make without constant supervision.

- *Hire the Right People. But* ... : In a targeted effort to build its capacity for breakthrough innovations, Tata Consultancy Services hired more PhD graduates. But broadly speaking, the processes are as important as the people when it comes to building a culture of innovation.

  General Electric (GE) values leaders and their criteria for hiring and evaluating leaders are fundamental to their innovative culture. They expect candidates to have:
  - The ability to stimulate and relish change and not be frightened or paralyzed by it; – Seeing change as an opportunity, not a threat;
  - A passion for excellence and hatred of bureaucracy and all the nonsense that comes with it;

   – Enormous energy and the ability to energize and invigorate others. They understand speed as a competitive advantage and see the total organizational benefits that can be derived from a focus on speed.
- *Build Innovation into the Organization*: A culture of innovation won't take root if you don't have clear systems for approving and funding ideas, for example, or an employee review process that includes innovation criteria.
- *Use Social Media to Tap Ideas and Encourage Collaboration:* In addition to IdeaMax, which will roll out to all Tata companies, Tata Consultancy Services has created Just Ask, a platform that allows employees to post and answer questions internally. Ten thousand questions were asked and answered within the first few months of its launch.
- *Celebrate Innovators:* In addition to the Tata Group-wide Innovista Innovation Competition, Jaguar Land Rover Chief Information Officer (CIO) runs annually what he calls the "Dragon's Den" Innovation Competition. Tata Consultancy Services runs its own Young Innovator Awards to reward and recognize successful innovators.

Key actions in leveraging culture

Organizational norms cover expectations about what are appropriate or inappropriate attitudes and behaviors, and socially created standards that help us interpret and evaluate behavior. However, important organizational norms that affect innovation culture are those attitudes and behaviors that can help or hinder the accomplishment of critical tasks, especially those which are rewarded or punished by group members and management. These typically include norms relating to performance, how we deal with people, and group or organization identity, and will also include the following:

- continuous improvement, innovation, and adaptation to change
- employee latitude and responsibility
- respect for people
- dedication to quality
- teamwork
- efficient and effective work flow.

Kotter and Heskett (1992) emphasize the importance of innovation and continuous improvement to long-term effectiveness by stating that "even contextually or strategically appropriate cultures will not promote excellent performance over long periods unless they contain norms and values that promote innovation and change". Their study over an 11-year period showed how a strong innovation-based culture outperforms a weak culture or a culture not focused on innovation. Their research proved the strong influence of innovation-based culture on a firm's long-term sustainability and economic performance.

Procter and Gamble (P&G), the worldwide consumer goods company, rewards innovation in several ways. First, it opened up the opportunity for anybody in the company to come out with new ideas. Employees whose ideas make it to the acceptance stage receive monetary incentives. The company also offers rewards to customers – virtually the rest of the world – for developing new product ideas.

To make sure that it captures ideas that will specifically work in emerging markets, the company has opened up R&D centers in emerging markets, including China, India, and Southeast Asia. As Bruce Brown, chief technology officer, wrote recently, "We don't want to count on serendipity as the basis for how we grow, because it's just too fundamental to how we do our work and drive our purpose". Whereas P&G used to take its standard American and European brands and figure out a way to reduce costs to tamp down product pricing elsewhere, now it wants to target new products specifically for newer markets.

A well-known luxury car manufacturer set up a competition among its staff who partnered with key vendors to help it build cars with better performance and mileage. The senior executive then brought together internal C-level people to short-list the ideas and allocated funding to the best ones. The vendors didn't do it for monetary reasons (although they received stipends for entertainment). They did it for the recognition factor – the winning ideas were announced across the organization and were funded.

A 2010 study of 1500 CEOs indicated that leaders rank creativity as the No. 1 leadership attribute needed for prosperity. It's the one thing that can't be outsourced, the one thing that's the lifeblood of sustainable competitive advantage. Unfortunately, most companies fail to unleash their most valuable resources: human creativity, imagination, and original thinking. They lack a systematic approach to building a culture of innovation, and then wonder why they keep getting beaten.

Josh Linkner (2011) identified seven key actions that organizations must carry out to develop a culture of innovation in their company:

1. fuel passion
2. celebrate ideas

3. foster autonomy
4. encourage courage
5. fail forward
6. think small
7. maximize diversity.

As an example of a key action we can see how a passion cultivated innovation at Shell. The Chief Scientist for Mobility at Shell, Wolfgang Warnecke, who has been passionate about cars and motorcycles since he was a boy, developed new, cleaner, and more efficient fuels which won him one of the car industry's top honors – the 2005 Professor Ferdinand Porsche Prize for innovation in automotive engineering. Wolfgang Warnecke was unique in the sense that his work brought the energy and the automotive industries together to work on the same strategy for the first time.

On the execution side of innovation discipline are idea generation, the building of business cases, and setting up suitable processes. Idea generation requires a willingness to engage in social computing. With current technology, social computing is the new knowledge and idea-generating domain. Some of the advantages include:

- value-add by connecting people
- ease of use
- minimal time commitment
- high visibility at low cost
- viral "word of mouth" can pay off
- the price tag – free!

Without opening itself to those newer forms of engagement, a company's idea generation might as well be stuck in the labs awaiting "Eureka!" moments. Innovative ideas also crop up in face-to-face activities – team meetings, brainstorming sessions, focus groups, and exhibit room aisles.

In both cases the company needs systems in place for managing the ideas, setting up some kind of vetting stage to winnow out the ones worth pursuing, and responding to contributors to let them know the status of their ideas. Those that make the cut will need to have business cases or justifications developed and processes mapped out for implementing the innovations. The itch of innovation provides the spark, but the discipline of managing innovation breathes life into it or determines that it's not the right idea right now.

Culture drives ideas

Organizational innovation is the successful implementation of creative ideas within the company. We can define creativity as "the production of novel and useful ideas by an individual or small group of individuals working together". This is not just a personality trait; a person's environment can significantly affect their creativity. Our experience has shown that creativity is more likely to occur when:

- people's skills overlap with their strongest interests, their deepest passions
- people have expertise about the problem or task
- people have developed personal characteristics such as independence, self-discipline, tolerance for ambiguity, perseverance in the face of frustration, and cognitive flexibility.

However, the most important predictor of creativity is the development of norms that support creativity in organizations. The cultural norms that support creativity are:

- Support for change
    - rewards and recognition for new ideas
    - positive attitudes toward change by management
    - people are expected to challenge the status quo
    - task-related conflict is encouraged rather than avoided
    - frequent constructive feedback on the work is provided.

As Michael Eisner, CEO of Disney, commented on innovative culture:

> This whole business starts with ideas, and we're convinced that ideas come out of an environment of supportive conflict, which is synonymous with appropriate friction. People at Disney are not afraid to speak their minds, be irreverent, and advocate strongly for ideas. That can be very noisy. It can be hard, too, because when you're loose, you say a lot of things, you challenge, you cajole, you provoke. Uninhibited discussion gets ideas out there so that we can look at them and make them better or just get rid of them if they don't work.

Established organizations are more likely to understand how to achieve success in each of their own areas within their unique cultures. They'll also understand what kinds of innovations have merit for their specific business models.

For example, Intel, a well-known global tech company known for its innovations in the microprocessor space puts in a great deal of effort to position its new products. It knows fairly precisely how to execute a given new product line and what resources and funding will be required to ensure success. Its company culture is predicated on supporting the development of new microprocessors.

Dell, another global company, also in the tech space, focuses its innovation energy on making improvements to its supply chain operations. For innovations in products, it generally relies on other companies to lead the way. So any product manager within that organization will have a tough time attracting the funding needed for innovating on the product side, but if an improvement can be made in how the company brings products to the market and gets them into customer hands, executive support and funding is readily available.

- Tolerance of calculated risk-taking
  - Mistakes are seen as a normal part of the job as long as the risk calculation was considered initially.
  - People are given the freedom to make changes.
  - Being "safe rather than sorry" is not always accepted.

The experience of Soichiro Honda, CEO of Honda is phenomenal as he continually took risk and failed so many times that his quote is an inspiration for all of us:

> Many people dream of success. To me success can only be achieved through repeated failure and introspection. In fact, success represents the 1 percent of your work which results from the 99 percent that is called failure.

Innovation requires freedom in many ways: the freedom to think out of the box, to explore and experiment, to venture – and most importantly to fail.

> If you give people freedom to innovate, . . . then you must also give them the freedom to fail. According to Deepak Seethi of AT&T, the organization of tomorrow will demand mistakes and failures. It is only by trying lots of initiatives that we can improve our chances that one of them will be a star.
>
> (Sloane 2006: 95)

Innovation is built on freedom – and freedom is built on trust. Without trust an enterprise will never be able to create an innovation culture. But trust, in this concept, is a two-way street: bottom–up employees need to trust their management. They need to be sure that lateral thinking and opposition is not fundamentally a bad thing that gets them a pink sheet. They need to know that management is open-minded and fair. On the other hand, management actually has to be open-minded.

What makes things even more complicated is that leaders witness their employees fail once, or more than once, but still need to keep up trust and motivation. Leaders should consider the wise words of Abraham Lincoln, "A man who is incapable of making a mistake is incapable of anything".

Leaders should do anything to avoid distrust, fear, and pressure. Instead, executives should get to know their employees better. Not in a classic fraud-prevention context (previous employment, education, certificates claimed, references to pre-hire drug screening), but personally. They can do this, for example, by walking randomly into their employees' offices and by engaging in small talk or by spontaneously crashing into project meetings. If they get to know the person behind the position better, building up mutual trust will be much easier.

The pace at which things move these days means that to ensure that organizations stay ahead of the pack, leaders need to embrace and encourage creativity. Sadly in some organizations there are real barriers to creativity. Some of those organizational impediments to creativity which we need to be alert to are:

- harsh criticism of new ideas
- intense internal competition
- avoidance of risk
- overemphasis on the status quo
- extreme time pressures
- unrealistic expectations for productivity
- distractions from creative work.

As Peter Drucker (1999) puts it: "Every organization – not just business – needs one core competence: Innovation." The core mission of any innovation leader should be the enhancement of a culture of innovation. Innovation depends on people and their personal skills, trust, teamwork, and commitment. Anybody improving these skills directly and indirectly helps to enhance a culture of innovation.

Organizational culture can be a powerful force that clarifies what's important and coordinates members' efforts without the costs and inefficiencies of close supervision. It also identifies a department or organization's distinctive competence to external constituencies. What do you want to be known for?

Managing culture requires creating the context in which people are encouraged and empower themselves to do their very best. Selection, socialization, and rewards should be used as opportunities to convey what's important to department members.

There is only one thing that is guaranteed in the organizational culture of a company, that is that a culture will form in your organization. The question is whether it will be one that helps or hinders your organization's ability to manage change and execute your strategic objectives. Thus, culture is too important to leave to chance; use your culture to execute your strategy and inspire innovation.

The rewards of rigor

Points to remember in deploying your innovation strategy

- Mix matters: Combine different types of innovation.
- Remember: Collaborative innovation is crucial. Great ideas can come from anywhere, including from employees, customers, and suppliers.
- Leaders must drive the creation of an innovation culture.
- Think broadly, act personally, and manage the mix of innovation. Broaden the discussion by figuring out how to address a single person's needs with a solution that will help a million people.
- Make your business model different: Don't just stick to what you've always done.
- Ignite innovation through business and technology integration.
- Defy collaboration limits: Truly think out of the box.

The rewards are numerous for putting in place a rigorous approach to managing innovation. A 2006 research project found that R&D investment alone could deliver a fairly level rate of return. But taking that R&D investment and adding a layer of innovation capability on top provides the potential for exponential growth. In particular, tying in holistic thinking and getting employees to participate increases company value.

Pcubed has developed a framework that identifies seven dimensions of strategic innovation that, when assembled, can produce a portfolio of outcomes that drive growth within an organization. These dimensions are:

1. *A managed innovation process*, which combines non-traditional and traditional approaches to business strategy.

2. *Strategic alignment* to put structures in place for making quick, smart decisions and executing effectively on them.
3. *Industry foresight* to understand emerging trends and identify the necessary success drivers.
4. *Consumer and customer insight* to understand both articulated and unarticulated needs.
5. *Core technologies and competencies* to leverage and extend corporate assets and capabilities.
6. *Organizational readiness* to help identify how ready the company culture is to take action.
7. *Disciplined implementation* to manage the route between inspiration and business impact.

It would be great if there were a shortcut to success – some implant technique to infuse an organization's culture with the discipline it needs to manage innovation in the same way it manages its other operations. Until that kind of innovative surgery has been perfected, an outside coach or advisor can help a company jumpstart the hard work of doing strategic thinking, developing a methodology, bringing experience to bear on the process, and assisting in execution.

The next chapter will discuss the launch of an innovation demand-capturing process that can be used in identifying ideas, selecting the ideas, and converting them into actions. As Drucker said, *"Creativity does not automatically lead to actual innovation"*, as such creativity, or ideas, generated without an investment case, business plan, and organizational structure to administer the plan (i.e., action-oriented follow-through) is meaningless. At best, creative ideas remain good intentions if not implemented.

CHAPTER 3

How Does One Architect an Organization's Innovation Landscape?

Currently, organizations seem quite captivated by the concept of innovation. Yet, as far as we know, innovation has been around as long as people have. So what's up with that? What's changed or what's missing in the corporate world or government that all this attention needs to be paid to innovation?

Certainly we can hardly read an article where a CEO or the president of an organization is not talking about innovation. And they need to. They need to look progressive and show that their organization is making strides in this area. The challenge we see is that many organizations don't have a strategy, formal process, or good evidence to support their claims. In order to gain better insight into their ability to drive innovation, organizations should be asking: What do we mean by innovation? What are we doing to foster a culture for innovation? What are we innovating around? What process do we have to ensure that our innovations are entering the market? Do we have an organizational structure to support innovation? Do we have the tools and technology in place to help manage the process?

The other thing we tend to see is that innovation is often equated with R&D. It's been proven in numerous studies that R&D is not necessarily a good indicator of successful innovation. In fact, there are well-reported examples of organizations that spend large sums of money on R&D, which are either no longer in business, or are going out of business, or are really struggling to distinguish themselves.

So, it's not that there's a problem with R&D in itself. Simply stated the process of managing innovation is intended in part to capture and manage the great wealth of ideas that were generated through formal research. The process can also be used to test new ideas against the corporate strategy in a meaningful way so that the organization can select the best innovations that are in line with its business direction.

This is really the discipline of managing innovation through a formal process, whereby an organization can gather a large number of ideas and systematically reduce the quantity and increase the quality or predictability of success. In other words select the best ideas, and nurture and develop them, while continuously testing and measuring these ideas against the business strategy or innovation success criteria. Developing the testing criteria could, for example, include asking questions such as: What is our business strategy? What is our innovation strategy? What does success look like? What markets do we serve in or want to compete in? How much of our budget do we have to devote to innovation? These are important considerations when it comes to thinking about how best to facilitate innovation. It's not simply a matter of saying, "Here's a great idea – let's run with it". It is about ensuring that good ideas can be systematically selected and tested to produce a more predictable business outcome within the prevailing organizational and market conditions.

Structured innovation approach: a project or an operational activity?

This is one of the great challenges among enterprises. Most people expect creativity to be unbounded, and you usually would not set parameters by saying, "We want you to come up with new ideas, great ideas – but follow these guidelines". It goes against the way most people think of and develop new ideas. I would like to believe that all organizations would want to embrace that creative spirit, but at the same time have a way to operationalize innovation at the back end.

When we think about putting a process behind innovation, we want to make it fun and easy at the front end – that is to say where people are able to capture their ideas very informally. And somehow we also want to grab all that information and start moving it into a very formal process – for example, a system inside your company that can quickly capture ideas. Maybe this can be done through a simple form on a website where a user writes up and saves a short description of their idea, which is then stored in a document library that's search-enabled.

From an organization or user standpoint, it will then be easy to search and find information about a product or project. The users of such a system can also broaden the search to selectively find related content, people, or communities. The system would also provide value to product managers who may only be looking for ideas that relate to their brand or product line and to harness the collective effort of many people.

We believe that providing a tool that's fun and easy to use will allow an organization to get broad participation in their innovation process and ideally allow every employee in the company access to the system. It has been proven that great ideas can come from anyone in an organization, especially if they're encouraged to participate in the process. It's highly unlikely that an organization will yield great results in the area of innovation if it identifies a few select individuals and appoints them to the position of innovators – "You are the great innovators. Go on and innovate!" An organization can certainly do that in the area of formal research, and you may have 20, or 30, or 100 dedicated researchers. The fact remains that any organization employing hundreds or thousands of people could have its next great breakthrough product, process, or service as the brainchild of one of these individuals. If you can't harness that, we think that's a big loss for the company.

One of the most intriguing things in today's world, with the emergence of social networking, is being able to share those ideas with communities. Community-driven innovation is a fascinating subject in its own right. You begin to see like-minded people in a company gravitating toward topics of personal or professional interest. The power of being able to share and collaborate with other individuals in a community who share these common interests most often produces great results. That kind of informal group behavior is very interesting, and is proving to be a source of some big innovations.

Crowdsourcing an upcoming approach

There are two forms of crowdsourcing: internal and external crowdsourcing. It is considered a form of internal crowdsourcing when some organizations want to keep the sourcing of ideas internal because they are very protective of their intellectual property. And then there are organizations today that have well-stated goals of wanting to include external crowdsourcing. For example, in 2006, Proctor & Gamble, an early and well-publicized adopter of crowdsourcing, stated in *Wired* magazine that more than 35 per cent of its new initiatives were generated from ideas sourced outside their organization. Today on P&G's website, their CEO, A.G. Lafley, shares that "external collaboration plays a key role in nearly 50 per cent of P&G's products".

Dell has an external website, called *IdeaStorm*, where its customers can post ideas. This is a public website and relies on social networking where a community can share comments and vote on the posted ideas.

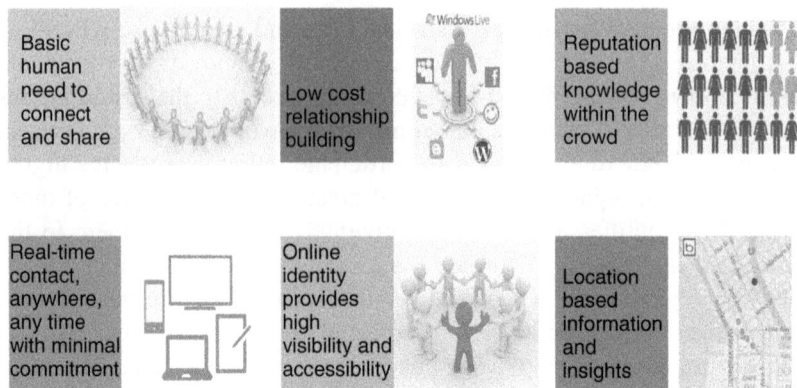

Figure 3.1 The new knowledge and idea-generating domain in social computing (*with the permission of Microsoft*)

People really are a company's greatest asset, and people innovate. If you make employees feel like they are part of the innovation process and make that process transparent, then individuals feel as though they are really contributing to the success of the organization, and they will make the time and effort to capture new ideas.

As social networking becomes more relevant, organizations should also consider implementing internal tools that provide similar capabilities to, for example, Facebook or Twitter. An individual that works, say, in sales or marketing, may have a great idea for a new product but may not know if it is technically feasible to manufacture. Imagine if that person could search on a few key words to identify people in the organization that have that required skill set. Using other collaboration tools such as instant messaging or email, they could easily arrange to meet over lunch and discuss the idea. That's a very powerful technique. Figure 3.1 (with the permission of Microsoft) above shows the new knowledge and idea-generating domain in social computing.

It also provides an organization with some interesting challenges: How do you take those tools that are very popular in the outside world and apply them internally to develop a strong community? We have seen customers who are expressing a lot of interest in these social networking tools, with a view to implementing similar capabilities within their companies.

Organizing the innovation landscape

We have found that the most exciting place and an area that gets the most attention from customers is the idea of a portal – a portal for any employee who has corporate web access to visit, and through filling out a very simple form to post their ideas. When that idea gets posted internally, a good ideation portal will typically create a community site where users can go back and look through the ideas, vote and comment on them, and add their own thoughts or suggestions. In other words, it's a very open, transparent site.

Many organizations start at that point. The downside of just implementing a portal is that in a short space of time a company could end up with, say, 10,000 ideas. At that point, how will they process so many ideas? What will they do with them? Are they intending to put individuals in a dark room and ask them to read every idea and make a decision? Individuals generally have their own perspectives, opinions, and biases that affect their selection criteria, so you can expect the system to fail over a relatively short period of time.

If the process can be partially or fully automated, then it becomes much easier for the innovation officer to focus on being a facilitator. The process in itself is not extremely complicated and can be likened to a series of filters. Let's say, for example, that the first set of filters is to test if an idea is in line with the company's overall business strategy. Let's say my company is in the business of making ski equipment – skis, helmets, boots, and accessories. I would logically expect to elevate ideas that are in line with the business and flag any ideas that are orthogonal as an exception. However, because all the ideas have been systematically captured, it would be possible to revisit a submitted idea any time in the future. An idea that is maybe today not in line with the company's core business may well be viable five years from now. By automating the process and testing against a predefined set of parameters, a company can come up with a set of ideas that are really aligned to the business strategy. Given below in Figure 3.2 is a screen shot of the Welcome/Landing page of an innovation process we configured jointly with Microsoft.

Ideally a company would have more than one core strategy and may include things like "Grow market share", "Grow revenue", "Delight customers", and so on. The company may well state these in its mission statement or guiding principles. By using modern techniques to search through all that posted information and by applying a set of filters, an innovation officer can very quickly produce a first pass that meets most of the set criteria and can then start looking closely at the innovation portfolio and manually intervening if necessary.

However, after we have used the system to expose the top ideas, we can still include and apply other types of tests to verify our idea: How much is this going to cost me? Can we create a good business case? Is there a market for this particular idea? At some point in the process you should

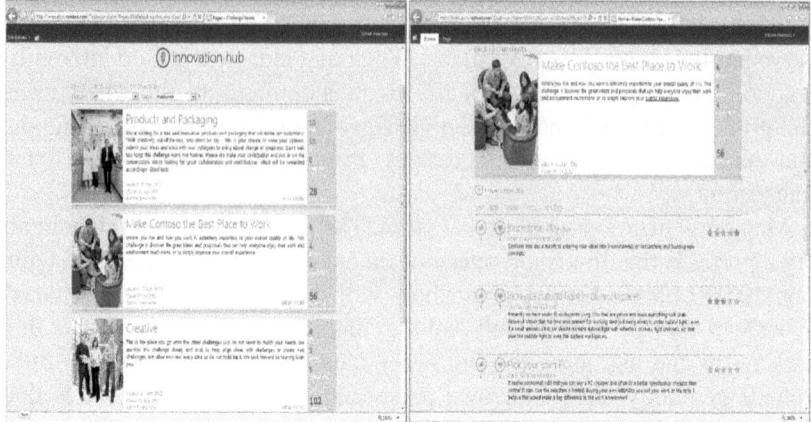

Figure 3.2 Screen shot of capturing ideas into Microsoft 2010 (*with permission from Microsoft*)

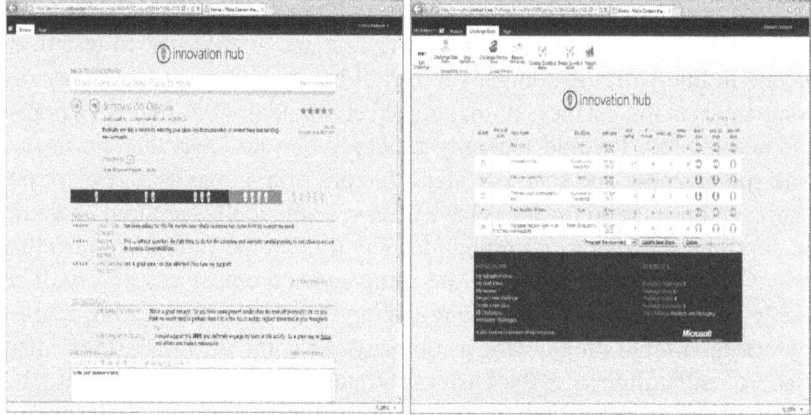

Figure 3.3 Screen shot of reviewing ideas, using Microsoft 2010 (*with the permission of Microsoft*)

expect to see prototypes and small projects develop in order to further validate the idea. The Figure 3.3 shows screen shot of reviewing ideas using Microsoft 2010.

Chief innovation officer's role in company's innovation landscape

A number of organizations are appointing chief innovation officers. I like to think of this role as being that of a facilitator rather than a manager – an individual who can collaborate well across divisional or corporate boundaries, look broadly across an organization to take advantage of many different corporate-wide initiatives and programs, and has the ability to connect technologies, people, and processes.

A skilled innovation officer who has the oversight of the full innovation portfolio and other corporate projects is in a unique position to connect the dots and provide the guidance necessary for the organization to combine new ideas, products, and services in order to create breakthrough innovations. There are many good examples of that happening in the world.

The ability to identify and combine separate and seemingly different ideas is proving to be an interesting challenge to businesses that may have traditionally separated products and services. An organization may have a good track record of delivering a specific product. Today we are continuously challenging our traditional thinking. For example, it's no longer enough to develop a good music player if there is no connected service for downloading music or developing a phone that has no web capability or embedded Global Positioning System (GPS).

A good example of how Microsoft benefited from combining seemingly different products and services can be seen with Xbox. The first high-definition console was Xbox 360. It was the first to digitally deliver games, music, TV shows, and movies in 1080-pixel high definition, and the first to bring Facebook and Twitter to the living room. And with Project Natal for Xbox 360, it was the first to deliver controller-free experiences that anyone can enjoy.

And in a world of software plus services, the groundbreaking part of Microsoft game strategy is Xbox LIVE. Today, more than 23 million people around the world routinely connect to the service to play games, chat, listen to music, watch movies, and much more.

Developing your innovation landscape

The business needs of today are changing in the approach to innovation. In the past, a company's thinking was that only the top minds can make meaningful contributions and that ideation is a strategy for innovation. This is an outdated concept. In today's practices we see the following:

- Ideas are potential investments.
- Ideas need to be managed.
- Everyone has a voice.
- Innovation is a process.

The Innovation & Portfolio Management (IPM) landscape will create an environment that fosters the flow of creative ideas across an organization while providing a structure to collect and evaluate investment ideas. Objective investment decisions maximize business benefits, balance risks, and address corporate constraints. Portfolio, program, and end-to-end product lifecycle management (PLM) processes provide the visibility and control necessary to achieve strategies and realize targeted organizational benefits, and drive sustainable market success. The IPM landscape is an integrated management discipline that applies to all forms of innovation.

The most difficult part of the innovation equation is not "what?" but "how to?"

The use of a collaborative consulting approach drives IPM delivery from existing organizational capabilities to provide immediate results. Other organizational enhancements – process, technology, capability evolution – can then be carefully planned and rolled out across the organization, creating the opportunity to benefit from more advanced management techniques across the IPM life cycle.

As innovation is the conversion of knowledge and ideas into new or improved products, processes, or services to gain a competitive advantage, businesses today face no shortage of ideas; rather, they lack the ability to determine their value in a systematic, timely, and cost-effective way. Developing an IPM process can help companies encourage people to share their ideas, rate them, and make critical decisions about their associated risks, benefits, and strategic value. Figure 3.4 below shows

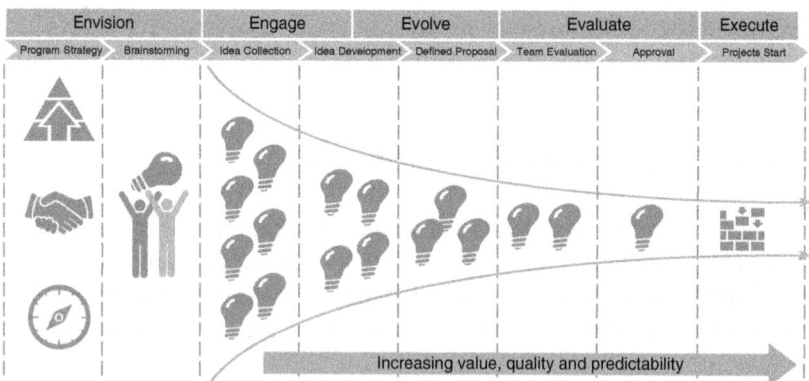

Figure 3.4 The pipeline approach to envision, engage, evolve, evaluate, and execute IPM process (*permission given by Microsoft*)

the process that aims to envision, engage, evolve, evaluate, and execute the ideas. These 5Es were developed by Microsoft, and Pcubed supports this process implementation with specific activities defined in the phases.

In order to facilitate the innovation process effectively, organizations need a solution that allows them to manage innovation in an objective, strategic, and scalable manner. Because organizations often lack the resources necessary to act on all contributed ideas, they must manage innovation through a systematic process that facilitates the selection of optimal ideas which have the highest strategic value.

The primary challenges associated with managing innovation processes are as follows:

- difficulty investing in the right ideas for the right market with the right resources
- no structured process in place to drive transparency, metrics, or cross-functional collaboration
- no good way to measure innovation
- difficulty selecting the right ideas
- little opportunity for all employees to contribute
- lack of coordination
- no way to socialize the idea with a wide audience
- limited customer insight
- long development periods.

Looking at these challenges, a common thread shows through: speed and coordination are very important. Thus, collaboration is essential. The second thread is the lack of good processes to turn insights into ideas into action.

Stages in envision, engage, evolve, evaluate, and execute

(The description of the 5E approach was written with the permission of Microsoft)

Consider a typical scenario, where an employee has an idea about a product's enhancement but there is no formal method or process in the company through which this idea can be captured and evaluated. Based on some assumptions, the employee brings the idea to his manager.

The employee's manager likes the idea and suggests that he should present it at the next leadership meeting. The leadership team also likes his idea but needs more business intelligence and creates a task team. Now this idea-generation and innovation process is fragmented. People are challenged to identify the right experts within the company to find what research may have already been conducted on the same topic. They don't have tools in place to develop a comprehensive business case. They can't socialize their idea with the entire company and also receive no rewards or incentives for the contribution and idea submission. It requires tremendous tenacity on the part of the person with the idea to push it through the organization.

If we consider that objectively, the entire process is shown to contain some of these top challenges:

- long lead times
- the involvement of a limited number of experts
- no structured processes in place to drive – transparency, metrics, cross-functional collaboration
- a significant amount of work is required by employees to refine their ideas
- no method to socialize the idea with a wide audience and no incentive to contribute

The IPM solution uses the Microsoft platform to help integrate the innovation funnel with R&D discovery or other investigative research to help customers address this end-to-end innovation management process through the following stages of envision, engage, evolve, evaluate, and execute as shown in Figure 3.5 below:

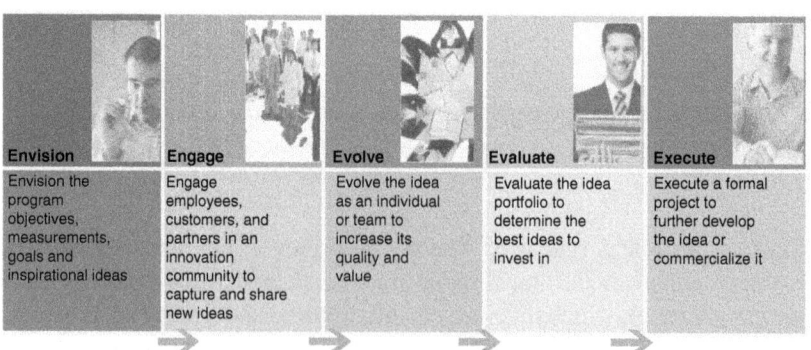

Envision	Engage	Evolve	Evaluate	Execute
Envision the program objectives, measurements, goals and inspirational ideas	Engage employees, customers, and partners in an innovation community to capture and share new ideas	Evolve the idea as an individual or team to increase its quality and value	Evaluate the idea portfolio to determine the best ideas to invest in	Execute a formal project to further develop the idea or commercialize it

Figure 3.5 Description of the envision, engage, evolve, evaluate, and execute approach (*with the permission of Microsoft*)

Envision

In this envisioning state it is important for the senior leadership team to inspire the innovation vision and set an expectation on the structure and mission of the innovation intended. This must be clearly supported by initiative objectives, measurements, goals, and underlying cultural inspiration for idea generation. If leaders only talk about innovation but do not really move in this envisioning direction, it'll be a big waste of time and a distraction for the company. It is best to know that up front.

Engage

In order to foster innovation, the organization must first establish and prioritize business drivers and metrics, as described in Part II of this book. It then engages employees, customers, and partners in an innovation community to capture and share new ideas. The ideas are captured through a centralized and collaborative portal. Employees can search to find experts both internally and externally, and they can search back-end systems to gather sales history data to develop a business case. Workflow and collaboration technology will then help create a cross-functional team and collaborative workspace for idea submission.

Evolve

The ideas can evolve because individuals or teams increase the quality and value of the ideas through interactions and secondary data. Mainly, ideas will be formulated according to business cases that include strategic impact, market potential, financial analysis, and Strength, Weakness, Opportunities and Threats (SWOT) analysis, and they can then be published for review. Other members of the community can provide ratings, reviews, and feedback to help determine the idea's priority and value.

Evaluate

Select ideas according to business parameters, analyze the portfolio, and objectively evaluate ideas. In this stage, high-rated ideas are approved for investment. A significant part of this stage is the feedback of ideas not accepted. Ideas can be on hold, postponed to the next investment cycle, or rejected; however, the reasons for the selections made must be transparent and visible to the participants and the organization.

Execute

Build the project team and execute the project while taking into consideration design, market potential, and legal evaluation. After the review is finalized, a design document is prepared that provides a project workspace for team collaboration. Assign resources and skills to projects in order to track project progress. Give the final funding approval to selected projects, and proceed to delivery processes such as New Product Development (NPD), enabling end-to-end project management and tracking, from idea to commercialization to retirement.

The focus Microsoft has on innovation process management solutions is built around three key aspects of the overall process of managing innovation. This process is facilitated by an integrated enterprise project management and business productivity infrastructure that includes collaboration, unified communications, business intelligence, enterprise content management, and enterprise search.

The three aspects of the overall process are:

- *Ideation and knowledge capture* helps you and your teams to share ideas easily and rapidly to promote a culture of innovation. This culture comes into existence by increasing participation and then the quality and quantity of contributed ideas. By collaborating to solve problems and develop ideas, teams can gain incremental benefits or create an entirely new product, service, or process. Collaboration encourages feedback, gauges interest, strengthens teams, and further develops concepts to transform them into well-thought-out ideas.
- *Process and knowledge management (PKM)* helps you to investigate, formulate, evaluate, develop, and promote an idea from concept to sanctioned project while involving key stakeholders internal and external to an organization. PKM provides you with the capability to enforce process structure and discipline without stifling innovation. In addition, you gain the ability to manage the lifecycle of all-digital content flowing in and out of the solution.
- *PPM* helps you to evaluate ideas according to governing strategic objectives, such as growth, globalization, innovation, and customer loyalty. PPM provides functionality to develop and implement operational parameters, such as workforce resource constraints, capital expenditures, project funds, and competing investments. PPM also

provides performance metrics capabilities, such as sales forecasts, inventory, and budgeted versus actual expenses. You gain the ability to analyze macro environmental factors, such as market dynamics, market size, and industry trends. You can also track up-to-date progress against forecasted metrics and make informed decisions to optimize budget, resources, and time constraints, so you can meet market demands, such as market windows of opportunity to gain first mover advantages.

Empowering innovation

People like to be involved. Employees who feel empowered and are recognized by their organization for doing great things motivate others to do great work. So I would encourage organizations, large and small, to invite employees to participate in their innovation efforts, develop internal innovation portals, make the process transparent, demonstrate that their input is valued, review ideas regularly, and reward people for successful efforts.

There are different types of reward programs that organizations can consider implementing. An incentive program in one organization may reward an individual or team by paying a bonus when a selected idea develops into a product, whereas an organization in another part of the world may offer a chairman's award. Incentive programs should, therefore, take into account different cultural and business environments.

When a company first creates an ideation portal, the site would probably do very well for the first five or six months while it's fresh and on everyone's mind. After that the site's usage will tend to decline like the old suggestion box in a corporate lobby, unless the site is continuously updated and new programs are put in place.

One technique that encourages employees to keep using the system is to issue what Microsoft refers to as a challenge. For illustration, a product Vice President (VP) may invite ideas for a new gaming console. In doing so, you achieve a number of things: The product group has set up some parameters as to the type of idea – in other words, this is inviting ideas for a console, not a controller. The invitation to participate may be sent directly to employees in that division to jumpstart the process. And each time a new challenge is issued, the site is refreshed.

Marketing the innovation programs internally, driving challenges, and managing the portal and submissions are some of the important responsibilities of the innovation officer. These will ensure that the innovation portal is not a one-time thing.

Let the innovative magic happen

I will go back to something I said earlier: people. Great innovations come from people in an organization. If a company does not recognize that fact and does not invite its employees to participate in the process or to capture the creativity, then they have a much greater challenge. There is no shortage of ideas, so that is not the root cause of the problem. The challenge is how to quickly identify the great ideas, nurture them, give your organization every opportunity to be innovation leaders, and – for most corporations, of course – drive revenue and profits. Try to leverage your people and their talents. If an organization can do that, then magic will probably happen.

CHAPTER 4

How Does One Launch an Innovation Process in your Organization?

Malcolm Gladwell, author of the wildly popular book *The Tipping Point* and other big idea bestsellers, recently spoke as the keynoter at the Project Management Institute's annual conference on the topic of organizational culture and innovation. During that talk he made the observation that there's a paradox with companies considered wildly innovative: "When you look closely at them, at cultures that seem to have what it takes, they're followers and borrowers, not leaders and inventors."

As an example, Gladwell cited Xerox PARC, the famous research facility in Palo Alto that in its earliest days pulled together dozens of distinguished researchers and gave them nearly unlimited funds to think up ideas. And this they did with a passion. They came up with a multitude of brilliant ideas: the idea of the computer mouse, the concept of the GUI, laser printing, and optical disk technology. But it took others – Steve Jobs is a famous example – to apply those ideas and make those innovations successful. They borrowed from the ideas that PARC thought up, tweaked them, and found much greater success.

I cite Gladwell because he recognizes a fundamental characteristic of innovation: "Innovation at its best is a mass phenomenon, not an elite phenomenon." The most effective innovations aren't typically totally new and untried ideas; they're ideas that already exist in some form that somebody adapts to their own purposes. Companies that want to instill innovation in their corporate cultures need to be able to capture those ideas and figure out how to apply them at the appropriate levels.

Pcubed has developed an approach that leads its clients through three phases to drive effective innovation management, superimposing on the 5Es approach given in the earlier chapter. The three phases are organizational awareness and innovation intent, innovation "ideation" and portfolio, and innovation delivery. Figure 4.1 shows the three phases with detailed activities.

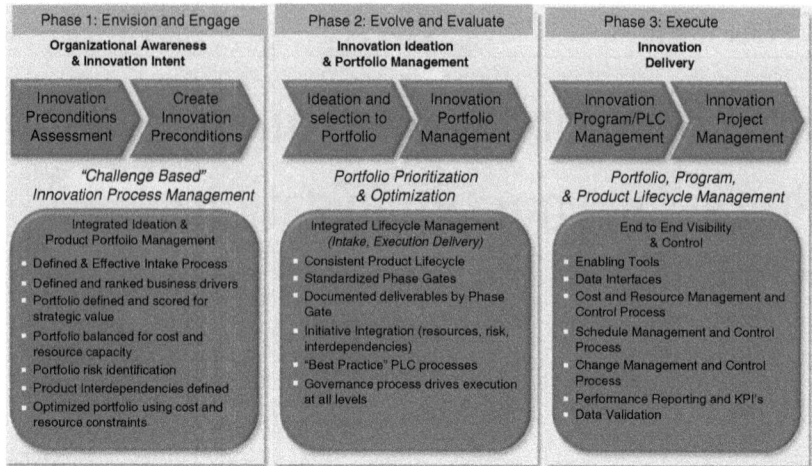

Phase 1: Envision and Engage	Phase 2: Evolve and Evaluate	Phase 3: Execute
Organizational Awareness & Innovation Intent	**Innovation Ideation & Portfolio Management**	**Innovation Delivery**
Innovation Preconditions Assessment / Create Innovation Preconditions	Ideation and selection to Portfolio / Innovation Portfolio Management	Innovation Program/PLC Management / Innovation Project Management
"Challenge Based" Innovation Process Management	*Portfolio Prioritization & Optimization*	*Portfolio, Program, & Product Lifecycle Management*
Integrated Ideation & Product Portfolio Management	Integrated Lifecycle Management *(Intake, Execution Delivery)*	End to End Visibility & Control
• Defined & Effective Intake Process • Defined and ranked business drivers • Portfolio defined and scored for strategic value • Portfolio balanced for cost and resource capacity • Portfolio risk identification • Product Interdependencies defined • Optimized portfolio using cost and resource constraints	• Consistent Product Lifecycle • Standardized Phase Gates • Documented deliverables by Phase Gate • Initiative Integration (resources, risk, interdependencies) • "Best Practice" PLC processes • Governance process drives execution at all levels	• Enabling Tools • Data Interfaces • Cost and Resource Management and Control Process • Schedule Management and Control Process • Change Management and Control Process • Performance Reporting and KPI's • Data Validation

Figure 4.1 Pcubed phased approach in supporting innovation with Microsoft Solution

Phase 1: growing innovation muscle

The first phase is what we call organizational awareness and innovation intent. You need the right culture to respond to innovation. And only by understanding how attuned the current culture is to innovation, will you know how far it has to evolve in order to sustain a culture of thinking about and supporting innovation.

An innovation precondition assessment examines a number of factors, such as what the senior leadership role is in guiding cultural change, who the key stakeholders are at all levels in the company (and externally), how diverse expectations are managed, and what the structure and mission of an innovation group would look like. If leaders are only talking about innovation but not really moving in that direction, it'll be a big waste of time and distraction for the company. Best to know that up front.

The critical success factors are a leadership-defined strategy for growing innovation muscle, a commitment to making innovation a core strategy for company growth and renewal, a pledge of long-term funding, and a time horizon that accommodates learning and adjustments to processes. Likewise, appropriate strategic, portfolio, and project metrics need to be tied to risk assessment. Also, the company's mainstream culture should accommodate the co-existence of an entrepreneurial culture.

Another critical step in Phase 1 is the conduct of innovation diagnostics by using a set of precondition assessment questions. Figure 4.2 shows the

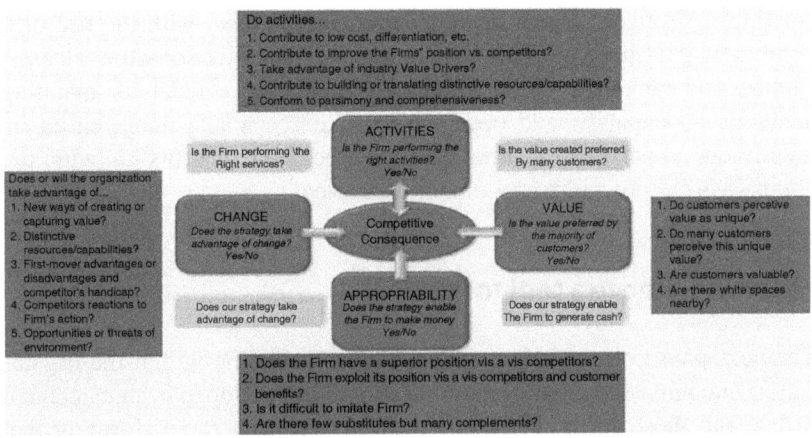

Figure 4.2 Innovation diagnostic with precondition assessment

innovation diagnostic with precondition assessment for companies. There are four key areas to assess your competitive posture:

- Activities – Is the firm performing the right activities?
- Value – Is the value created preferred by the majority of customers?
- Appropriability – Does the strategy enable the firm to generate a revenue stream?
- Change – Does the strategy take advantage of change?

Another critical factor is geography. As an international company we've seen the impact of a country's culture on the outcomes of these innovation assessments too. In the United Kingdom, for example, there's a bias toward being employed. The innovations that people come up with will be company-directed for that reason. In Asian countries, people tend to be much more entrepreneurial. I've had many conversations with people in Hong Kong and Taiwan who tell me, "If I come up with a good idea, why should I contribute that to the company?" The United States, on the other hand, prefers to use legal structures to ensure that innovations stay within company boundaries; American operations seem not the least bit squeamish about taking current and former employees to court to retain the ideas they've developed, presumably during company time. Innovation strategy needs to take into consideration cultural elements to drive the "right" behaviors.

One company we worked with wanted to bolster its R&D operation to better align it with the overall corporate budget and strategies. After assessing the current state of R&D, the leadership team set a goal of creating a stronger "return on innovation investment" with the use of a systematic decision tree. This would help it to prioritize product releases, capture and rank new ideas, develop a governance model for mapping demand and capacity, and optimize its resource management based on investment opportunities. The decision-tree approach fits in with the company's culture and management processes.

Phase 2: we have a tool for that

The next phase of executing an innovation discipline within the organization encompasses creating new ideas and using portfolio management to manage those ideas. PPM provides an approach for performing that prioritization as well as managing benefits realization – making sure your company is gaining the benefits promised by its investments in innovation.

Idea generation is an area that frequently requires a tool. Software can be used effectively to create campaigns or challenges across the organization to promote idea generation, to accept and save those ideas in a repository, to categorize them by particular parameters, to set up a notification system for sub-committees to review ideas, and to post ideas in a way that allows employees to vote on them so that the best-ranked ones rise to the top of the slush pile for a short list.

Imposing a portfolio process on the management of innovation ideas allows you to figure out what the right innovation portfolio mix is, whether radical or incremental, and whether aligned to specific corporate strategies or unaligned.

The critical success factors for Phase 2 are these:

- the designation of governance roles in place of hierarchy
- a transparent evaluation and prioritization process
- the compilation of an innovation portfolio that hedges bets linked to strategic intent while leaving room for opportunism
- having people for new roles with the competency requirements, especially in areas of high uncertainty innovations
- maintaining a balance between incubation and interaction with mainstream business, which includes consistently "seeding" incubation of ideas and performing joint acceleration activities.

You may find that you'll want to manage the two primary innovation strengths independently – incremental innovations versus more "destructive" ones – to make sure each has a place within the portfolio. The former frequently has immediate business value; the latter, while higher-risk, may have greater ultimate value that's worthy of funding. By separating their management, smart companies don't have to worry about pitting one directly against the other.

Pcubed worked with an automotive intelligence company to deploy an ideation and portfolio management process. A key element of the system was to capture cost improvements, which went into the business case for each idea. We developed a "hybrid" approach to ensure that ideas and projects were assessed not just on their own merits but also based on how they fitted in with the overall portfolio mix. As part of that project Pcubed developed detailed processes from inputs to gateways to outputs; each stage had clear roles and responsibilities so that nothing fell through the cracks. That commitment to follow-through is important for earning employee trust within the innovation discipline.

Another R&D environment company we worked with came up with a portfolio mix based on five classifications of R&D projects. The first level targeted projects that catered to client needs for the existing market. The next level had "anticipative" types of ideas, which proposed projects that anticipated the new needs of the client and/or market. This level could be influenced by changes that were legal, political, or technological. The middle level was "prospective", where the projects targeted new or different market segments that involved the creation of new service lines and new technologies. The fourth addressed issues or specific risks in existing services and existing markets in the same industry. The fifth covered "blue sky ideas", the riskiest of the lot.

Here's how the five categories were invested:

- application: 60 per cent
- anticipative: 15 per cent
- prospective: 10 per cent
- secure, more risk-based: 5 per cent
- innovation: 10 per cent

Once the client created these groupings, the categorizing and management of ideas for innovation became much easier for them.

Phase 3: delivering on the promises

The final phase is managing innovation delivery, including tracking and promoting innovation projects. The unique nature of innovations – things that haven't been done before – calls for an organization to sort out its project management strategies when there's a high level of uncertainty in areas such as technical know-how, market need, and resource expertise. Also, it's essential that the company have a mechanism for motivating entrepreneurial teams and individuals. Frequently, the people who thrive in innovative environments aren't inspired by the same rewards as people who work on the day-to-day operations side. While the motivations may be different, both need to have a place at the table.

The critical success factors for instilling innovation discipline are these: an innovation-driven reward structure, staging investments tied to project milestones – especially important for more complex and radical innovations – and systems for building the organization's learning-based processes and tools for reducing uncertainties. Figure 4.3 below shows the integration of Microsoft and PTC technology with the Pcubed innovation, portfolio and program management process (PTC is a cutting-edge PLM tools company, which is a global partner with Pcubed and Microsoft).

One Pcubed client in the financial services industry used a portfolio management tool to optimize its portfolio of innovation-related projects. The company achieved a 27 per cent savings on resources by managing the delivery process of those projects more efficiently.

Another company, this one in the luxury automotive sector, turned to Pcubed to develop a system for capturing new ideas. (It didn't use the term "innovation", but still the focus was on new ideas.) One such idea turned

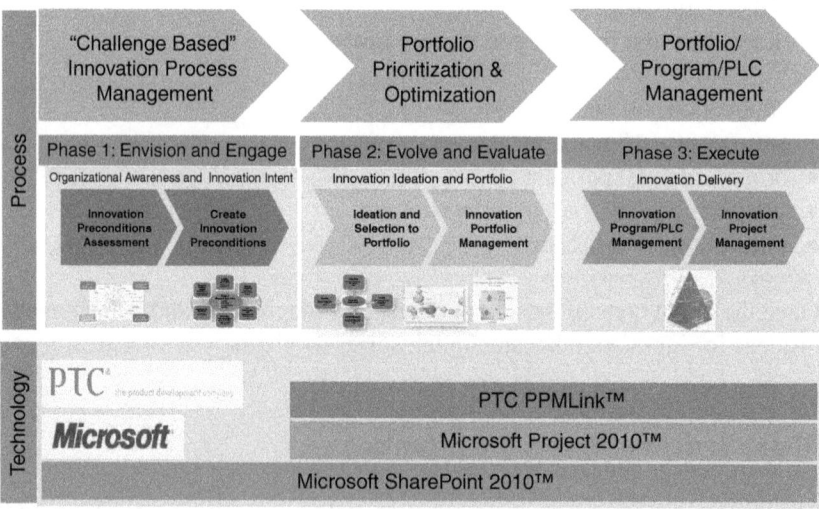

Figure 4.3 Integration of Microsoft and PTC technology with the Pcubed innovation, portfolio and program management process (*written with the permission of Microsoft and PTC*)

out to be a process whereby the person ordering a car would be invited to come to the factory to watch a portion of the manufacturing process and to choose the colors of the seats and the body. This VIP treatment fit in nicely with the "secure" innovation mold and turned out to be quite popular with customers.

We can't do everything!

Tips for creating an effective innovation culture

Align growth and innovation strategy: Pursue several alternative growth platforms. Ensure the innovation strategy is well defined in the areas of performance, metrics, and goals.

Practice portfolio management: Create a closer cross-functional process with specific steps and transparent decision criteria for assessment, selection, decision-making, governance, and balancing the mix of projects; use "internal discipline".

Manage the pipeline: Continue managing after a project enters the pipeline.

Let the market help you innovate: Reduce market research, release more products, and let the market dictate which ones are worth major investment.

Instill innovation as an organizational discipline: It requires the same processes and forethought as any other management practice within the organization.

You may be wondering what happens once the pipeline is brimming with ideas? How do you prioritize your innovation ideas to focus on the ones with the most promise? PPM, of course, plays a role in this. Pcubed advises organizations to consider four broad areas in determining the rank order: activities, value, appropriateness, and change. Each area feeds into competitive consequence, which is also part of the prioritization process. Let's go over each area.

First is the activity itself. Is the firm performing the right activities? These are activities that contribute to low cost, differentiation, or the like. They contribute to improving the firm's position compared to competitors' positions. They take advantage of industry value drivers (the areas that expose where opportunities exist that can help a company improve its business). They contribute to building or translating distinctive resources and capabilities. And they conform to parsimony or cost-cutting imperatives and comprehensiveness.

Next is value as perceived by the majority of customers. Would the customer perceive the value of the innovation as unique? Do *many* customers perceive this unique value? Are the customers who would consider it unique valuable to the company? Are there white spaces nearby – responsibilities related to customers that aren't "owned" by anybody in the company and which therefore get insufficient attention?

Third is appropriateness. In the commercial sector, would the innovation allow the company to make money? In the public sector, would it provide a vitally needed service? In both scenarios, would the innovation provide a superior position compared to competitors or alternative services? Does the firm exploit its position compared to competitors? Would competitors have a difficult time imitating the firm's innovations? Are there few substitutes but many *complements* to the innovation?

Finally, there's the change aspect of the innovation. Will the idea enable the organization to take advantage of new ways of creating or capturing value? Does it require distinctive resources or capabilities? Will it provide first-mover advantages or disadvantages and will it handicap competitors? What will be the reaction from competitors? Does the innovation represent an opportunity or a threat in the environment in which the company operates?

Sustaining your innovation practices

I've seen many companies pick up innovation as a fad and then dump it when it falls out of favor as a business magazine cover theme. By doing the hard work and following the phases I've outlined here for executing innovation within your organization as a true discipline, you'll be assured of its sustainability.

If we take the example of the manufacturing sector, to empower excellence and sustain performance the enterprise needs to look at four key performance networks:

- Customer network – This is growing customer relationships by observing and serving customers globally to drive growth with profitable proximity.
- Innovation network – This is accelerating innovation by managing innovation across boundaries to accelerate the time taken to reach the market.
- Value network – This is managing the global supply chain so that it is orchestrated to an agile and responsive network which maximizes efficiency under dynamic market conditions.

- Manufacturing network – This is improving operations that drive flexibility and integrated manufacturing to deliver operational excellence.

These performance networks are depicted in Figure 4.4, where the innovation network helps to accelerate managing innovation across boundaries to meet the time-to-market-launch dates.

In the manufacturing sector the innovation life cycle and product life cycle are well integrated to convert the ideas into a competitive and sustainable advantage. Figure 4.5 below shows the innovation network as part of the company's performance network that depends on the critical interrelationship between the innovation and product life cycles. It also depicts how the innovation network converts ideas into products that give a competitive advantage or a strategic leverage in the market.

If your investment in innovation is strategically relevant, it will align with your business model, operations, and products or services and markets. By tying your portfolio of diverse innovation investments to strategic intent and level of risk, you'll be exploiting new opportunities without "betting the farm". Your company will be able to navigate the divide between innovation and dominant operational excellence cultures. And

Figure 4.4 Excellence and sustaining performance network in manufacturing sector (*with the permission of Microsoft and PTC*)

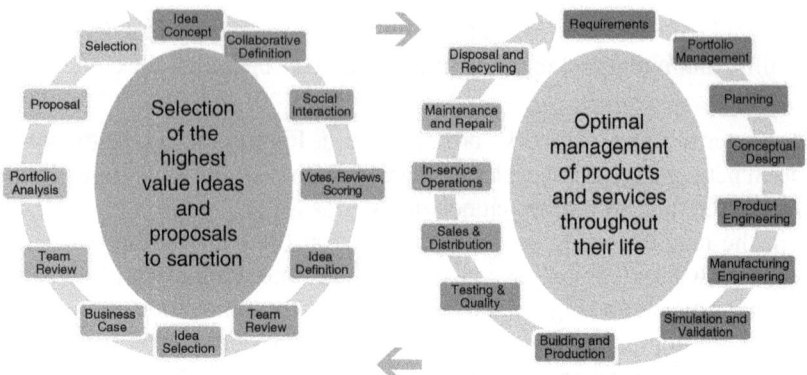

Figure 4.5 Innovation network showing the conversion of ideas into products for gaining market advantage (*with permission from Microsoft*)

your leadership team will be prepared to bring a new discipline to the chaotic, uncharted waters of new ideas.

As Charles Darwin famously pointed out, "It's not the strongest of the species that survives, nor the most intelligent either, but the one most responsive to change". Innovation calls for change. By wrapping that into a management practice you'll ensure its continued success. My own experience has shown that companies which can develop resilience, both in the organization and its staff, have the essential ingredients for business survival in this rapidly changing world. These key ingredients are:

- *Attitude toward change* – perceived as challenge rather than threat, therefore accompanying anxiety is lower. Supports change and development in staff and has a more positive attitude toward lifelong learning.
- *Quality of communication* – direct and frank, with low levels of subversive rumor and gossip. Makes the implicit explicit where possible, so there is less chance of misunderstanding. Staff comments are welcome.
- *Staffs see themselves as part of the organization* – have some ownership of corporate goals, while retaining their identity and individuality.
- Clear about flexible power structure – people remain clear about their changing roles and responsibilities as the company responds to changing conditions.
- *Sense of reality* – an accurate self-image of the organization exists, together with a good level of understanding of the marketplace and its implications for the company and its staff.
- *Quality of relationships* – high level of trust, as hidden agendas and covert expectations are minimized.

Learning to act and work in an innovative way

The last four chapters provided a holistic view of how companies can adopt a disciplined way of thinking for their people, process, and the utilization of technology to enhance their market positions. We are responsible for what we are, and whatever we wish ourselves to be, we have the power to make ourselves.

If what we are now is the result of our own past actions, it certainly follows that whatever we wish to be in future can be produced by our present actions, so we have to know how to act and work.

You may say, "What is the use of learning how to work and act? Everyone works in some way or other in this world". But there is such a thing as frittering away our energies … by knowing how to work, one can obtain the greatest results. You must remember that all action and work are aimed at bringing out the power of the mind, which is already there, or at waking up the soul or the creative energy in oneself. The power is inside every one of us, so is knowledge; the different kinds of work and actions are like blows to bring them out, to cause the "brilliancy" to wake up inside us. The next chapter will dive into how we can enable good innovative habits within ourselves and in our organization.

CHAPTER 5

How Does One Enable Good Innovative Habits?

Have you ever looked at super creative or innovative people and felt they are special beings blessed with gifts? Have you felt that you are not as fortunate? I used to feel this way. I have since learned that creativity is more about psychology than intellect, and there are no secrets to being creative. Actually, there is no such thing as "being more creative"; you are already a "creative being".

Swami Vivekananda stated in a speech that "Knowledge is inherent in man. No knowledge comes from outside, it is all inside. What we say a man 'knows' should, in strict psychological language, be what he 'discovers' or 'unveils', what a man 'learns' is really what he discovers by taking the cover off his own soul, which is a mine of infinite knowledge".

We say Newton discovered gravitation. Was it sitting anywhere in a corner waiting for him? It was in his own mind, the time came, and he found it out. All knowledge that the world has ever received comes from the mind; the infinite library of the universe is in your own mind. The external world is simply the suggestion, the occasion, which sets you to study your own mind, but the object of your study is always your own mind.

The falling of an apple gave the suggestion to Newton, and he studied his own mind. He rearranged all the previous links of thought in his mind and discovered a new link among them, which we call the law of gravitation. It was neither in the apple nor in anything in the center of the earth. All knowledge, therefore, is in the human mind. In many cases it is not discovered but remains covered, and when the covering is slowly taken off we say "we are innovative or creative". Thus, ideas are the source of innovation and the vital spark of all human change, improvement, and progress. Creating an innovative culture and managing the ideation process in a purposeful and systematic way will advance knowledge through this process of uncovering.

I'm sure we can all relate to moments when we felt stuck trying to tap into our own creativity. Did you know that this block is merely your mind at work? Your mind is creating all sorts of assumptions, self-imposed constraints, and self-limiting inhibitions. I have found that we can remove these assumptions just by being in the moment; start doing and stop thinking.

How to change oneself to uncover the potential

In my workshops I normally pose this question to my audience, "Do you know why snakes have to lose their skins?" I normally get a range of answers; however, some get the right answer which is "If the snakes do not shed their skins, they cannot grow. As such they will suffocate in their old skin and die".

My asking that question was to enlighten the audience that "shedding of the skin" is equivalent to the ability of the human to "unlearn the past" in order to grow and achieve success in the present. According to the *Oxford English Dictionary*, the word "unlearn" – a verb – means an attempt "to discard (something learned) from one's memory". The *Cambridge Advanced Learner's Dictionary* defines it very suitably to meet the present-day understanding of "unlearn". It says that to "unlearn" is to make an effort to forget your usual way of doing something so that you can learn a new and better way.

Habits help us do everything, every day. Our unconscious mind eliminates the need for us to think consciously about each small step and action involved in everything from making a latte to operating the photocopier. Our mind wants to make a memory and make the thinking and behaviour automatic so that our conscious mind can deal with more immediate and complex things. That's the good news. The bad news is that habits can also have a negative grasp on our mind and behaviour. Bad habits die hard, are easy to resume, even when we think we've stopped them, as many reformed smokers or alcoholics will attest. So to unlearn is to remove, discard, forget, and expel undesirable things from our minds. It also means keeping the mind free from unwanted information, deleting irrelevant data from the memory, and having more free space in the mind for future thinking. Unlearning is the way or path to move from self-defeating methods of performing something to different methods, leading to the road of success. Unlearning is the method of preparing a list of parameters that have to be discarded from life for a better life.

It is important for all of us to learn more about unlearn to live a better life in this century. Irrespective of the country or place, individuals will have to unlearn to have more happiness and success in life. By unlearning today we can change, grow, and uncover our full potential.

There are many books and studies on innovations leadership and what it takes to be innovative. Dyer, Gregersen, and Christensen (2011) in their book identified five effective habits that are fundamental building blocks for becoming more innovative and changing the world. These are:

1. associating – being able to connect the dots between disparate phenomena
2. questioning – being able to question the unquestionable
3. observing – and taking pleasure in the unexpected
4. experimenting – an ability to try out new things
5. networking – being able to embrace people from disparate backgrounds

It is important to understand that every work that we do, every movement of the body, every thought that we think leaves an impression on the mind-stuff; even when such impressions are not obvious on the surface, they are sufficiently strong to work beneath the surface, subconsciously. What we are every moment is determined by the sum total of these impressions on the mind. What I am at this moment is the effect of the sum total of all impressions of my past life. This is really what is meant by character; each person's character is determined by the sum total of these impressions.

These are the characteristics that anyone from a creative background would exhibit, maybe not all the time, but at least intermittently. So when one is consistently engaged in these actions – associating, questioning, observing, networking, and experimenting – they create strong impressions which form the person's creative character through repetitions. Habits are created by repetition and habits reform character. All the actions we see in the world, all the movements in human society, all the work that we do are simply the display of thoughts, the manifestation of the will of the person.

Most of us think creativity is an entirely cognitive skill; it all happens in the brain. A critical insight shows that one's ability to generate innovative ideas is not merely a function of the mind, but also a function of behavior.

Scott Berkun (2007) identified seven habits found in highly creative and innovative people. These are:

Persistence and determined will

In willpower lies the germ of success. Innovative habits involve more than just great ideas. They need faith, hard work, and a laser-sharp focus for the end result to keep our vision persisting in the face of roadblocks. Most people become extremely nervous or tense when they are trying to accomplish something that means a great deal to them. Anxious, nervous actions do not draw the power of the Universe; but the continuous, calm, powerful use of the will can shake the forces of creation and bring a response from the Infinite.

The germ of success in whatever we want to accomplish is our willpower, which is what makes you innovative. You must believe in the possibility of what you want. If you want a home, and the mind says "You simple guy, you can't afford a house", you must make your will stronger. When the "can't" disappears from your mind, the infinite power comes. A home will not be dropped down to you from heaven; you have to pour forth willpower continuously through constructive actions.

When you persist, refusing to accept failure, the object of your will might materialize. When you continuously work that will through thoughts and activities, what you are wishing for has to come about. Even though there is nothing in the world to conform to your wish, when your will persists, the desired result will somehow manifest itself. We tend to see the end result of a creative idea in awe, but what we don't see are the actions, hard work, and persistence behind the scene to make the vision a reality.

Nothing in the world can take its place – talent will not; nothing is more common than unsuccessful men with talent. Genius will not; unrewarded genius is almost a proverb. Education will not; the world is full of educated derelicts. Persistence and a determined will alone are omnipotent. In the confrontation between the stream and the rock, the stream always wins, not through strength but by perseverance.

George Bernard Shaw stated, "When I was a young man, I observed that nine out of ten things I did were failures. I didn't want to be a failure so I did ten times more work." Thomas Edison famously stated, "I had to succeed because I have run out of things which didn't work."

From these statements and many more, we know what type of substance men of persistence are made of. It's small wonder that "reward" tends to crown them in the end. I would like to share a not so well-known story which I read in a book by Billi Lim (1996), which concerns the inventor of the telephone. To many of us the inventor is Alexander Graham Bell. Well that is the story that we know now. But what we have not been taught, I am afraid, is the real great lesson.

During that time there was a person by the name of Philip Rice who actually challenged Bell about his claim to be the inventor of the telephone. What Rice had done by that time was that he was able to transmit musical notes and tones through the wire. And he claimed that Bell had actually studied whatever he had discovered up to that date and used it to transmit voices through the wire.

He therefore claimed that he should be recognized as the rightful inventor of the telephone. Finally, the case went to the Supreme Court of the United States of America. The answer as we now know is in the history book. How did the Supreme Court come up with the answer? Well, what they found out was that Rice's invention could only transmit musical notes and tones and not voices. "Something more" had to be added for it to be able to transmit voices – and Alexander Graham Bell did exactly that.

Rice actually didn't fail – he stopped! If only he had persisted like Bell, today his name would have gone down in history. The difference was only a "screw" which converted the tones into voices. As the saying goes, "People don't fail, they quit".

Remove self-limiting inhibitions

Under the spell of inhibition, we feel limited and stuck. We need to free ourselves from these mind-created constraints by removing assumptions and restrictions. This is what we refer to when we say, "Think outside the box". We should encourage ourselves to be open to new ideas and solutions without setting limiting beliefs. Remember, innovation is more about psychology than intellect.

As Ford stated, "If You Can't, You Can't". We need to cauterize the "can'ts" in our brain. A weak person's brain is full of "can'ts". Being born in a family with certain characteristics and habits, one is influenced by these to think one can't do certain things; one can't walk much, one can't eat this, one can't stand that. Those "can'ts" have to be cauterized. You have the power to accomplish everything you want; that power lies in the will.

Whoever would like to develop willpower must have good company. If your desire is to become a great mathematician and your customary associates all dislike mathematics, you will most certainly be discouraged. But when you mix with accomplished mathematicians, your will is reinforced; you think, "If others can do it, I can do it". Company has the greatest influence on will. Your willpower is definitely inspired or weakened by the company around you. If you want to be innovative, surround yourself with creative people.

Take risks, make mistakes

I believe that part of the reason why there is self-imposed inhibition is due to our fear of failure. As Abraham Lincoln stated, "A man incapable of making a mistake is incapable of anything". Expect that some ideas will fail in the process of learning. Build prototypes often, test them out on people, gather feedback, and make incremental changes. Rather than treating the mistakes as failures, think of them as experiments. "Experiment is the expected failure to deliberately learn something" (Scott Berkun 2007). Instead of punishing yourself for the failures, accept them, and take your newfound knowledge and use it to find the best solution. Live up to your goal of producing the best result, but understand you might hit roadblocks along the way.

Escape

Our environment can and does affect how we feel. The more relaxed and calm we are internally, the more open we are to tapping into our flowing creativity. This is why ideas sometimes come to us in the shower or while we're alone. Each of us has different triggers to access our creative energy. I get into the "creative zone" from sitting at my dining table, with a warm cup of chai, and my noise-canceling headphones. Many great thinkers go on long walks to help them solve problems. Experiment and find what works for you.

Writing things down

Many innovators and creative people keep a journal to jot down ideas and thoughts. Some keep a sketch book, scrap book, post-it notes, and loose paper. They all have a method to capture their thoughts, to think on paper, to drop their inhibitions, and start the creative process. Leonardo Da Vinci's famous notebook was purchased by Bill Gates for $30.8 million dollars.

Find patterns and create combinations

Ideas come from other ideas. Did you know that Edison wasn't the first one who came up with the invention of the light bulb? He was the first to build a workable carbon filament inside a glass bulb that made light bulbs last longer. You can increase your exposure to new ideas, look for patterns, and see how you can combine ideas to improve upon existing solutions.

Curiosity

Many innovators are just curious people who are inquisitive, and like to solve problems. Practice seeing things differently. For example, when seeing the solution to a problem, ask yourself, "What are some alternative ways of doing this?" Ask a lot of questions and challenge the norms or existing methods.

Personality is defined as the type of person you are; it shows the way you behave, feel, and think. It's the whole nature or character of a person. How a person behaves, feels, and thinks, and how he conducts himself in a given set of circumstances are largely determined by the state of his mind. A person's external appearances or speech or even mannerisms are only fringes of their personality. They do not reflect the real personality.

Practices in cultivating creativity and the power of concentration

Tina Su (2007) shared nine practices which she found useful in "cultivating" creativity. I believe these practices are used by many of us and you need to find a practice that will let your "creative juices flow".

- being relaxed
- gratitude
- tickling your imagination
- being in the moment
- being inspired
- drawing
- seeing alternatives
- being open
- thinking on paper.

Chapter 2 discussed how culture influences innovation and ideas. In this chapter we again emphasized the human element that is more significant in idea generation. With the right culture and the right environment and with the tools and process rightly in place, do you believe we can achieve an innovative organization?

Throughout Part I, where I have emphasized innovation as a discipline for business success, you will notice that I have revolved around the power of the mind to generate ideas. To control the mind we need to develop the power of concentration.

The power of concentration

All success in any line of work is the result of the power of concentration. Everybody knows something about concentration. We see its results every day. High achievements in art, music, and so on are the results of concentration.

The difference in the power of concentration constitutes the difference in achievements among individuals. If you compare a successful executive with an unsuccessful one, the difference is in the degree of effort toward concentration. Everybody's mind becomes concentrated at times. We all concentrate upon those things we are passionate about, enjoy, or love, and we love those things upon which we concentrate our minds.

The trouble with concentrating on things we love is that we do not control the mind; it controls us. Something outside of ourselves, as it were, draws the mind into it and holds it as long as it chooses. We hear a melodious tone or see a beautiful painting, and our mind is held fast; we cannot take it away.

If I speak to you well upon a subject you like, your mind becomes concentrated upon what I am saying. I draw your mind away from yourself. Thus our attention is held, our minds are concentrated upon various things, in spite of ourselves. We cannot help it.

When our mind is focused or concentrated, our energies are not dissipated on irrelevant activities or thoughts. This is why developing concentration is essential to anyone who aspires to take charge of his or her life. This skill is essential for every kind of success. Without it, our efforts get scattered, but with it, we can accomplish great things.

Concentration has many uses and benefits. It assists in studying and understanding faster, improves the memory, and helps in focusing on any task, job, activity or goal, and achieving it more easily and efficiently. It is also required for developing psychic powers, and is a powerful tool for the efficient use of creative visualization.

Now the question is: can this concentration be developed, and can we become masters of it? The Yogis say yes. The great Yogis say that we can gain perfect control of our mind. There is no limit to the powers of the human mind. The more concentrated it is, the more power is brought to bear on one point, and that is the secret to success. By having the right environment and culture with a systematic process of capturing ideas and guiding the workforce to concentrate on the areas of innovation, an organization can rightfully channel the organizational energies toward being imaginative and creative.

Concluding remarks for Part I

In Part I of the book we covered innovation as a discipline for business success. We discussed what innovation is, where ideas come from, and how corporate cultures can support creativity in an organization. We also reviewed what is required to architect your innovation landscape and identified methodology that you can adopt to launch the innovation process in your company. We discussed the need for one to change in order to uncover one's potential, and we also identified the power of the mind and the power of concentration to tap the library of universal knowledge that is within us. This ability to seek knowledge internally will enable good innovative habits among your staff, colleagues, and peers.

As you attempt to deploy the approaches to innovation and creative imagination as a discipline within your organization, you will discover that it will be a change management initiative as it covers people, process, and technology. The process and technology are the easy part and not as important as people with ideas, who will be the main asset you will need to harness. Whether you are raising new questions and new possibilities or regarding old problems from a new angle, you will require a creative imagination. In fact the ability to use the human mind to create success marks the real advances in science. With this, Albert Einstein's words come to my mind; he had said, "Innovation is not a product of logical thought, although the result is tied to logical structure". With this statement I will proceed to Part II of the book, where we will explore strategy and portfolio investment decisions.

PART II

Strategy, Project Portfolio, and Benefits Investment Decision

Portfolio management for innovation has surfaced as one of the most important senior management functions for research and development (R&D) organizations. Faced with rapidly changing technologies, shorter product lifecycles, and heightened global competition, more than ever, how an R&D business spends its technology, money, and resources is paramount to its future prosperity – even its survival. Indeed, we believe that portfolio management is the manifestation of the R&D business strategy. It dictates where and how a company will invest for the future. Portfolio management treats R&D investments much like a fund manager in the stock market treats financial investments. It deals with issues such as maximizing the value of the portfolio (hence, the return on R&D spending), compiling an appropriately balanced portfolio, and developing a portfolio investment strategy that is aligned with the company's overall business strategy. Logically you will think that I will spend more time on portfolio within R&D organizations. However, based on my definition of innovation and with the emphasis on ideation, I will devote Part II of this book to reviewing strategy and project portfolio investment decisions across all business sectors.

The innovation demand decision established in organizations will monitor the pipeline of ideas and will help to generate a portfolio of initiatives. These ideas can be further evaluated to ensure that there is alignment with the overall business strategy. These portfolios of initiatives can be prioritized and then optimized to help maximize the investment, and delivery performance is tracked for the business benefits. Don't forget that the basic principle behind this discipline is to gain competitive advantage, and it can come from both new ideas and continuous improvements. As a desired state for an ongoing continuous portfolio management process, we

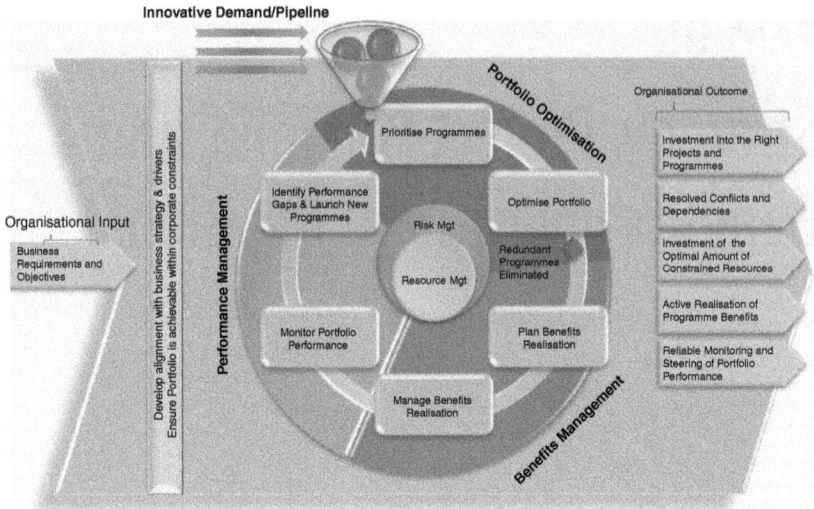

Figure II.1 Ongoing desired portfolio management process

have represented the process as circular and continuously ongoing. This is shown in Figure II.1.

The vehicle of investment decisions will have to be fueled by the firm's strategy and tuned by experienced leadership to ensure that better mileage of returns and performance are realized from the projects.

Investment versus value

The prevailing economic climate forces organizations to restrain their investment while at the same time securing their future viability. Even organizations less affected by the current events revisit and realign their strategy to ensure their ongoing productivity. Whatever the motivator, these are the times that organizations revisit their practices and launch change initiatives to implement new ones. You need innovative ideas to change, and in its simplest terms, innovation, investment, and implementation management are practices that coordinate the creation of idea, successful selection of the idea or initiative, and implement the company's programs and projects. It achieves this through an approach to filtering all innovative ideas – evaluate what innovative projects should be launched based on what the organization needs. It also helps to evaluate projects in flight and steer them to deliver the benefits they were launched to deliver.

A recent IDC Survey (2011) of Organizations that had invested and been successfully using project portfolio management (PPM) illustrated the following benefits:

- Effective use of budget: cost per project reduced by 37 per cent
- Delivery of projects with real business value: redundant projects dropped by 78 per cent
- Effective use of staff resources: IT staff productivity increased by 14 per cent
- Improved project success: project failure rate dropped by 59 per cent
- Return on PPM investment: payback occurred in 7.4 months.

An investment versus value analysis can represent how PPM process and tools can pull data from multiple sources and provide analyzed information that can be used to maximize value for investment decisions. Measuring and managing benefits of a portfolio of projects can effectively give a good value for moderate investment, and hence good value for money.

Portfolio management includes:

- Defining initiatives – initiatives must be properly defined to have a chance of being launched and will then compete against each other for the limited resources in organizations.
- Launching initiatives – initiatives are not launched on a "who shouts loudest" basis, but they are the result of an objective check against what the organization needs.
- Steering initiatives – current initiatives are scrutinized for their capability to deliver the benefits and needs of the organization. Where gaps are detected, change projects are launched and unnecessary projects are halted.
- Ending initiatives – initiatives are not finalized once their main products are delivered. They are finished when the change they were meant to support has been implemented. Portfolio management ensures that we focus on the long-term outcomes of our initiatives and not short-term outputs.

Through this commonsense approach, portfolio management coordinates the delivery of corporate strategies through the execution of projects. You will realize that the PPM process is well accepted and established within the IT functions of many industries as IT gains greater recognition at board level. As such you will note that the examples given in this part of the book are more IT related than specific businesses, but this does not mean that the PPM process does not apply to businesses. In fact the examples given are IT-enabled business projects which have turned failing business into successful ventures. Part II of this book will investigate the following:

- In Chapter 6, we will explain what portfolio management is and why it is relevant. Why projects fail, the root causes for this failure, and what remedies portfolio management provides are also studied. We also give a short introduction to the history and evolution of the discipline, explain portfolio in relation to established program and project management, share some examples of success stories in the corporate world, and introduce the portfolio themes and process and how these interact and are best applied.
- In Chapter 7, we will investigate the process of converting strategies into actions. Portfolios of projects are created to deliver change. Before these are launched, an organization must understand what it seeks to become and what are its goals. How does it want to create future value and measure its success. This chapter introduces business drivers as the currency to use to launch, steer, and measure projects. It introduces how to make the drivers tangible. Portfolio management provides guidance on how to define drivers, define their impact, and prioritize them. We also elaborate on other techniques, especially categorization, as a means to structure and manage portfolios of projects.
- In Chapter 8, we will explore the key areas of resource management (RM) and investigate how they can be conducive to making plans achievable. RM's associations with portfolio management are explored. The resource manager's role is examined as the forgotten link to portfolio management. This is achieved by assessing whether we have the right people with the right skills to execute a project that goes in as a prioritized part of the project portfolio. We then throw more light on resource planning to emphasize its role in successful portfolio execution.
- In Chapter 9, we take a good drive through the tunnels of benefit management. Starting from defining and understanding benefits, we further investigate why benefits and their measurements are needed. To understand this, we explore different indicators to measure benefits, such as net present value (NPV), return on investment (ROI), and break-even period. We also look at what is needed as breakdown for ultimate investment decision.
- In Chapter 10, we focus largely on the assurance and realization of benefits for the innovation and portfolio investments made. This is done through the set-up of a portfolio management office (PfMO). PfMO

involves assuring stakeholders of the overall health of programs and projects in the portfolios. This chapter talks about the various elements involved in the set-up, implementation, and running of a PfMO, including roles and responsibilities in the PfMO team, PfMO reporting and other challenges that involve organizational and behavioral change during the transformation of a PfMO. The key factors to ensure success of a PfMO are discussed.

CHAPTER 6

What Is Portfolio Management, What Are the Trends and Benefits?

Project portfolio management (PPM) is a disciplined approach to overseeing the collection of projects and programs in which an organization invests. These initiatives are intended to realize the organization's strategy in order to maximize business benefits, and each is undertaken with a certain level of risks and constraints. A PPM process and governance framework uses various techniques to provide tangible results for businesses, ensuring that project investments contribute directly to realizing corporate goals.

The ultimate outcome of portfolio management efforts depends on the type of organization. Experts who have studied the use of portfolio management within companies have identified several elements that influence the portfolio environment:

- *cultural*, particularly with respect to the readiness of the organization to work in a more structured, disciplined, and transparent way
- *environmental*, including political, legal, and mandatory conditions
- *maturity level*, to manage expectations for outcomes and understand the appropriate place to begin in the portfolio management process
- *executive buy-in,* the collective will of the leadership to adopt a more systematic and accountable way for managing project selection.

Many organizations "flirt" with PPM. They try out formal numerical or measured assessments for project prioritization and selection and then quickly reject it as being inflexible, time-consuming, or providing faulty results. This outcome often comes out of a failed first attempt to develop and use a prioritization tool. While many of these first attempts do fail, and many of the instruments that are designed to support them produce incorrect and meaningless results, the approach itself shouldn't be rejected out of hand. The "Operational Efficiency Programme: final report (PDF)", issued by HM Treasury in 2009, recommends that public sector organizations "implement portfolio management processes to prioritize projects and resources and to reduce overlap and duplication in IT-enabled change projects".

For an organization to create a viable solution for effectively prioritizing and selecting projects, it must first define a framework within which it will operate. For many organizations, this framework is created within an umbrella concept of PPM – simply put, the concept of dealing with all of an organization's projects as a single portfolio. While the projects within the portfolio are still managed as individual initiatives, from a senior management perspective they are viewed in the aggregate as a collective means of establishing the organization's goals.

We encounter one of the biggest challenges of portfolio management right up front: Which projects should be included and which ones shouldn't? Given that a portfolio management approach should encompass all the initiatives an organization is undertaking, this really becomes the question: Which projects are we going to do and which ones should we reject? More than any other question about a portfolio of projects, this is the hardest to answer but also the most meaningful.

The act of prioritizing and selecting projects is hard, not necessarily because of the mechanics of the process, but because it demands that we make choices. For every project that we do take on, there may be five, ten, or a hundred that never see the light of day. We must make choices with imperfect information. We can never be quite sure whether the results of one project will better serve the organization than those of another, or whether the estimates of cost and benefits provide a truly accurate picture of organizational return. Choosing the right project is what allows an organization to succeed and thrive. The wrong projects can take a successful, high-flying organization into a death spiral from which it may never recover.

Why portfolio management

In our fast-paced business world, choosing the right things to do and doing them in the right order is what distinguishes leading organizations from followers. With product lifecycles decreasing and the pressure to churn out more innovative products at an ever quickening pace increasing, the margin for error in selecting the right initiatives is shrinking.

To complicate matters, the current economic downturn brings additional need to deliver substantial corporate cost reduction. Companies now more than ever need to understand how best to balance investment risk and execution, optimize their shrinking project, and make the "right" cost reduction or reallocation decisions.

Table 6.1 Summary of project failures report in the IT sector

Corporate reality	<ul><li>24% of projects fail – Standish Group 2009</li><li>49% of projects experienced budget overruns – Dynamic Markets Limited Survey 2007</li><li>62% of organizations experienced IT projects that failed to meet their schedules – TCS Survey 2007</li><li>41% of IT projects failed to deliver the expected business value and ROI – TCS Survey 2007</li><li>44% of IT projects are challenged from a cost, schedule, or expected functionality perspective – Standish Group 2009</li></ul>

Executives have a different view of project success than project managers. Here are some of the things they tend to ask:

- What mix of potential projects will provide the best utilization of human and cash resources to maximize long-range growth and ROI for the firm?
- How do the projects support strategic initiatives?
- How will the projects affect the value of corporate shares?
- What mix of projects will take us to a desired future state?

Within the IT context, we have seen leaders in IT portfolio management who have demonstrated ways to cut IT costs by 2–5 per cent, improve productivity by 25–50 per cent, and shift 10–15 per cent of the IT budget into more strategic projects.

An inconvenient truth

While the case for portfolio management appears to be evident, the reality of most corporate portfolios looks sobering. Table 6.1 summarizes some studies on project failures within the IT sector.

Common root causes

The causes for corporate project portfolios failing to achieve organizational goals are often similar across industries:

- Poor portfolio planning at a strategic level – a lack of top–down direction leads inevitably to projects not delivering expected results.

- Managing too many of the wrong projects – a huge amount of resources deliver projects that have become obsolete or are not any longer aligned to changed corporate priorities.
- Unable to prioritize critical projects or kill the unnecessary ones – these decisions are difficult to make and often highly political. Only an established, fact-based, and objective methodology can succeed.
- No defined processes for reviewing ideas and business cases – without these organizations are unable to prioritize projects and weed out potential failures early.
- Senior executives driving personal agendas – prioritization based on individual departmental agendas alone leads inevitably to a less effective portfolio at corporate level.
- Attempting too many projects simultaneously – scarce resources are spread among too many initiatives, jeopardising delivery of key projects and the achievement of corporate goals as a whole.
- No process to measure strategic alignment – without this process it is difficult to justify stopping or changing projects, and it is highly probable that many initiatives deliver value not based on current organization priorities.
- Lack of overall visibility of risks, issues, and conflicts – focusing on individual projects alone, without understanding the context and interdependencies of the portfolio, will lead to suboptimal decisions.
- Over-reliance on financial measures as portfolio selection basis – financial measures are important but increasingly depend on highly volatile variables (e.g., interest rates, exchange rates). as such if projects are selected based on their contribution to strategic goals will yield better results.
- Lack of alignment of technology initiatives with business strategy – without clear top–down direction and a proper understanding of technology's contribution to wider organization goals, technology projects are doomed to waste resources without creating the benefits required by the company.

Benefits of portfolio management

Properly executed portfolio management helps to overcome the root causes for portfolio failure. Once established portfolio management addresses three fundamental questions:

- Are we doing the right projects?
- For the projects that we have chosen, are we confident that they will be delivered well and meet their goals?

- For the projects that we have completed, are we consciously changing how the organization operates in order to realize the value we expected?

These are obviously fundamental yet simple questions. Portfolio Management goes also deeper to answer more complex questions like:

- How do we know we are doing the right projects?
- What criteria do we apply?
- What judgments do we make?
- Right projects as compared to what?

Once established and operational, portfolio management provides organizations with:

- Maximum value – an optimized portfolio to achieve maximum strategic value and financial ROI under any given constraints.
- Improved visibility – a shared understanding of what the organization is doing and why; objective, fact-based, less political decision-making; ongoing insight into the status of initiatives and their joint impact on the strategic goals.
- Improved effectiveness – ongoing evidence of project performance, benefits realization, and achievement of organizational change.
- Reduced execution risk – upfront investigation of investment risk, launch of projects with a high likelihood of success, and allocation of resources to prioritized initiatives; partnered with comprehensive monitoring and control at portfolio level, projects are provided with the best possible environment for successful delivery.

Shifting focus in portfolio management: "triple constraints" within project and portfolio

The traditional measures of project success cover scope, schedule, and resources which are the components of the project objective, rather than independent measures of success. Does this miss the true business objectives?

We always aimed to meet or exceed the targets for scope, schedule, and resources. But even achieving all of these did not always equate to benefits for the enterprise. This conventional wisdom does not make sense as there was something more to project success than the time-honored triple constraints. Figure 6.1 shows the triple constraints in project and portfolio which are tightly linked and integrated.

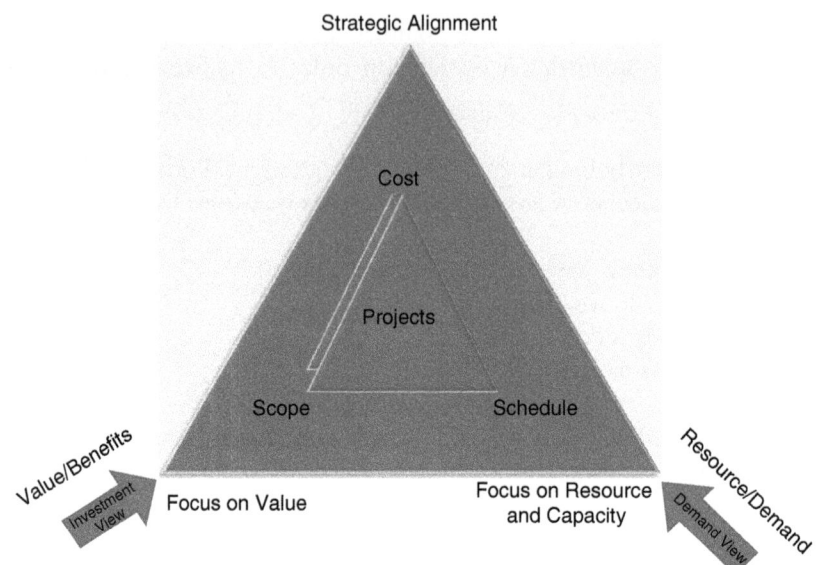

Figure 6.1 Triple constraints in project and portfolio tightly linked and integrated (Adapted from Harvey Levin)

In this instance project lifecycle is expanded and the old "project" triple constraint now is a component of wider "portfolio" triple constraint. The demand management becomes one of the three major components of the new triple constraints.

The old triple constraint still applies for each project. But the portfolio addresses a much larger picture. The portfolio triple constraint deals with C-level issues and goals. With this larger focus, projects must be more than "successful". They must contribute to the corporate welfare. PPM is designed to support this objective.

The portfolio is a packet of investments, most of which are projects. Like any investment portfolio, such as we might have in a retirement portfolio, we look for the best possible return on the resources (cash) that we have available for investment. And we moderate our potential return objectives so as to stay within a comfortable risk position – accepting something less than the maximum gain while limiting exposure to undesirable losses. We develop an investment strategy, and we confine our potential investments to support that strategy.

The ground rules for a project portfolio are essentially the same. From the demand angle, our focus is primarily on *resources, capability*, and *capacity*. From this point of view, the available resources, capability, and capacity are defined. Capable resources are allocated to projects until the capacity is reached. The issue is "which projects get the limited resources?" With structured, integrated demand management, we can develop a portfolio of high-value projects while staying within the defined capacity.

One of the great benefits of having a PPM process is that these two angles are fully integrated and interdependent. It is like looking at the portfolio as a prism. It is a single unit that can be viewed from multiple perspectives. The investment and demand facets are so tightly linked that it is virtually impossible to consider demand without value and vice-versa.

Trends influencing portfolio management

According to META Group research, half of global 2000 companies have adopted some form of portfolio implementation. In about 6 per cent of those companies, the implementation of PPM drove portfolio value up by as much as 30 per cent; attempts at many of the remaining companies became just another failed project!

In this section, I like to examine why so many organizations in a multitude of industries are prime candidates for tapping into the power of PPM. Where at one time IT decisions were based on what IT demanded or felt would add value to the organization, today IT has become the backbone that can make or break a company. Consequently, the demand by strategic leaders and stakeholders from the business side to gain a clear view of the "state of the union" has catapulted the rise of the PPM market and its sub-components (including application portfolio management).

PPM basics – and why companies need it

Companies that implement PPM effectively show characteristics worth listing. For one, there's considerable cost avoidance from stopping the funding of high risk, poorly aligned, low projected return projects. Companies see an increase of 5–40 per cent in projected return (whether measured by internal rate of return, NPV, or earnings before interest and tax) of the project portfolio for the same budget by funding high-value projects and eliminating high cost, low-return projects. And these operations improve resource utilization by 5–15 per cent due to more effective resource planning and scheduling optimization.

PPM is an organization's process of making and managing project investment decisions to maximize business benefits, both financial and strategic in nature, at a certain level of risk (the likelihood of delivering benefits within the expected time and budget), given constraints such as financial and resource capacity.

In the face of that 6 per cent success rate, we have to ask, "why do so many organizations fail in their portfolio efforts?" The most common causes of failure include one or more of these challenges:

- lack of senior stakeholder buy-in or alignment
- lack of data or avoiding facts, which are too painful to face
- too much difficulty in showing results or a lack of agreement on success measures
- low maturity; they try for too big a jump or have poor discipline
- lack of alignment across silos
- enterprise project management offices lack a view of the enterprise; roles and responsibilities are unclear
- stepping from annual to in-year management regimes
- business cases are viewed internally as an approval hurdle, not as something real
- rationalizing assets isn't done; the project roster never really changes
- benefits management is lacking
- cultural change is weak; the organization is too tools-centric or won't commit enough budgets for change.

The kinds of symptoms shown by these "failing" organizations include a habit of giving into "he who shouts the loudest"; a continuation of projects that still have budget whether or not the projects are still justified; outdated project data fresh off the printer; a hazy understanding about how a given project aligns strategically; and budget overruns that only show up after the event has passed.

Those rare companies that succeed (only six in 100!) have mature PPM practices in place and have learned how to take into account four significant elements:

- the environment in which they sit (including laws/regulation)
- the scale of the organization and the challenges and changes it faces
- the culture of the organization and its readiness to work in a more robust and transparent way
- the collective will of leadership and their key stakeholders to work in a more systematic and accountable way.

These companies have figured out how to gain involvement at all levels of the company through integration of projects, programs, and the portfolio.

Trends affecting portfolio management

We are at an interesting time in the evolution of PPM. Organizational and technology-driven aspects of the discipline are undergoing transformation, which affect the readiness of companies to adopt its practices and principles. Since my involvement with portfolio management for the last two decades, I have observed changes that are strongly influencing the direction and maturity development of PPM practice. The trends observed are given below:

Trend 1: no longer just nice to have

No longer a leading-edge practice, PPM has started to transition from a "nice to have" into a "must have". In the private sector, PPM will become a competitive necessity, especially in sectors where time-to-market, quality, and cost control are key success factors. In the public sector, PPM will raise the bar for financial accountability for programs and projects, and that new level of visibility will become expected by constituencies. In fact, in some cases it has already become a mandate.

Senior managers will begin to expect a certain level of visibility and accountability for the project portfolio. They'll grow increasingly accustomed to reliable reports and metrics that tell them what's going on as of right now, as well as providing a predictable pipeline of what is coming up next. The lessons learned in the leading-edge organizations will begin to carry forward, not just through case studies and press coverage, but through the migration of experienced leaders who have seen the value and the impact. Experienced leaders will carry those tools and techniques with them from one assignment to the next.

Trend 2: PPM implementations are becoming predictable

Early stage PPM implementations were all unique. There were very few best practices in place and organizations were still learning about the impacts that PPM would have. The pioneers were learning as they went, which is typical in a newly developing market discipline. Increasingly, we will see much of the mystery of PPM transition into standardized implementation approaches. Predictable and standard patterns for successful PPM are emerging, and these patterns mitigate both risk and cost.

Trend 3: enabling technologies and analytics

As the PPM market matures, technology companies are working closely with best practices organizations developing enabling technologies to support the advancement in portfolio requirements. The very good example is Microsoft Project tool 2003 that is so vastly different for its Project Portfolio Sever 2010 which has best practices on portfolio optimization, benefits tracking, and RM embedded in the software. The dashboards and reports are also of the highest standards which give management live data so that they make meaningful decisions.

Trend 4: software as a service

As Software as a Service (SaaS) continues to move from interesting to viable to a competitive threat, PPM solutions are ideally suited to run as SaaS applications, otherwise known as "PPM On Demand". There are several reasons why SaaS is so well suited for PPM: rapid deployment, team collaboration, reduced risk of failure, tighter vendor/customer relationships, and reduced cost of implementation and support. But perhaps the biggest reason is the rapid innovation cycle. It is at least twice as fast to deliver innovations to customers in a SaaS model, and as a result PPM using a SaaS model is evolving rapidly.

Trend 5: collaboration across boundaries

Collaboration means communication. It is now a well-known phenomenon that communication is one of the key success factors for projects and project teams. Because PPM solutions involve a large number of team members who are working together on tasks and deliverables, PPM solutions are beginning to drive more and more collaborative capabilities. But these collaborative capabilities aren't just unstructured chat sessions. They are fully integrated into the work plan and the reporting systems, so that the knowledge is captured and available to broader audiences. What we are seeing is what I call "collaboration beyond your own domain".

Trend 6: connecting to benefits tracking and realization

This is the fastest growing expectation from senior executives. Companies are investing millions in systems and are demanding ROI through tangible and intangible benefits. Both benefits management process and enabling technology are working hand in hand to provide benefits tracking and real- ization capability. We for one are currently working with Microsoft to embed this capability into the Project Portfolio Server 2010. The integra- tion of cost management and tracking to strategic drivers, value metrics, key performance indicators (KPI), and performance indicators (PI) either process or financial based are enabling organizations to tie projects and programs to the benefits reaped.

Trend 7: connecting to the web and web services

The World Wide Web offers an almost limitless field of information ser- vices: intelligent search, web-based education, research into standards and best practices, and much more. Also, as a technology, web services have moved into the viability stage and more examples are beginning to emerge in the software market as a whole.

PPM is no longer a little-known specialty. Customers – that 6 per cent of successes alluded to earlier – are now sharing their stories. PPM has emerged as the next generation of project management. PPM tools and techniques will continue to mature and stabilize, and the supporting pro- cesses and content will mature as well. As PPM matures, project managers will spend less time on overhead and more time delivering high-value projects. And organizations will get more disciplined in how they spend money on discretionary projects and programs.

Building a business case for strategy and portfolio management

As stated in previous sections, the main objective for PPM is to deliver maximum value for organizations, and it is imperative to ensure that your portfolio is aligned with overall business strategy. Therefore, I believe that there is a strong case to build your strategic drivers in your PPM to ensure that portfolio represents projects which are delivering maximum value for business. Further, PPM – which helps ensure that the right projects are being done right – is moving from the nice-to-have realm into the "must have" category.

A client once told me that portfolio management provides a platform on which to negotiate. Participants in the decision can talk about a given set of projects at a strategic value level. The use of the portfolio approach removes the sheer emotion from decision-making. Another client in the financial sector calls it a "trading platform": These are the projects we have agreed to, based on a systemized way of thinking. It is important for organizations to care and know how to sell internally and start making portfolio process work within the organization.

Everybody's doing it

In 2007, according to a Forrester research project, only a third of companies were doing portfolio management. But another 56 per cent said they were developing a portfolio management effort. I see four reasons for this dramatic uptake:

- Government sectors have raised the bar of financial accountability for programs and projects, and in some cases this accountability is mandated. This has given a new level of visibility to portfolio management within government agencies.
- Senior executives are now demanding greater visibility and accountability for their portfolio of projects. That encompasses the availability of reliable reports and metrics that can lay out what's happening right now and what's coming next. As these managers move to other positions, they take their knowledge of the portfolio tools and techniques with them because they understand the impact on the organization. As a result, the expectation for portfolio management is going up.
- Now that portfolio management has been around for 10–12 years, a lot of research has gone on, best practices have surfaced, and implementations are becoming more mature.
- The technology offerings too have matured and become quite adept at helping organizations create the kind of visibility and accountability those executives want. Those systems have become a key driver in moving the portfolio forward.

Portfolio management, which is an organization's process of making and managing project investment decisions to maximize business benefits given risk constraints, aids the business or agency in measuring three broad areas:

- Benefits, to understand the project's financial and strategic impact on the organization.
- Risk, to understand the project's likelihood of delivering benefits within the anticipated timeframe and budget.

- Constraints, to understand the resource capacity for the initial and ongoing investments required by the project.
- The ultimate outcome of your portfolio management efforts will depend on the type of organization you are in. Those who have studied the use of portfolios within companies have identified several elements that actually influence this portfolio environment:
- cultural, particularly with respect to the readiness of the organization to work in a more robust and transparent way
- environmental, including legal and mandatory conditions
- maturity level, to manage expectations for outcomes and understand the appropriate place to begin in the portfolio process
- executive buy-in, the collective will of the leadership to adopt a more systematic and accountable way for managing their project selection.

Counting up the benefits of portfolio management

Understanding what your expected benefits will be can be a painstaking job. First, you need to apply industry benchmarks against your company's own values in areas such as project costs, project resource costs, project cost overruns, and so on. Those numbers help you develop your "benefit pool". The benefit pool defines the benefits you expect as a result of applying industry benchmarks to organizational metrics. Determining your expected benefits from a portfolio management initiative requires you to measure how much of a benefit pool is no longer available based on past success in implementing and adopting project and portfolio management processes.

If this sounds complicated, it doesn't have to be. We have access to well-tested metrics and tools for determining expected benefits by measuring your company's current state based on its process maturity. The benefit opportunity is calculated by combining the results of that process and a value assessment process. Those results go into building the roadmap that lays out your organization's priorities for achieving portfolio nirvana.

The portfolio cost and its payback

Undertaking the journey into portfolio management for an enterprise isn't inexpensive. A rough estimate of what your organization will spend as an initial investment is $450,000–$500,000.

But likewise, the payback when portfolio work is done correctly is impressive. Both Forrester and Gartner have studied this among IT organizations specifically and have come up with fairly comparable numbers:

- You'll see a 1–5 per cent reduction in annual project costs.
- You'll see a 1–5 per cent reduction in annual resource costs.
- You'll gain a 15–30 per cent reduction in project cost overruns.
- You'll gain a 20–30 per cent reduction in project- and portfolio-related operational costs.
- You'll see a 5–8 per cent reduction in lifecycle investment costs.
- And you'll see a 10–20 per cent reduction in application maintenance costs.

Those are tangible benefits, but intangible ones accrue as well:

- Improved decision-making and improved success of decisions.
- Reduced risk.
- Improved resource utilization and satisfaction.
- Improved organizational agility and improved operational efficiency.

Starting on the road to portfolio excellence

Implementing a portfolio management program is a multi-pronged effort that requires a holistic approach encompassing processes, enabling technology, and organizational change.

It starts with the definition of an "improvement initiative" to help prioritize your organization's needs. The point of that initiative is to get a clear, objective sense of what your organizational maturity level is compared to the rest of your industry and to develop a quantifiable measure of expected benefits.

Out of that a roadmap will result to lay out how the portfolio management effort will unfold over time, for example, "In the next six months it will focus on demand management and risk. Next, it will focus on portfolio selection and then resource management, and so on ...".

We have advised companies on the process of integrating portfolio management into their operations, using a fairly straightforward set of Excel-based tools with potent, complex algorithms behind them to help an organization assess its current maturity level and develop its future state.

Although the tools aren't 100 per cent foolproof, we have tested them across a number of different industry segments – government, oil and gas, financial, manufacturing, and others – and I have found that our results do provide a good rule of thumb to indicate where the organization's maturity is and – as a result of that – what kind of benefits you can expect from a portfolio initiative. In a lot of situations the assessment process and its results have gone far in helping to define the business case for the portfolio approach.

If your company is new to portfolio management, it is time to start building your business case and to leverage independent assessment tools to uncover your portfolio maturity and next steps.

If you are in an organization that already does portfolio management, it is time to assess your level of maturity to start improving that. Portfolio maturity assessment can help you prioritize next steps.

Portfolio management is no longer in the backseat. It is coming to the front because a lot of senior executives are moving it forward. If you want to drive your company in a way to say where it needs to go, this is a powerful approach.

In this chapter, we have defined portfolio management and its benefits. We have also explored the triple constraints in PPM and discussed the trends influencing PPM. We also discussed the business case for aligning strategy to the projects and programs. The next chapter will investigate in detail a methodology used by us on how to convert business strategy and the innovative demands captured into actionable plans. We will find that PPM helps in strategy implementation through its strategy formulation process and translating strategy into actionable strategic drivers and capturing the benefits' impact as business case for use in projects.

CHAPTER 7

How to Convert Strategy and Innovative Demand into Actionable Plans?

Portfolios of projects are created to deliver change to an organization. Before any project or program can be launched, it is important that we define, understand, and communicate the benchmarks we will use to evaluate them. The company must find or define answers to questions like:

- What is the organization seeking to become?
- What is the company trying to accomplish for its stakeholders?
- What key decisions have been made to help the organization reach its strategic goals and objectives?
- How does the organization want to create value?
- How will success be measured?

Many projects fail to deliver success because there is no easily describable organizational strategy in place to align project scope as:

> PPM is not strategic management. The determination of corporate direction and deviation of strategy takes place outside the remit of portfolio management.

Portfolio management supports strategy formulation and implementation through two key processes:

1. Providing the strategy formulation process with ongoing information on strategic goals and benefits generated by existing change initiatives. The strategy process can incorporate any gaps into its considerations.
2. Helping to translate or convert strategy into executable strategic drivers for usage in projects and programs and ensuring application of these drivers in creation of new change initiatives.

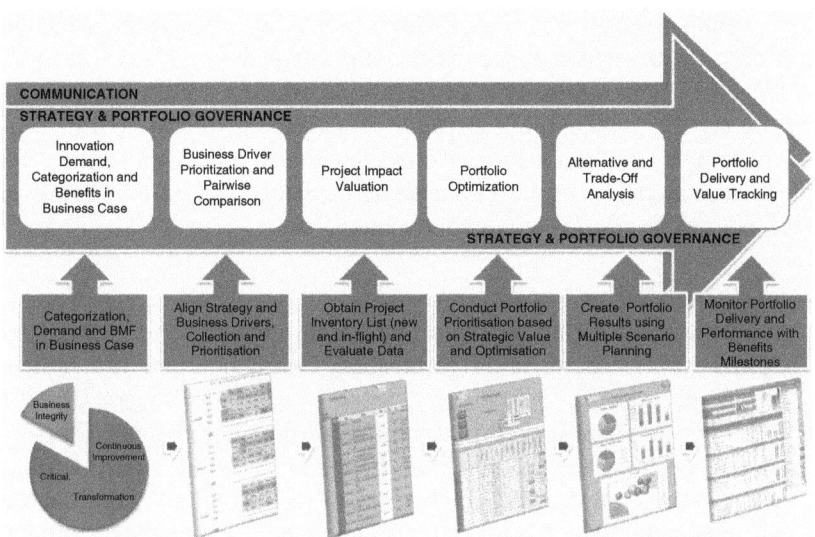

Figure 7.1 Pcubed strategy, portfolio, and benefits (SP&B) management best practice framework

Figure 7.1 shows our strategy, portfolio, and benefits (SP&B) management framework and steps involved in implementing this robust and predictable process for organizations. This SP&B framework is a cutting-edge management approach that helps organizations achieve maximum performance from investments in internal improvement and innovation initiatives. This is done by employing a standardized governance model throughout the entire lifecycle of a business investment from the very early stage of idea generation through continuously evaluating investments against key measures and strategic business objectives and finally tracking their execution and benefits realization in a centralized fashion.

Portfolio management has a broader reach than project management, in the sense that project management addresses the efficiencies of delivering scope based on defined timelines, budget allocations, and resources, while portfolio management employs standardized processes that lead to enhanced visibility into the entire business investment plan. Ultimately, these consistencies support the decision-making process to properly plan and govern key investments based on their value to your organization.

This framework addresses the alignment of projects and programs to business strategy, evaluates the benefits statements as business case, and supports investment decision through prioritization and optimization of the initiatives using the strategic value defined. This is followed by the portfolio performance delivery and value tracking. Details of setting up the portfolio management office (PfMO) to monitor, track, and control the portfolio delivery activities are discussed in Chapter 10.

The goal of our approach is to achieve an effective PPM capability by first laying the foundation of portfolio management within the organization and implement best practices into their existing processes, people, and governance models. The creation of the development plan will be based on the four key capabilities of portfolio management:

- Innovation demand/pipeline management, categorization, and benefits in business case – this involves innovation, initiative and project categorization, standardization of business cases, program and project governance models.
- Portfolio optimization – this comprises of defining strategic/business drivers, prioritizing the drivers and aligning with the business strategy, capturing the benefits impact statements of the projects from the business cases, prioritizing the portfolio, identifying the organizational constraints and creating multiple scenarios in optimization based on constraints, and making decisions based on trade-offs presented.
- Benefits management – this involves supporting ways of capturing and estimating the benefits at the business case, defining the value metrics of measurement in line with key performance indicators (KPI) and performance indicators (PI) either as process performance indicators (PPI) or financial performance indicators (FPI).
- Portfolio delivery and value tracking – this involves portfolio tracking and reporting, including benefits dashboards.

Innovation demand/pipeline management, categorization and benefits in standardized business case

Defining innovation demand/pipeline management

One of the primary objectives of portfolio management is the creation of a centralized inventory of investments, which includes both existing investments that are currently being implemented in the form of projects and new investment proposals regarding new or innovative areas of improvement and change. A single repository of investments allows for increased transparency, visibility, and control and provides decision-makers with a summary view of the current investments and potential future investments.

Categorization

Categorizing projects is an important way to facilitate project selection. There are many different ways to categorize projects and it can include some of these examples: strategic, key operational, support, and high potential; or by regulatory, improvement, replacement, and operations; and even by major projects and small projects.

Specifically where the portfolio contains a vast number of initiatives, categories help to break it down into more digestible units. Organization can use categories to:

- Define overall composition of the portfolio pre-selection: a company interested in growth could, for example, stipulate that a certain percentage of the portfolio needs to support this objective, independent of whether there are more attractive projects in other categories. Such a policy helps to ensure that simpler, more predictable projects (support, operational) do not completely dominate the portfolio and choke any investment into more risky endeavors.
- Allocate different optimization procedures and governance rules to categories: small projects are treated differently than major initiatives; regulatory projects are checked with less rigor on their strategic value, but even stronger on their risk (as they must not fail), and so on.

Categories are not meant to replace assessment of projects against strategic drivers or risk, and organizations that do will see their portfolio not delivering to strategic goal. But categories bring structure in an otherwise complex discipline. Figure 7.2 shows an example how a company can categorize its portfolio spend.

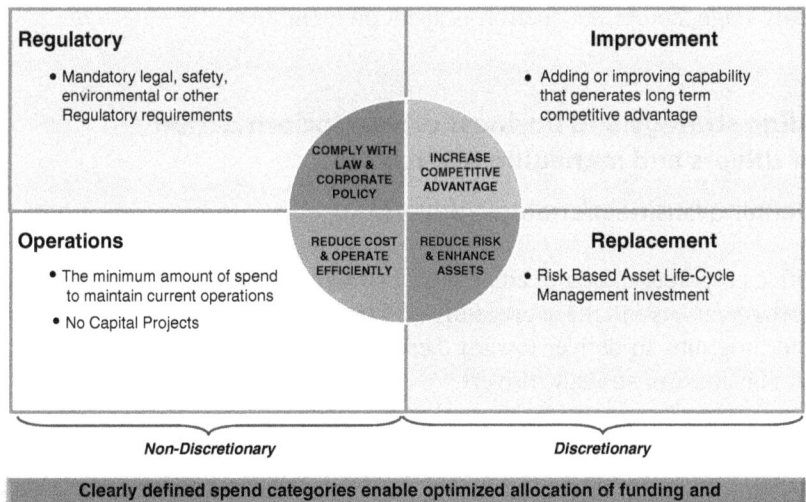

Figure 7.2 An example of clearly defined portfolio spend categories

Benefits in standardized business cases

Within the portfolio management process there is a need to define the validity factors for a new investment idea (i.e., what are the minimum characteristics that define an investment proposal) and utilizing a standardized method for capturing investment data. Capturing the data in a standardized business case format creates a common language for reviewing investment proposals throughout the organization, making it easy to understand and compare information in an objective way.

Here are some example elements that a business case format may contain:

1. scope of the investment
2. estimated cost of the investment
3. estimated benefits the investment would bring to the organization (financial and nonfinancial)
4. dependencies on other factors or investments
5. risk profile (based on current organization factors and market conditions)
6. strategic objective alignment (degree of support toward realizing the strategic plan).

The ability to see and manage all investment proposals in a single place and using a common taxonomy of terms provide great value, making it easy to spot duplicate efforts and possible redundant requests at a very early stage, before much effort is spent on them.

Align strategy and business drivers, prioritization of drivers and managing divergence

Defining business/strategic drivers

Often corporate strategies are highly abstract and visionary and with a time horizon far beyond the average life of a typical project. To enable projects and programs to deliver toward these strategies, they must be translated into business or strategic drivers.

Business drivers are measurable, attainable, and actionable objectives.

Business drivers enable management to prioritize corporate objectives and align projects/investment decisions to corporate strategy. Business drivers

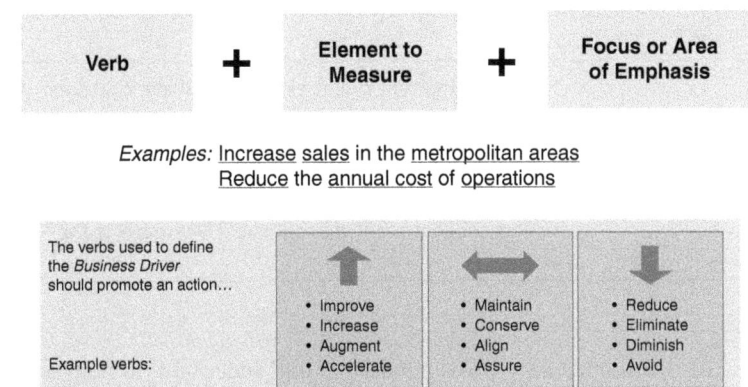

Examples: Increase sales in the metropolitan areas
Reduce the annual cost of operations

The verbs used to define the *Business Driver* should promote an action...

Example verbs:

• Improve	• Maintain	• Reduce
• Increase	• Conserve	• Eliminate
• Augment	• Align	• Diminish
• Accelerate	• Assure	• Avoid

Figure 7.3 Syntax rules to simplify business driver name

help to "operationalize" the business strategy. The strategic value or attractiveness of any initiative will be determined by how many strategic drivers it supports and to what extent.

To help in the translation of strategy into business drivers, it is recommended to follow some simple syntax rules: an actionable verb; a clearly measurable, preferably quantified objective; and well-defined constraint to keep the objective attainable. Figure 7.3 shows how to simplify a business driver name following the syntax rules.

There are best practices to support the successful definition of business drivers:

Business driver definition: best practices	• Driver definitions should be clear to everyone
	• Keep in mind the ultimate application of these drivers – if the portfolio is to cross multiple business units then effort should be made to make driver definitions general enough to apply everywhere while still being specifically measurable within a given business unit.
	• Should tie in closely to existing business strategy but need not directly reflect it; oftentimes business strategies are very abstract, whereas business drivers should be quantifiable and specific.
	• Involve the right people from the get-go: whoever defines strategic drivers must have the authority/understanding to determine company strategy.
	• Driver definition does not happen rapidly. Enough time should be scheduled to understand strategy and agree to business drivers and their weightings with senior executives.

(Continued)

> - Never assume that senior executives all interpret their company's strategy in the same way – strategic driver definition and prioritization will reveal differences and facilitate convergence
> - More than seven drivers are difficult to work with from a timing/concentration perspective. Five–seven is the "sweet spot".

Three key techniques have proven valuable and successful to help organizations develop strategic drivers:

- *Individual interviews*: meeting with the executives of each business unit to define and/or validate their business drivers. Downside: does not encourage cross-business unit collaboration; executives may not have sufficient time to invest in process.
- *Strategic planning meetings*: Work with a senior sponsor, paired with company employees involved in strategic planning to define drivers based on corporate strategy. Downside: does not guarantee executive buy-in; many companies do not have staffed strategic planning positions.
- *Combination of both*: The business units or sponsor individually define the business drivers and then these are discussed and validated with senior management. This provides the best nexus of focused planning paired with executive socialization of the intended drivers.

The outcome of business driver definition is a list of five–ten drivers, well described, measurable, attainable, and actionable, agreed by all key executives and also well communicated to the organization.

> A dedicated Portfolio Manager or Portfolio Management Office is best positioned to facilitate the Driver Definition Process; capture the outcome in a Business Driver Log; and ensure appropriate communication of these drivers to Project and Programme Managers, tasked with designing new change initiatives.

Defining business drivers and benefits impact statements

Benefits impact statements are metrics designed to track implementation of strategic business drivers. Business drivers help to translate strategy into more tangible objectives for business or change initiatives. When initiatives are prioritized later during portfolio prioritization and optimization, the prioritization will be based on:

- the weight of the strategic drivers a project supports and
- the impact the project has on each of these drivers.

In simple terms, the higher the weight of the driver and the greater the impact of a project on the driver, the higher is the strategic value of the project and higher is its rank in the portfolio. To ensure projects do not define their impact on driver subjectively and randomly, it is important to define these as detailed as possible. Figure 7.4 shows a sample business driver with the benefits impact statement.

Well-defined impact statements bring several benefits to project creation:

- objectivity and consistency in impact assessment
- accountability
- drive behavior and performance through organizational focus on key business metrics
- standardization of metrics across projects
- managing the bottom line.

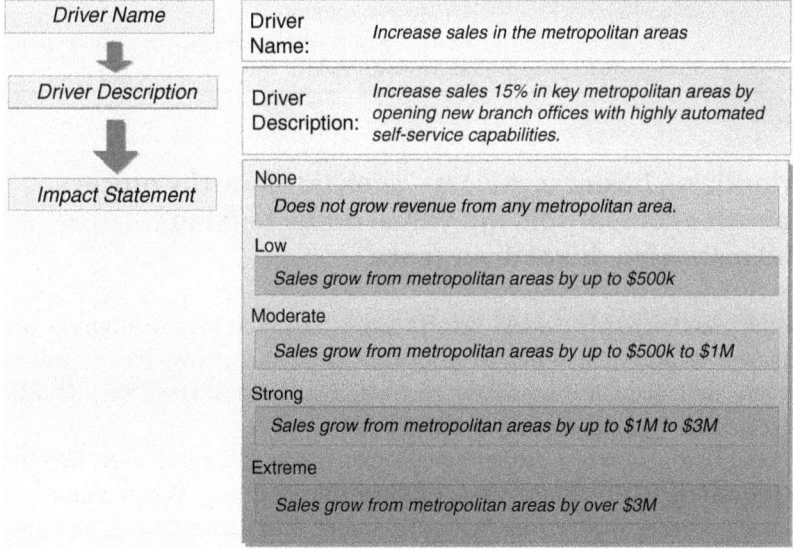

Figure 7.4 Example of formatted business driver with benefits impact statements

There are best practices to support the successful definition of benefits impact statements.

Business driver benefits impact statements: best practices	• When creating impact statements, ensure that all drivers have consistent "weight". An "Extreme" rating in Driver A should deliver the same value to the company that an "Extreme" in Driver B provides. The relative value between multiple drivers will be handled by the pair-wise comparison.
	• Once drivers are agreed to, start the impact analysis in parallel with pair-wise comparison meetings and executive/stakeholder socialization.
	• If soliciting information from multiple business units (KPIs, impact assessments, etc.), ensure to allow sufficient time for data to be completed and returned.
	• It is recommended as a best practice to collect metric actuals as well as impact assessments. The ability to track actuals on a portfolio is a powerful way to measure the success of executed projects.
	• Determine ahead of time who will be reporting on actuals/impact assessments, and bring them up to speed on the new process prior to data collection. Ideally, schedule a working session to socialize the new process with every person responsible for submitting data.
	• Ensure that impact assessment requirements are clearly communicated.
	• Consult your holiday schedule when planning due and delivery dates.

Prioritizing business drivers – analytic hierarchy process, pair-wise comparison, individual driver ranking, and managing driver divergence

Defined and agreed business drivers are an essential step in aligning with business strategy. In order to prioritize these initiatives, these business drivers first need to be ranked and weighted themselves. This is what business driver prioritization achieves.

Deciding which one of the two alternatives is preferable over the other is something most humans are easily capable of doing. When it comes to ranking several alternatives, with all kind of interdependencies and combinations possible, most struggle. This is where analytic hierarchy process (AHP) process helps the decision-making.

The Analytic Hierarchy Process (AHP) is a multi-criteria decision making methodology designed to make complex decisions easier to address, particularly where achieving consensus is important.

The methodology was developed in the 1970s by Dr Thomas L. Saaty who saw a need for a methodology that simplified the process of synthesizing both quantitative and qualitative information in reaching decisions. Saaty leveraged psychological studies that analyzed how the human brain deals with complex decisions and also the mathematical theory of consistent matrices to address a fundamental flaw he saw with group decision-making techniques while working for the Arms Control and Disarmament Agency at the US Department of State. He observed that there were effective techniques to analyze data but no pragmatic methodology to help synthesize the results and then use that information to prioritize criteria.

There are many other formal decision-making approaches, but none of them as useful as AHP:

- multi-attribute decision-making – MADM
- MADM variant – weighted-product method (WPM)
- MADM variant – forced decision matrix (FDM)
- MADM variant – weighted sum method (WSM)
- ELECTRE
- PROMEETHEE
- TOPSIS
- Decision trees
- Plus–minus-interesting (PMI) charts
- six thinking hats
- PARETO
- pros and cons analysis
- maximin and maximax methods
- conjunctive and disjunctive method
- lexicographic method.

There are three reasons why AHP is more effective than other decision-making methodologies:

AHP advantages	• **Structuring complexity**: AHP breaks a complex decision down into hierarchies, mirroring the way the human brain intuitively copes with complexity. A decision as to which car to choose, for example, is broken down into a series of hierarchies for criteria, sub-criteria, and alternatives.

(Continued)

- **Measurement on a ratio scale**: AHP uses "pair-wise comparisons" of criteria to determine the ratio of relative importance for each criterion versus every other criterion. The resulting ratios allow weightings to be derived that reflect this relative comparison. The technique allows numerical weightings to be applied to both quantitative and qualitative information. Using a systematic methodology to convert the experience, intuition, or "gut feel" of experienced managers to a numeric measurement of the relative importance of criteria is a powerful aspect of AHP.
- **Synthesis**: Complex decisions often involve too many dimensions for humans to synthesize intuitively and often result in senior executives interpreting differently the analysis they consider in making decisions, leading to impasse. The impasse is often due to inability to synthesize rather than poor analysis. The hierarchy structure in AHP facilitates easier analysis but the pair-wise comparison and conversion to a ration scale facilitate synthesis of the many different factors in those hierarchies. There are lots of methodologies that help with analysis but few that help to synthesize and even less that do both!

Decisions made using AHP are much more difficult to overturn as they are based on facts and criteria that have been carefully discussed and agreed. The concept of "pet projects" and the associated emotion is eliminated from the decision. Process "buy-in" from both decision-makers and those impacted by decisions is much easier to achieve because the decisions are supported by robust data and methodology and all of the decision-makers participate in the pair-wise comparison. The prioritization achieved using pair-wise approach is often very different to that arrived at by other decision-making methodologies as it forces the relative importance of criteria to be considered carefully.

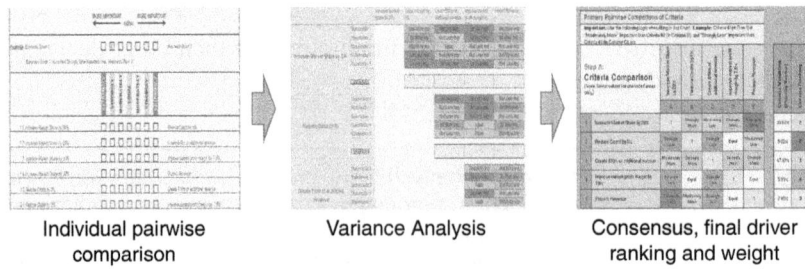

Individual pairwise   Variance Analysis   Consensus, final driver
comparison   ranking and weight

Figure 7.5 AHP steps in business driver prioritization

AHP is best applied using adequate software to facilitate the pair-wise comparison. Figure 7.5 shows the steps that a pair-wise comparison should follow, and these are as follows:

- Individual "pair-wise" comparison sessions with senior management: Each of the interviewed executives will define his/her priorities by comparing the defined business driver against all other drivers.
- Variance analysis of the individual prioritization results: The results of the individual interviews are captured with key discrepancies in the assessment of priorities between executives identified.
- Facilitation of consensus-building session on business driver prioritization: The workshop with all executives focuses on the areas of divergence and assures that at the end a common set of priorities is accepted.

It is common for executives in prioritizing drivers tend to give importance to their areas of interest. As such it becomes necessary during a drivers' definition exercise to understand why each driver is more important than the other among the executives and an independent advisor arbitrate the discussion so that a consensus is reached in alignment with the business strategy. Figure 7.6 shows the divergence that can occur and how getting a consensus is a very important part of the process as we gain buy-in from all executives. Acceptances by key stakeholders provide visibility and transparency on why the projects are selected from the portfolio and how the projects are aligned with the strategies.

Based on the above steps, we can demonstrate how business strategy is aligned to the business drivers which are ranked and weighted and aligned to the benefits impact statement from the projects. Figure 7.7 shows the alignment between business strategy, business driver, and the benefits impact statements.

Portfolio prioritization and optimization: options and trade-off analysis

Typically in any situation, resources are inherently scarce and not one organization can undertake all the desired initiatives on its "wish-list" at any given point in time. There will always be investment ideas which are not being pursued or are postponed due to insufficient resources. Portfolio selection is the part of the SP&B management process that assists organizations in choosing the most valuable group of investment proposals to be pursued. The decision to select a proposal should account for

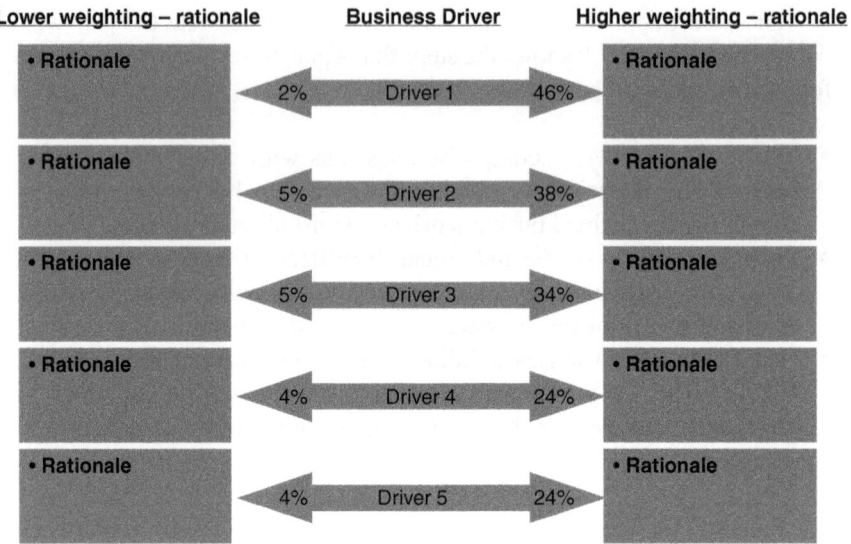

Figure 7.6 Business drivers with divergence – understand why to reach consensus

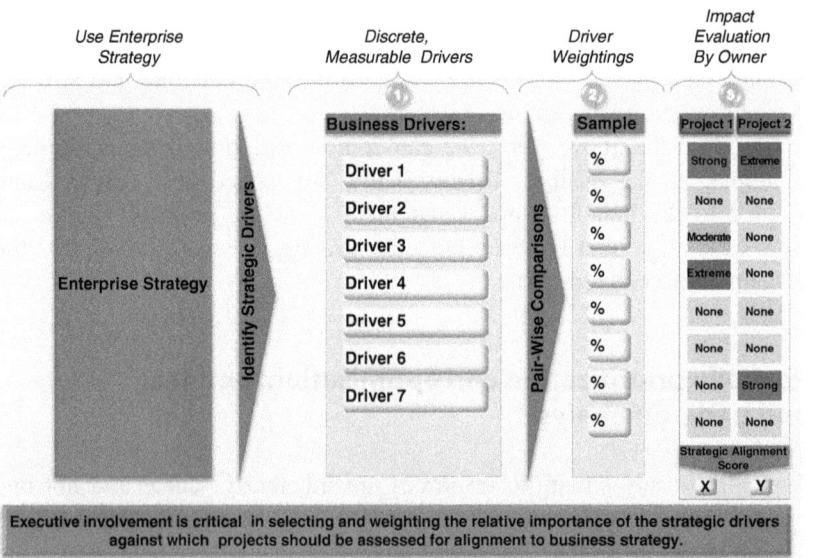

Figure 7.7 Alignment of business strategy to business driver to benefits impact statement for projects

current business climate at the moment of analysis, among other factors. Having the inventory of projects and new proposals created through the innovation demand and pipeline management, the next step in the process is to decide on the ones that should be approved for implementation and granted funding. The SP&B management process suggests that the decision should be made after looking at the entire group of investments as a whole (portfolio), as opposed to analyzing them on a "one-by-one" basis.

Portfolio prioritization

There are several different perspectives when analyzing the collection of investments and ranking them based on the value they provide to the organization:

1. *The subjective decision perspective* (investments are ranked based on the subjective opinion of one group of high-ranked individuals)
   This perspective provides good results in few cases, when the individuals making decisions are objective, experienced, and knowledgeable about the organization and industry. It usually does not provide the best outcome as the decision-makers are likely to treat their "pet projects" preferentially, disregarding the "big picture".
2. *The financial value perspective* (investments are ranked based on financial indicators such as net present value (NPV) or investment rate of return (IRR))
   The financial value technique measures everything in dollar currency and ranks proposals based on their profitability (NPV or IRR). It offers an objective view and therefore better outcome than the "subjective decision" perspective, but it tends to lose sight of the intangible but important benefits that could be gained when implementing some proposals that have a more strategic importance, as the financial valuation focuses only on monetary figures.
3. *The strategic value perspective* (investments are ranked based on their impact on the business drivers)
   Analyzing proposals through a business strategy lens and prioritizing them based on their strategic value (contribution to achieving the organization's objectives) provides an objective way of selecting projects, without limiting itself to a noncomprehensive, hard-currency perspective, alone. Sometimes this method may incorporate a degree of subjectivity when it involves internal experts on the culture and dynamics of the organization in the process.

Portfolio optimization and selection – decision-making support

When carried out properly, portfolio management process removes the subjectivity associated with selecting investments by aligning new investment ideas to previously agreed strategic objectives. When agreed by most of the stakeholders in the organization, this method drives adoption and further ensures a successful portfolio management implementation. Part of the portfolio selection process allows for the ability to model multiple scenarios based on various project dimensions, all of which serve as decision-making support material for portfolio selection. Examples of such analysis can include one or more of the following constraints:

- financial constraints
- resource constraints
- project priority (based on strategic impact)
- risk level
- project financial benefits.

In 1952, Harry M. Markowitz published an article called "Portfolio Selection" in the *Journal of Finance*. In it, he demonstrated how to reduce the standard deviation of returns on asset portfolios by selecting assets which don't move in exactly the same ways. Markowitz showed that, by choosing assets whose returns are not perfectly positively correlated, the risk of a portfolio can be lowered while maintaining or increasing the expected return. The article defined a Markowitz Efficient Portfolio as one with minimum risk for a given level of return, and maximum return for a given level of risk: no additional diversification can improve a Markowitz Efficient Portfolio for a given return or a given level of risk. The set of all Markowitz Efficient Portfolios constitutes the Markowitz Efficient Frontier: risk/return combinations above the Frontier are not possible, and risk/return combinations below the Frontier are not efficient.

He laid down some basic principles for establishing an advantageous relationship between risk and return, and his work is still in use 40 years later where the Markowitz Efficient Frontier is used in project portfolio optimization calculation. Microsoft in their MS Project 2010 uses a linear programming module originally written by Lindo, who uses a mathematical technique to maximize an objective variable, subject to a constraint (e.g., maximize value, subject to a budget constraint). This is depicted in Figure 7.8, which shows optimal portfolios that meet key strategic measures and satisfy business constraints constructed.

This is a graphical representation of how optimization can be used to ensure that the projects that generate the most value per unit of constraint

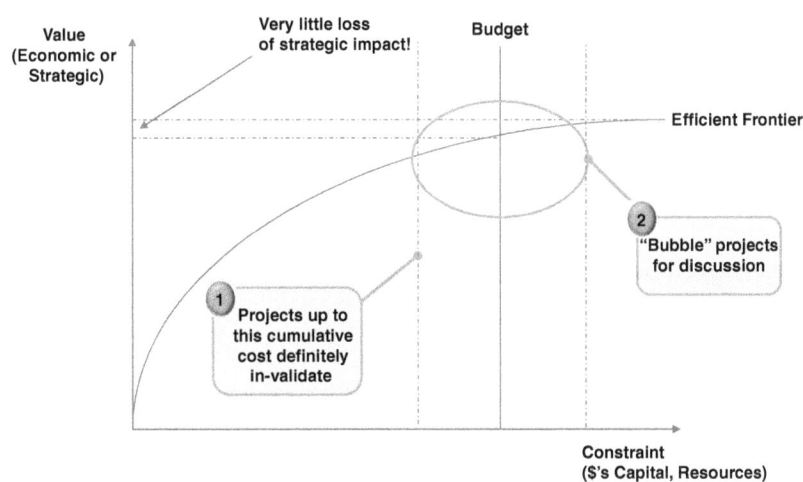

Figure 7.8 Optimal portfolio to maximize benefits value for business: Markowitz Efficient Frontier

($'s, resource, risk) are done first. The flatter part of the curve shows portfolios that include projects that are less efficient in generating value – these are the ones to cut first, especially if they are resource intensive or high risk. Note that the curve is a smooth one because the x-axis units are cumulative.

We have often helped clients to maximize value variables for portfolios such as:

- Measurable strategic value/benefits
- NPV
- Benefit-to-cost ratio (an efficiency measure as it considers how much value is generated per $ of cost invested)
- Discounted profitability index (also an efficiency measure as it considers the amount of NPV generated per $ of cost invested).

Typical constraints will include:

- Budget or cost
- Resources (transferable between locations or projects)
- Risk (acceptable level of overall execution risk in the portfolio).

Additionally, project selection should also take into account the compliance (mandatory) initiatives, project inter-dependencies, and project achievability when making decisions on which investments to pursue.

Graphs and charts showing the multiple dimensions of a project portfolio should also be used in order to facilitate sound decision-making. This approach provides quantitative insight into an investment's effectiveness and control over project budgets and is based on objective criteria rather than personal preferences.

Portfolio delivery with benefits and value tracking

Benefits and value tracking

Benefits and value management allows organizations to quantify factors like growth and improvements in certain existing processes or areas in a standardized fashion, and keep internal investment requestors accountable for their ideas and business cases for new funding areas. The two main areas of a benefit management methodology are benefits estimating and benefits realization.

Benefits estimating

Estimating the benefits that could be derived from a new internal investment is not easy. In order to ensure consistency and accuracy, standardized estimating models should be employed by the organization, allowing all project requestors to use the same approach and assumptions when providing financial or nonfinancial benefit estimates.

Benefits realization

Benefits realization is the process where during and after initiatives are implemented, the actual benefits derived from their implementation are tracked and compared with the estimated figures, for a predetermined time period. The variance between these two numbers is used to determine the effectiveness of the investment and ultimately of the business case, providing real historical data that can be used when new and/or similar investments are being proposed. At the portfolio level, the benefit realization element assesses the capability of achieving strategy. On a secondary level, tracking the actual benefits realized against the estimated figures for each investment leads to better future estimates by requestor(s), while also setting up an accountability mechanism for delivering according to plans.

Benefits and value management will be discussed in greater detail in Chapter 9 of this book.

Portfolio delivery tracking

After the optimal collection of investment ideas has been selected for implementation and funding has been approved, the strategy portfolio and benefits management methodology recommends tracking initiative progress with periodic reviews. The reviews should occur at equal intervals of time (monthly, quarterly, etc.) and should include status reports on progress (in terms of money spent, resources utilized, and schedule completion). Actual spends should be captured for each reporting period and measured against the planned figures. Additionally, progress of the implementation against the initially defined scope for a set of initiatives is a proven method for identifying problems early. When tracking the portfolio, the portfolio management and project management methodologies complement each other. On one hand the initiatives are split into small portions of work – project tasks carried out by small teams and managed following project management guidelines. On the other hand, the progress of each task is aggregated up to the initiative level, for portfolio status reporting against portfolio management principles. Employing both of them in parallel provides organizations with a robust delivery capability (on time, on scope, and within budget) and guarantees that the work is in line with strategic objectives.

The benefit of monitoring progress and expenditures at an aggregate level (for all the initiatives grouped together within a portfolio) is that it facilitates the review process for meeting the organization's strategic objectives. The implication of an initiative being off-track during implementation to an organization's objectives is easily determined and quantified during this activity and allows for appropriate measures to be taken. A secondary benefit is enhanced visibility into the dependencies between initiatives being implemented across different parts of the organization, when the areas implementing the interdependent initiatives lack visibility into each other's progress (program management).

Portfolio recalibration

SP&B management is never a static process. The phases presented above occur on an ongoing basis, with new proposals being added to the portfolio all the time, and approved work being tracked until completed. A mature SP&B framework should result in portfolio re-assessments or re-calibrations occurring at equal time intervals (often on a quarterly or semi-annual basis) where the portfolio is re-prioritized and aligned with potential changes in organizational strategy. As a result of the re-prioritization, some existing projects may be suspended or reduced in scope, as they no longer add value or are significantly out of alignment with initial estimates, and replaced with new investment proposals that better serve the business objectives.

In this chapter, we have demonstrated the ability to align strategy with portfolio investment decision using our SP&B management framework. We have explored using the AHP as a multi-criteria decision-making approach designed to make complex decisions easier to address, particularly when achieving consensus is important. We used the pair-wise approach (one to one) to convert the experience, intuition, or "gut feel" of experienced managers to a numeric measurement and manage any divergence so that the business drivers are ranked in alignment with the strategy. We also explored the portfolio efficient frontier as a mathematical means to optimize and select your investments based on your constraints. In my experience I have found that lots of people know what to do, but only few people do what they know, and these few are successful because knowing is not enough but taking action is what matters. The next chapter explains in detail how RM is essential for delivering and achieving your project outcomes. The reason why I am emphasizing it is because RM is commonly forgotten as it involves actions to be taken by people.

CHAPTER 8

What Is Resource Management? Is It the Forgotten Link to Achievability of Actionable Plans?

Ideally we should manage portfolio triple constraints strategic alignment, value/benefits delivery, and resource capacity simultaneously; however, in the corporate world it is a huge challenge to balance these three constraints. I believe that this chapter provides us a relevant framework and best practices to help organizations manage these triple constraints which fit the purpose of their operations.

When you read "Resources", think Humans. The textbooks define resource management (RM) as the management of humans, cost, and materials. While this is true, our experience says that 60–70 per cent of the resources for a project tend to be of the human variety.

While other types of resources – cost, systems, material – are project ingredients too, the human resource (HR) is more elusive and more laden with variables. What are the planning and forecasting abilities? Do we have the skills needed? What are those resources working on right now? How good are they at achieving their deadlines and deliverables?

As we think of answers to the above questions asked, we may realize that effective RM and portfolio management go hand-in-hand. What's difficult about RM is that most organizations don't have the information they need to do it in one place. In order to evaluate demand against capacity, we need a portfolio view of projects, current and future. Unless you have a view of what you need to deliver over the next 6 or 12 months, it becomes virtually impossible to do effective planning or know what capacity you have.

A lifecycle for RM can be broken into four key areas:

- *Definition*: HR/resource policies, rates, and supporting fiscal periods, as well as the definition and identification of the key components and levels of the organization/resource breakdown structure.

- *Development*: Entry and ongoing maintenance of resource plans and assignments, including baselining and versioning, as well as support of a top–down or bottom–up planning approach.
- *Delivery:* The collection, either manually or automatically, of the actual; and, conversely, the provision of configurable reports and views to support the entire process.
- *Drive:* A series of what-if modeling scenarios and variance analysis to drive ongoing decision-making and performance tracking, involving resource demand versus capacity analysis.

Have a view of your project portfolio: define resources upfront

Say someone has an idea for a new project that he/she believes business should embark upon. At that point you'll start to do a high-level assessment about what it's going to cost you to deliver this. That encompasses a high-level estimate of the total resources you might need. Note that I say "estimate". This means you simply identify the generic roles required. If you have a view of your portfolio of projects and their respective resource role requirements, you'll be able to assess whether the organization can take on the new project or not.

How easy is it to gain visibility as a resource manager?

Visibility into what a resource is currently scheduled to work on, what the person is actually working on, and what he/she should be working on is a complex matter and depends on the relative maturity level of the organization and the processes enabled to support it. Being able to effectively track time and expense, as well as overall progress, is the key to ensuring the capture and aggregation of performance metrics. Moreover, this data provide real-time visibility into how much capacity an individual or group of individuals have at any given time so that informed decisions can be made about re-assignments and re-prioritization of work.

Execution and tracking begins at the most basic level with the assignment of team members to project tasks. The RM solution should provide visibility into the current capacity and allocations for resources across all work, including projects, work items, administrative tasks, and so on. Integration with other systems such as timesheets and Visual Studio may warrant additional investigation, in that effective RM must take into account all work (demand) and all availability (capacity).

Remaining work can be re-scheduled and re-assigned as required and should be reflected in real-time to the system to identify over- and under-utilization scenarios. The objective is to maximize effort on those activities that maximize value or ROI and those that are aligned to both the strategic objectives of the organization and the individual as well.

In summary, a solution addressing resource execution and tracking needs to encapsulate the following:

- assignment/work item management
- progress tracking
- status reports
- time and expense collection
- utilization.

Mature management

Effective RM takes a collective view of your portfolio of projects and considers what your resource demand will need to be to deliver them successfully. It enables management to make better decisions by letting them know which projects they can undertake and in what order, based on current capacity; allows project owners to make a business case for funding to get more resources where necessary; and helps the organization clarify which projects need to be delayed or killed for lack of resources. You'll know you have RM right when you have visibility into the requirements for work that needs to be done over the next three to six months. That level of maturity allows you to plan for the future and not simply be reactive.

This visibility also increases the achievability of the plan and induces the much needed confidence in management in seeing its portfolio succeed in execution.

Resource manager: forgotten link to portfolio management?

The typical practice of portfolio management involves a meeting of senior management to evaluate (and, in some organizations, prioritize) a list of projects – given a number of factors – to provide the greatest value to the company. They then communicate project approvals to the organization and hope for the best.

Projects enter this process with or without project plans. In some cases there are detailed, carefully constructed Microsoft Project schedule plans;

in others a "to-do" list in document or spreadsheet form. Some companies have a mix of both types; others may be all one or the other.

But most companies don't systematically ask the resource managers – line or functional managers – about the availability of resources and skills to support the projects. These resource managers are the individuals who have broad responsibilities in areas such as HR, technical competency, and balancing project and nonproject demand. (As I like to say, resource managers have a "day job".) Without this missing ingredient, portfolio planning ultimately has little credibility.

How does this play out? Let's say the organization has 50 projects in its portfolio. Someone comes up with a great project worth more than any other project in the portfolio. Those senior leaders say, "Hey, this is great. We really should do this." So they make it priority number one. They make an educated guess about the effect the new project has on the portfolio, but they don't have the data or analysis to fully understand the impact.

Management teams are making important decisions with fuzzy and unreliable data about resource supply–demand balance. Before putting in a project and assigning it a priority based on its known attributes, decision-makers need to consider a fundamental question: Do we have people available with the right skills to do it?

Figuring out the answer to this question is where the resource manager's insights are essential.

You can follow a number of approaches to facilitate resource planning and the budgeting process, as well as the staffing and subsequent scheduling process. For the most part, any combination of bottom–up and top–down planning can be used, each most likely addressing the needs of different constituents, for example, providing the ability to plan at the role level versus the individual or "named" resource level. Resource plans provide an early mechanism to extrapolate resource demand even before a project has commenced, thereby providing the necessary level of insight into overall capacity relative to demand. The forecast should be enabled by entering full-time equivalent (FTE) units, hours, and dollars, with a possible translation from dollars to units based on the role/individual resource selected. The planning period should be flexible so that varying levels of granularity can be accommodated (weeks, months, quarters, years, etc.) and so that a conversion from one to another can be automated (such as viewing by week or by year). Some products offer a posting process to extrapolate values from one planning period to an entirely different planning period.

To facilitate the planning process amid the reality that not everything is a sure thing, you'll want the ability to identify whether or not resources are committed or proposed. You'll want to be able to filter out each of these to see what is actually committed and what is being planned or proposed. You'll also want to be able to invoke a requisitioning process, especially within matrix-organizations, to ensure that a formalized request, proposed and committed, is tracked and that the staffing process has some level of approval. Any solution must be able to start with an abstract or high-level estimate and subsequently be expanded as more information becomes available and as the relative level of maturity within the organization or individuals increases. Notifications, alerts, and workflow should all be enabled to ensure effective use and collaboration throughout the workforce planning process.

The overall solution must be able to analyze and assign resources to projects based on skill, availability, and location, as well as a host of other criteria. Automated and manual matching and searching capabilities must exist to facilitate the assignment of resources at both the plan and schedule levels. When scheduling an organization's work, managing resources wisely helps ensure that capacity and capabilities align with current and future needs.

Optionally, the solution should provide for manual and automatic leveling or optimizations that take into consideration the best available candidates, as well as potential cost implications (to enable the organization to leverage the best skills at the most advantageous cost). The leveling should transcend projects, programs, and even portfolios, as well as lines of business. This entails making sure that the right resources are working on the right projects at the right time.

Another aspect of RM is career development through the alignment of individual goals with that of the line of business or organization. This functionality provides for performance appraisals, status reports, and other performance tracking mechanisms to ensure that all information is captured (or accessible) in one central location. Having this type of information provides visibility into what skills the organization has now and well into the future.

In summary, a solution addressing resource planning and scheduling should encapsulate the following:

- resource plans for the top–down approach
- assignments/work (project/web planning for the bottoms up)
- resource leveling/optimization (for advanced portfolio integration)
- substitution wizards and team building (for search and automated matching of skills and availability)
- a resource negotiation process (for notifications, alerts, and workflow enablement)
- resource development plans.

A major factor in project failure

Almost every project-driven company in the world has a resource planning problem. Typically, resource managers are off doing their own resource planning in Excel spreadsheets. Most resource managers don't use scheduling tools such as Microsoft Project because the tools are too detailed or complex or are otherwise inappropriate for the type of resource planning they need to do.

The result is that the organization has a bunch of scattered Excel spreadsheets being maintained by individuals. Trying to consolidate those spreadsheets for the purposes of portfolio management activities is a nightmare: The data are inconsistent, consolidation is difficult and time consuming, and updates occur at different times.

Project managers complain that they are not getting the staffing and support they need, and that is a major reason why their projects are failing. On the other hand, the resource managers are saying, "This is crazy! Management has no idea what my people are working on. They think we can do everything, and they keep adding more and more to the workload – and they never prioritize any of it."

Does the ultimate resource planning solution drive portfolio execution?

Although implementing portfolio management begins with the inventory of projects and their attributes, the biggest payback comes from integrating systematic resource planning into the process.

The basic premise of a RM solution is the centralization and – more importantly – standardization of resources and resource-related information. Many applications today provide a central resource pool from which all activity is assigned and tracked. For example, Microsoft Project offers a shared resource pool and Project Server provides an enterprise resource pool. To provide governance over the process, the system should also work with local rules and regulations and be aligned with corporate HR and business polices. Policies such as statutory holidays, working hours (resource calendars), units of measure, and applicable rates should be captured and assigned and governed accordingly. Moreover, the information about resources is typically stored and maintained in other systems such as HR, payroll, inventory, fixed assets, and directory services such as Active Directory. Consequently, any RM solution should provide some level of integration with any or all of the applications mentioned. For example, the solution should obtain skills and certifications from the HR application so that these values can be used in search and matching algorithms with the staffing and planning processes.

In summary, a solution addressing resource policies and profiles should encapsulate the following:

- HR/Active Directory interface
- types: resource, material, equipment, expense, other
- capability: skills capture, including competency levels and proficiency
- availability: resource calendars, holidays, self-service time-off
- rates: billing, costing, planning, and so on
- categorization: Internal/external/other
- roles
- alignment: for instance, organizational structure/line of business.

The Portfolio DecisionWare is an advanced portfolio management tool which provides an Excel interface in which resource managers maintain their forecast of how resources will be used. Because it is Excel-based, most users are comfortable with it. But unlike Excel, this Portfolio DecisionWare software tool consolidates that data into a central relational database that enables analysis and reporting at any level, global to individual. The analysis highlights – well in advance – staffing conflicts and problems that could send a project off the rails. This allows management to act rather than react.

As an example, the resource manager would use this Portfolio software tool to enter forecast demand, by role/skill or resource name, for each project the manager's team is supporting. The resource manager has to own that data, since he/she is responsible for delivering those resources. The use of the tool allows the resource managers to update their forecasts, save it to the database, and thereby make that information available to the project teams.

Another key tool from Microsoft is the Project Server 2010 which manages project portfolios effectively. The Project Server derives resource requirements from the resource plan created and feeds into the portfolio analysis using resources as constraints. Figure 8.1 shows resource availability over project requirements. This depth of visibility through early resource planning helps analyze and optimize the portfolio by applying resource constraints. Portfolio managers can now build multiple scenarios based on various combinations of resources available against each project in the portfolio being analyzed.

In some organizations RM is about commitments and the ability to deliver, while to others it may involve simply assigning resources to a task. But fundamentally it is an issue of balancing and optimizing supply

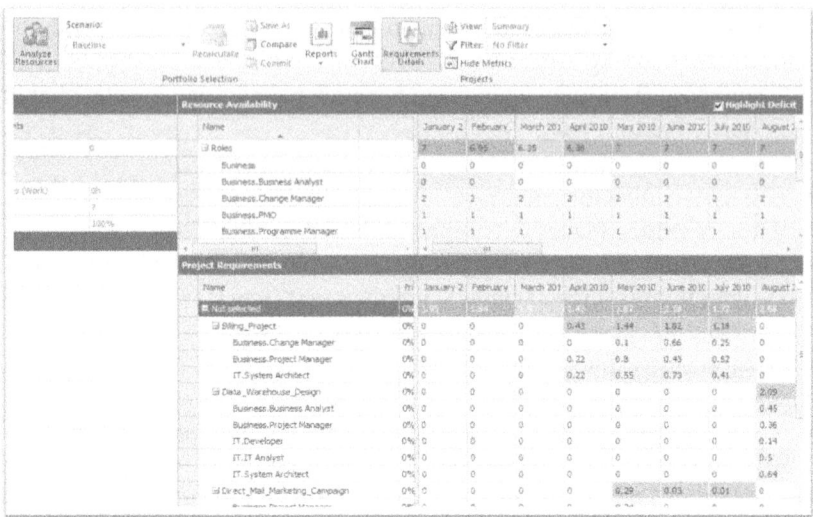

Figure 8.1 Resource planning helps in resource constraint analysis during portfolio optimization (*with permission from Microsoft*)

versus demand. We have found that the right combination of technology solutions and process cadence can automate and enhance the definition, record-keeping, planning, tracking, and optimization of most RM efforts.

The functionality and capabilities essential for an effective RM solution was reviewed in earlier sections of this chapter. Depending on the relative maturity of the organization and the constituents responsible for the process, appropriate solutions can range from simple Excel worksheets that allow users to monitor available resources to more complex enterprise tools such as Microsoft Project Server 2010, which enable the organization to perform what-if scenarios and sophisticated resource assignment based on business drivers and their consensus-based priorities. This overview of capabilities presumes the most mature organization, since that is where the smart application of these technologies can really deliver value.

What-if and scenario-based analysis and modeling based on KPIs and targets is almost a given for any RM solution. Users need the ability to slice and dice through the information, based on varying levels of granularity. They also need to be able to aggregate and roll up any level of reporting structure (such as the organizational breakdown structure or work breakdown structure) using both planned and actual data. Much of the analysis in Microsoft products is provided through integration with SQL Analysis Services (OLAP) and most recently with Excel Services, which will only gain in popularity and use. Modeling can be facilitated through interaction with Microsoft PerformancePoint, Excel, and application functionality.

In modeling, the premise is to align resources with key initiatives to maximize capacity and ensure that you have the right resources working on the right deliverables. Scenarios as well as the targets should be savable and usable in comparisons.

Demand and capacity planning gives you visibility into your entire resource pool, helping you deliver the highest return from your workforce. Project managers should be able to use real-time "what-if" modeling to measure new project requests against current projects, capacity, skill-sets, and projected costs/return. They can also evaluate resource capacity based on available hours and full-time employees (FTEs) and compare all project requests against overall capacity. Capacity planning should also provide a compelling, visual representation of the opportunities within and limits of your workforce.

Demand management focuses on the evaluation, prioritization, and funding of new business initiatives. This allows executives to involve business counterparts for more collaborative decisions-making, align with business priorities, and communicate value.

Supply management focuses on the management of delivery capabilities, spanning project and portfolio management as well as RM. This allows executives to reduce costs, allocate resources according to business strategies, and deliver projects reliably.

In summary, a solution addressing resource execution and tracking needs to encapsulate the following:

- demand versus capacity analysis
- resource plan analysis and aggregation
- resource usage and assignments
- resource allocations
- time-phase analysis and modeling across varying planning periods
- identification of current and long-term skill gaps
- alignment of resources and project investments with strategic objectives.

A better way to do portfolio management: make planning pervasive

You won't be successful if you do portfolio management once a year at operating plan time. Nor is it enough to do portfolio management once a quarter during portfolio and strategy reviews. Every project phase gate review must have a portfolio component – what effect does this project have on other projects in the portfolio and what effect do they have on this one?

We recommend resource managers do a rolling three-month forecast each month (or more frequently if appropriate) and that company leaders require a resource demand forecast for the remainder of the project at each phase gate. That way, when the big exception occurs (and it will), you won't be scrambling like Indiana Jones in front of the giant rolling ball. You'll know what the impact is, and you'll have credible data with which to build alternative responses.

Approaching a phase gate review, the project team will have updated its project plans. Likewise, the resource managers will have updated the forecast of how their resources are going to be used and that data will be rolled into the project plans. At the phase review, neither resource managers nor project managers should be surprised by the resource plan; either they are in agreement that the plan is good or they are jointly raising an issue for senior management to resolve.

If the resource expectations are different from that specified at the beginning of the project, it will have an impact on other projects in the portfolio that are of lower priority than the one under review. The portfolio team needs to assess the impact to decide what gives schedule, scope, cost, and hiring. That kind of discussion needs to happen as a portfolio discussion.

I view the key attributes of an effective, sustainable portfolio management process thus:

1. Capture project schedule and status data from project managers periodically.
2. Capture fresh, credible demand data from first-level (By this, I mean resource managers who have no resource managers reporting to them; they have individual contributors as direct reports) resource managers periodically.
3. At phase gates, require concurrence by project managers, resource managers, and portfolio managers that the resource plan is realistic and the project plan is achievable, and baseline everything – the "contract".
4. Demonstrate with prioritized resource/skill supply–demand analysis that you can finish everything you start.
5. Keep it simple, and use the kinds of tools that users are familiar with.

The portfolio software enables and embodies all five of these attributes.

Project management alone is not an effective method for portfolio planning. It is fundamentally incomplete because resource managers are not formally responsible for creating and maintaining project resource plans. It is too complicated to be widely and uniformly used well. As a result the resource plan data are unreliable. By bringing resource demand forecasting into the planning process and including everyone in a simple process, organizations can stay ahead of the big problems and create portfolio plans that will be respected.

As in the previous chapters we realize that the human element is the one thing we commonly forget. From creative imagination to implementing project portfolio successfully, we need the right resource to act with the right focus and energy. The human resources are our intellectual capital who add value and create success for our organization. If we do not manage and harness this intellectual capital well, we are for sure to spiral down to an inevitable death.

The next chapter will discuss the benefits and value management as part of the SP&B management framework.

CHAPTER 9

Where Are the Business Benefits Invested? Are We Tracking and Realizing Our Benefits?

Benefits are an often talked about thing within the portfolio, program, and project environment. But what actually is a business benefit?

One definition offered by the Office of Government and Commerce in their Managing Successful Programs guidance is:

> A benefit is an outcome of change that is perceived as positive by stakeholders.

(OGC Definition)

What is clear from this definition is that benefits are an outcome of change. Organizations tend to manage change through programs and projects and it is these that will deliver the benefits to the organization. Business benefits describe the value to an organization that a change provides. This can be described using a variety of measures and will include tangible and intangible benefits, both financial and nonfinancial.

One thing in business is certain and that is the need for change and as these changes deliver value to the organization in the form of benefits it is in defining and measuring these benefits that we can assess this value. This must be balanced along with cost and risk so that we have a true understanding of the ROI. It is also the case that many changes will be running at the same time in an organization, so benefits will play an important part in decision-making across the portfolio to select the project investments that will give the optimal return considering the organizational constraints on money and resource capabilities on which investments to initiate given the organizations constraints.

Benefits tend to be either tangible (measurable – usually financial) or intangible (less measurable nonfinancial). For benefits management to be valuable it is best to apply measures to all benefits. Usually a good starting point is to use the existing organizations' KPIs to look for the types of measures that are important to the business and then a set of benefit categories to cover the portfolio can be constructed around this.

Why even consider benefits?

Are benefits just the latest management buzz-word or can they actually provide value to the organization? Organizations measure the performance of their operations, so why would they not need a measure for how successful their investment in change is? Some of the reasons for considering benefits are:

- Benefits are the fundamental reason for initiating change programs – it is the measure of the value of business change to the organization and the ROI;
- Benefits are a fundamental part of the business case and therefore investment decision;
- Robustly defining benefits will enable prioritization of the portfolio, allowing comparisons between programs and projects using a consistent measure and therefore enabling the highest ROI;
- Once a program has been initiated, it should continually be reviewed for its ongoing value and validity of its business case. Tracking benefits delivery of the program is a key indicator of whether an investment will succeed;
- Benefits can provide a way of describing and communicating the value of investments to shareholders and stakeholders.

As per the definition of benefits, they are the outcome of change in an organization. Therefore, in order to decide which change to undertake benefits with measures are required to enable the correct investment decisions. For a portfolio of change programs and projects defining benefits for each of them will allow the comparison of their corresponding value or return to the organization. Ensuring benefits are defined and measured is also a way of ensuring that investment is not wasted.

Benefits should form part of the business case and justification for investment and this should be constantly reviewed during the execution of the change program to make sure that the investment is still valuable and will deliver the anticipated level of value to the organization. If it is not then it should be considered for termination and launch of another programs of higher value. External factors may reduce benefits, so ensuring the benefits are still a valid key, otherwise the investment may be best placed elsewhere.

The nature of program and projects and the portfolio optimization and program initiation processes will often mean that it is difficult to accurately estimate benefits before the program has moved into execution and detailed planning has been carried out. This is okay for the initial investment decision, as all programs will be in this position with often only a high-level estimate of cost, benefits, and risk available for selection decision. As a living artifact the business case including its costs, benefits, and risk should be continually refined throughout the programs' execution so that it can be continually reviewed for its value, justification, and position against competing programs in the portfolio. Figure 9.1 shows an example of how the SP&B framework can integrate with a company's project lifecycle to support the Benefits Tracking and Realization after execution.

It is also the case that as programs and projects are temporary vehicles to deliver change to the business, it may be that the program structure has long disappeared when benefits are still being realized. For this reason it is important to have a clear definition of how the benefits will be measured for realization with handovers to appropriate operational resources who can continue to monitor benefits realizations after

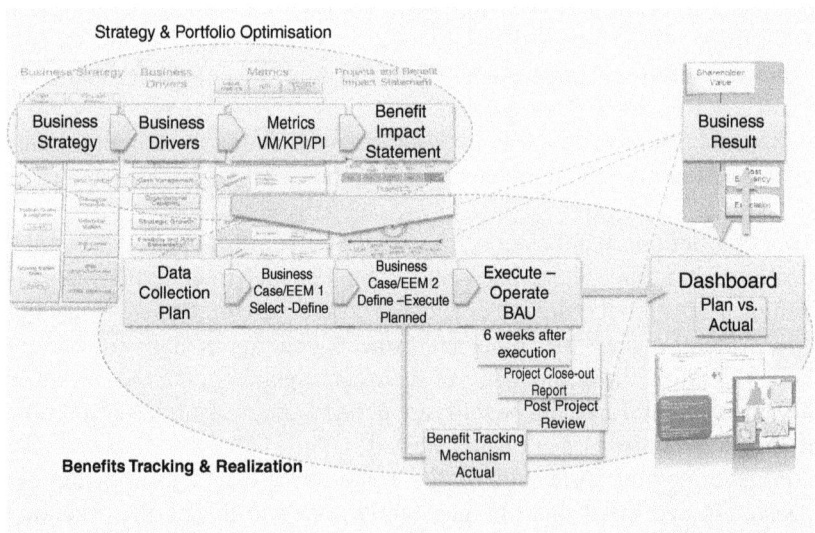

Figure 9.1 An example of end-to-end strategy, portfolio, and benefits management framework with project life cycle

the program has completed. Continued adjustment and identification of further opportunities will also be required.

When do we tend to use benefits?

All good Program and Project management theory will stress the importance of a business case. This could be at program or project level but when talking about large change benefits tend to be defined at the program level. The benefits in a business case will demonstrate the value or return to the business from successfully executing the program along with other information such as risk, cost, timeline, and dependencies.

Business cases will be built prior to the initiation of a program right upfront in the program lifecycle and hence at this point the data may not be the most mature. It will be used to inform the investment decision and compete in the portfolio against other investments.

Once initiated the business case should be constantly reviewed and updated with changes and at gateways to ensure that the investment is still valid in returning value to the organization. Benefits should be monitored for their realization during and after the program, maximizing any opportunities for further benefits.

Benefit categories

In large organizations with multiple large change programs happening at once it is good practise to develop a consistent set of benefit categories which can be used across the full portfolio of programs and projects to define benefits. Using an organization's existing strategy and KPIs can be beneficial in defining these categories. For example, most organizations particularly in the current economic climate will have some form of efficiency/cost reduction KPI measure – therefore cost reduction would be an obvious choice as a benefit category. Similarly, perhaps an organization has increase in revenue as a key part of its strategy – therefore an increase revenue benefit category would be another choice. Defining a set of benefit categories will enable:

- each program to define their benefits in a clear and easy manner;
- Consideration of benefits in the portfolio optimization process to ensure selection of the highest value investments through apples to apples comparison across the portfolio;

- Demonstration of the impact of the portfolio against the categories and the link back to the organization's strategy and KPIs.

Benefits can be tangible or intangible; therefore, the set of benefit categories should cover these types. Some example benefit categories are given below to cover both public and private sector organizations:

- Cost reduction – cost saving direct from the bottom line based on outcome of the program (e.g., automation, efficiencies from improved processes). Measured financially and is likely to be the easiest to track for its realization due to it being tangible and visible in the accounts.
- Example: Decommissioning legacy un-needed IT applications to reduce hardware, software license, and support costs.
- Cost avoidance – investments made to avoid future costs. For example, investing in a program to re-locate premises due to future rent increases.
- Increase in revenue – benefits that will increase revenue for the organization. Most likely to be expressed in financial terms but can also be linked to sales targets and market growth KPIs.
- Maintain revenue – in most industries investment is required to maintain a revenue stream and remain competitive in the market. The benefit will relate to the current level of revenue and its maintenance. Similar to increase in revenue, this can also be measured financially and linked to KPIs such as market share.
- Improvement in quality – manufacturing organizations may use this in particular. This tends to be a nonfinancial measure and is related to product or service quality.
- Reduce risk – a difficult category to measure but one that a lot of organizations will want to improve. A good guide is to use the organizations risk strategy for pointers on how risk is measured and use these as measures for this benefit.
- Improvement in customer satisfaction or service levels – often applicable instead of increase revenue for public sector organizations.
- Improved capacity – investments made to increase the capacity of the current IT systems, for example, increase possible size of positions, daily number of transactions, number of clients, and so on.
- Improved security – investments made to IT/Technology Security to improve the protection of the bank against internal and external threats.
- Improve control – investments made to reduce operational risk or the overall control framework of the operations.
- Improve stability – investments made to improve the stability of systems and reduce the outage time.

Most organizations will have specific regulatory and mandatory programs that need to be initiated. Although these will most likely be classed as "Force-in" to the portfolio – that is, they must be initiated and will consume a level of resources and budget – they could actually have benefits associated that will also need to be considered. If regulatory changes were not carried out, this may attract fines, hence this could be classed as a cost avoidance benefit by avoiding the future fines. There may also be other impacts like enhancing security or stability, so these programs and projects should also have a business case which can then provide a basis for optimizing the benefits of these mandatory programs and making the most out of the investment.

All benefit categories should be defined with measures which may be financial or otherwise. Some measures may be simple to define such as a cost reduction benefit, and in these cases further detail can be captured, such as where the saving will be made (cost center, budget area etc.), for ease of tracking of realization.

When a business case is being constructed, the benefits defined should be defined with measures that are realistic and with timing that will relate to the deliverables triggering the benefits. For example, a new system may provide efficiencies in an accounting team which can save two hours per week for each staff member. This can be quantified with a financial value as a cost reduction benefit; however, a saving of two hours per member of staff in a team will not truly deliver any cost reduction benefit as the members of staff will remain just with two more hours available! So in order to truly realize the benefit, changing the roles should be considered so that a full head could be redeployed elsewhere.

Dis-benefits should also be considered in any program – most common will be the increase in cost due to a particular action – for example, a new IT capability that will incur additional maintenance/support and license costs. There can also be other dis-benefits that are intangible, such as increased training costs, dip in service levels due to new processes/technology, and dip in staff morale because of this; these also need to be captured for the program so that they can be taken into account in the value calculation.

How does an organization measure business benefits?

Measurement of business benefits can often be a difficult process with a number of challenges:

Defining the measures

Most benefits can be defined with a financial value, even if this means using assumptions for costing purposes. However, some benefits cannot necessarily be defined in financial terms and need other measures. This is often the case for soft factors such as staff morale or brand image. In these situations it is often necessary to define a measure and take an initial measurement as a baseline. Then periodic measures can be taken during the program to determine whether there is a positive increase against the baseline. For example, if a benefit is defined as improving staff morale, taking a measure of staff morale through some form of survey before a program has begun and then taking at regular periods during the program to assess the change is a good way of measuring the benefit. Often such KPIs exist in an organization that can be used to both define the benefit and measure progress and realization. In some cases it can be difficult to assign the change in a KPI to just the delivery of a program as many other programs will be running in the organization, and other factors may also affect the KPI. However, in understanding which programs may impact on a particular KPI, reviews across the programs can take place to see if the group of programs contributes to this KPI.

For example, let's take a KPI of an organization of system downtime. The current measure could be an average of two hours per week. A program may have a benefit that will improve system availability, and we can estimate that this could impact by 30 minutes improvement per week. We now have a baseline and measurement against which to track the benefit. The complication comes when other programs also impact that particular KPI, and then the attribution of benefit to program can become difficult. Deliverable timings can be used to demonstrate the impact. For example, Program A delivers a capability that should impact downtime. Taking a view of the current KPI values at a period before and immediately after the deliverable can give an indication of whether the program delivery actually did have an impact on the KPI.

Complex interdependencies of benefits between programs

Large-scale change in an organization is often complex with multiple dependencies between programs. Getting a handle on these dependencies will allow an understanding of risk in delivering the benefits. If there are dependencies between programs, it can be good to roll these up to initiatives for better tracking. A benefit dependency framework can also be a good way of understanding the dependencies. A benefit dependency network maps out the relationships between the benefits in a program and how they link to the deliverables.

Multiple external variables impacting programs/organizations

Programs are not run in a sterile environment. Factors beyond those of the program and even organization can impact whether the benefits can be delivered and how they may be measured. For example, perhaps a program has benefits that will increase revenue to the organization in a certain function. However, the increase in revenue in that function could also be impacted by other factors such as market conditions or competitor's positions, so attributing the value of benefit to the program and measuring the benefits can be difficult. Careful thought must be given to the correct measure in this case.

Up-front benefit estimation is difficult given the amount of unknowns

Benefits form part of the business case, and although analysis and preparation go into the development of the business case as a base for investment decisions, not all unknowns can be eradicated at this point. It will often be through the execution of the program and detailed planning that the benefits can be refined along with the costs and risks. Optimism in defining benefits can be a risk. There are several ways of trying to analyze this risk. It can be useful to look at different what-if scenarios using a best case, worst case, average spread to show the level of risk. A tool that can be used here is the NPV Sensitivity to Benefits Optimism chart. This plot NPV against percentage of benefits realized is a good way of illustrating at what point the NPV becomes negative if benefits are lost. Figure 9.2 illustrates an example, and in this case it can be seen that NPV becomes positive when 30 percent of benefits are realized. This can also be replicate with cost optimism and can be useful indicators as to the sensitivity of the program benefits to changes in benefits or costs.

Use of historical data in estimating benefits is also a good method of quantification. Looking at similar past programs for their benefits realization can be a good measure. An organization which can do this will be at high level of benefits management maturity!

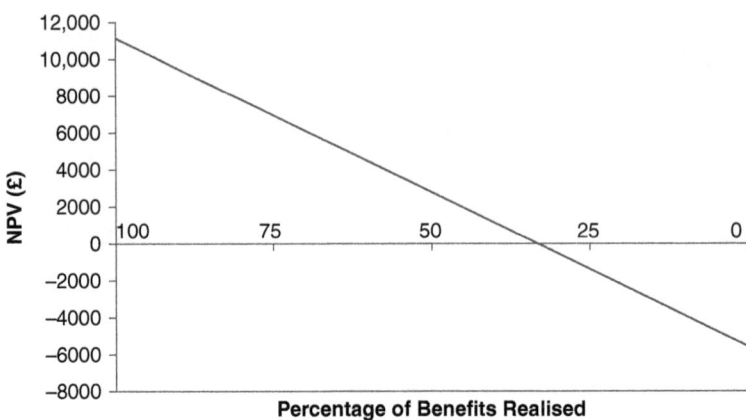

Figure 9.2 NPV sensitivity to benefits optimism graph

Existence of organization measures

Determining whether a benefit has been realized will often require an initial baseline against which to measure. It can often be the case that these measures and baselines don't exist in the organization, so a method of measurement and initial baseline will need to be put in place. For example, a program is being launched to improve program and project management capabilities in the organization, including tools and processes. This will have the anticipated benefit of reducing program and project overrun and overspend. However, prior to the launch of the new program the organization does not currently measure the amount of project/program delay and overspend, so no baseline exists to measure from. In this scenario it is useful to use external examples to define the benefit – that is, similar programs in other organizations implementing program and project management tools and process improvements reduced project delays and overspend by 10–20 per cent. External organizations often have these types of benchmark measures available as a guide. Then monitoring future projects and programs post-implementation will compare how this program fared against the external benchmarks.

Comparing program benefits for investment decisions

Programs in their very nature can be very different in terms of timespan, value, and benefits. Comparing them can be like comparing apples and oranges unless a framework for comparison can be put in place. As well as having a defined set of benefit categories or a value assessment to the organization based on organizational strategy, it can be useful to compare anticipated benefits over a specific period. This is particularly useful for financial benefits where comparisons can be made using formulae as described below. It is necessary to bound the period in which benefits are going to be captured and tracked – for example, a program that will reduce cost can do so by removing from the budget in one year and equally it will not be there the year after – yet for how long after the program will we claim these benefits. A good guide would be five years and comparing benefits over this period.

Example: benefit measurement metrics

Benefit measures can come from a number of places across the organization such as:

- definition from senior leaders in the business who will set the program goals, targets, and objectives;
- brainstorming with program stakeholders who will be impacted by the program;
- historic knowledge of similar program run in this or other organizations in the past;
- KPIs that are already in place in the business often linked to an organization's strategy and will be impacted by the program;
- external industry benchmarks.

Some example benefit measures are provided here as a useful guide:

Cost reduction/savings

Cost reduction is possibly the simplest type of benefit to track, due to its tangible nature. The measure is in financial terms and can be tracked for realization by analyzing the impacted budgets to identify the saving. The savings should be baked into future budgets through the budget setting process to truly realize the benefit.

Increase in revenue

Measures for increase in revenue will include direct financial measures through increases in sales. The difficulty in this measure comes from the attribution of the increase in sales to a particular program. Using the timing of the program outputs as indicators can link the increases back to the program; or alternatively by being more granular in the benefit – so rather than just increasing sales specify what type of sales and where will they be felt (increase in sales of Widget A by 3000 in the United Kingdom). Other revenue increases might come from things such as asset sales that might be defined and measured as a one-off benefit.

Business key performance indicators

There are many KPIs of a business that may be useful in defining and measuring benefits. Revenue, sales, profit, customer satisfaction, brand image, and staff morale are all examples that an organization may have defined as a KPI with associated measures. Similarly in IT organizations there will be operational performance measures that can be used as a base for defining program benefits such as stability, risk, capacity, usability, and system performance. It can be possible to identify a KPI that the program will impact, and then it will be necessary to determine by how much will the program impact the KPI. Also the impact of other programs in the portfolio on the KPI should be taken into account and a method of attribution. is to assess the trend of the KPI before and after program deliverables so as to see if the program has affected the KPI. Review of the KPI and measure of realization can be tied into program gateways.

A mixture of both financial and nonfinancial benefits can be used to define a program's benefit. The advantage of using financial measures is that they can also be used in other value measures to compare across multiple programs in the portfolio to enable selection of the highest value programs. Some examples of these financial measures are as follows:

Return on investment (ROI)

This takes into account the financial investment (costs) and the financial return (benefits) as a ratio. Once an ROI has been calculated for a program, it can be used as a factor for comparison in investment decisions:

$$ROI = \frac{(Benefits - Costs)}{Costs}$$

Net present value

Net present value (NPV) is typically used to assess the value of projects and programs at specific points in time as their worth to the business. It can also be used as a metric to compare investments and their value at a certain point in time. So if we were looking at a point five years ahead and wanted to compare the NPV of programs as a guide to how much they would be worth to the organization, we could use this measure.

$$\text{NPV} = \sum_{t=0}^{n} \frac{(\text{Benefits} - \text{Costs})_t}{(1+r)^t}$$

where:
$r =$ discount rate
$t =$ year
$n =$ analytic horizon in years

Note that the NPV formula uses a discount rate which can be set by the individual organization depending on the expected return they would have if they had used the investment budget elsewhere.

Break-even period

Figure 9.3 shows an example of a break-even analysis. This can be used to compare when an investment will start to pay back to the organization. The breakeven point is the point where the accumulation of benefits goes above the invested cost. A break-even period is the time required by the net cash flow (total revenue – operating expenses) of a project to offset the project cost or investment. Any benefits that received after this period are direct value contribution to the project.

Total cost of ownership

This is often used in investments that will be purchasing an asset such as buildings or software as this takes into account the future operational costs along with the initial investment.

Although these formula tend to be emphasize the monetary value but they can be used alongside and in conjunction with the nontangible benefits. Again confidence in the estimation levels must also be taken into account in any investment decision.

Once benefits are defined, this is far from the end of the process. A business case is a living artifact and should be constantly refined and reviewed through the life of the program with reviews at key gateways. Along with benefits values a plan for realization should also be produced, and it will be against this plan that benefits are tracked. Benefits will be triggered by

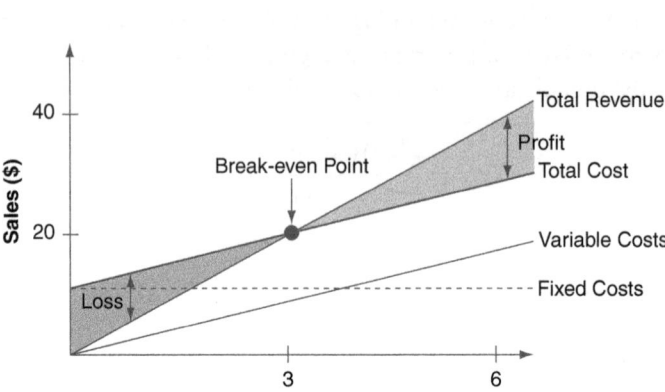

Figure 9.3 Break-even period illustrated with profit as benefit (Adapted from: 12manage.com)

a deliverable in the program and hence can be tracked once the deliverable is complete. A benefit owner will also be required to track the realization. As it is often the operational areas that will feel the benefit these are best placed to track and measure the benefits. For financial benefits, for example, it is useful to enlist the support of finance staff who have access to the organization's financial systems to track the costs. This could be looking for items such as invoices from suppliers whose services have been removed or staff time bookings or salary costs.

Is there a single benefit's model or framework that can be used?

A recent study performed by the Association of Project Management (APM) relating to benefits management found that 60 percent of respondents described their benefits management processes as either informal or incidental. This is interesting as we have discussed in the rest of this chapter the importance of benefits as a key measure of successful organizational change. A good start to implementing benefits management is using a simple benefits framework along with the benefit categories described earlier. In terms of benefit frameworks – there are many defined but they all share the same basic principles of benefits definition, monitoring and realization with an emphasis on identification of further benefits throughout the process. The benefits management framework used by us is shown in Figure 9.4.

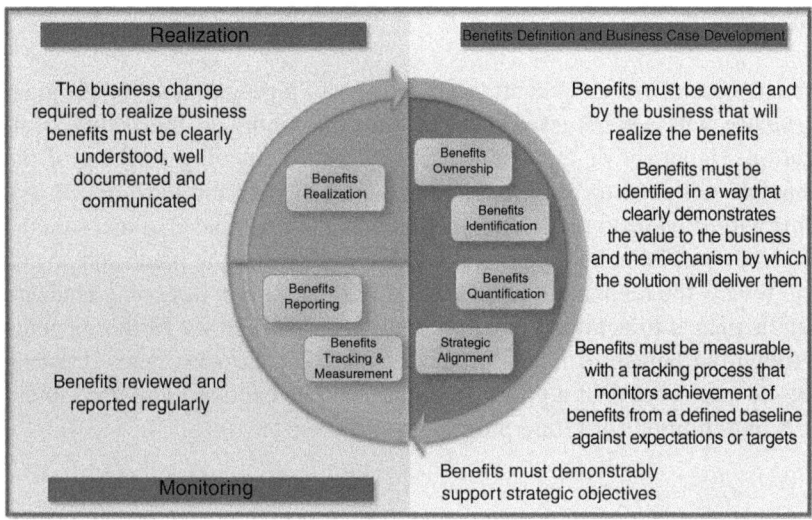

Figure 9.4 Benefits management framework: "Cradle to Grave"

Benefits definition and business case development

This will include the definition categorization, and realization planning of the benefits. The initial definition of the benefits will be the input to the investment decision and portfolio optimization/selection processes. The definition of benefits needs to include any future uplift in operational costs, either as a cost or dis-benefit. Other dis-benefits should also be taken into account and included in the business case. Outputs from this part of the process will include the business case, benefits plans, and benefits profiles.

Monitoring

Once a program has been initiated, during program execution the benefits will need to be monitored and refined as part of the business case and regular reviews. During the program execution change management should be in place to assess the potential impact any scope or timing changes may have on the benefits and business case. Portfolio governance should be in place to review the programs and how they are performing in terms of delivery and benefits realization. Some benefits can be time sensitive – for example, launching of a product before a competitor to increase revenue, and hence this must be taken into account and acted upon during execution. Business cases should be updated with future forecast of benefits delivery ready for the governance reviews.

Realization

Benefits are often realized after the delivery of a program, so the program structure will not necessarily be in place to report on the benefit realization. Handover of the responsibilities for the ongoing tracking of the benefits will need to be completed as a part of program closure process. This will often be to the operational area that is best placed to measure the realization of benefits. In general a PfMO will still be in place and so can still review the realization of benefits after the program has completed and can be placed to act upon any opportunities identified for further benefits through the launch of a new project or program. Lessons learned during the closure process of a program should also be captured and used to aid benefit definition for future programs.

What's the ultimate breakdown of what's expected in the investment decision?

The portfolio can be optimized based on a balance of return for the investment at a certain level of risk given constraints (funding and resources). Benefits are a key part of this equation, providing a description of the return of investment or value to the organization. As described previously measures can also be used to compare one investment to another, but taking the nonfinancially quantified benefits into account can be difficult. Another method of describing the value of the investments is by tying the programs or projects in the portfolio back to the organizations strategy. In this way, it is possible not only to get a feel for how the investments tie to strategy but also to include all benefit types in the comparison by using a variety of measures and KPIs.

A set of measures based on the organizations strategy can be constructed and then each of the individual programs or projects can be assessed for their contribution to the measures. Summing across all measures and applying a fixed scoring system, a value can be calculated for each program and project and used as an initial aid in ranking the portfolio. The measures used can be a variety of financial and nonfinancial elements that describe the benefits of the investments.

When considering an investment case the following elements should be considered:

- Do the benefits look realistic in both value and timing, what assumptions have been used in their calculation and can they be tested?

- Does it follow that the benefits can be delivered based on the description of the investment?
- Do the benefits and their timing align to the program deliverables?
- Is there any independent validation or assessment? Who was involved in defining the benefits, and do the major stakeholders who will feel the benefit sign up to them? – Particularly for cost savings where their future budgets will be reduced as a consequence.
- Does it stand up to historical evidence of the benefits from similar programs?
- How risky is the investment and what is the sensitivity to reduction in benefits? Are there any particular critical timings or dependencies with other investments?
- Have future operational costs been considered and included in the analysis?

Thus, this chapter brings us to terms with tracking and measuring business benefits obtained as a result of investment decision made by the management. However, we have to ensure that these investments are realized according to plan, and the innovative project ideas included as part of the portfolio are successfully implemented as projects with realizable business value. The assurance of innovation and investment realization needs strategic governance of portfolio. The strategic objective is achieved through a portfolio management office or a PfMO, a set of governance processes to support, drive, and deliver this change.

The next chapter explains in-depth the assurance and governance of portfolio investment benefits through the set-up of a PfMO. The chapter comprehensively explains the people, process, and tools that make up the PfMO and emphasizes the need for this level of governance to achieve change in the organization through effective portfolio management.

CHAPTER 10

How to Establish Portfolio Management Office for Strategy, Portfolio, and Benefits Governance? How Do We Assure Innovation and Investments Are Realized?

Innovation is a multi-disciplinary group process that is supported top–down and driven bottom–up. Innovation process needs to be systematic and structured but at the same time it must give freedom to an individual's creative imagination. Aligning innovation to the portfolio process needs an optimum portfolio governance model for coaching and decision-making.

We have learnt that practising portfolio management is instrumental in creating an effective innovation culture in an organization, creating closer cross-functional process with specific steps and transparent decision criteria for assessment, selection, decision making, governance, and also balancing a mix of projects well. Figure 10.1 shows how Strategy, Portfolio and Benefits (SP&B) management approach influences from top to bottom, and how a governance process drives execution at all levels. Innovation process management is illustrated to comprise of integrated ideation and product portfolio management.

We have understood PPM as a product development process that drives product innovation by optimizing the collective value of a set of development initiatives through regular, informed trade-off decisions across development programs, projects, and new ideas. This is how we can visualize the dynamics of influence of innovation in portfolio management, and in PPM decision-making.

And then there are enablers that help PPM drive innovation. These can range from technology to sheer methodology in product development, which can cause innovation. The SP&B management framework

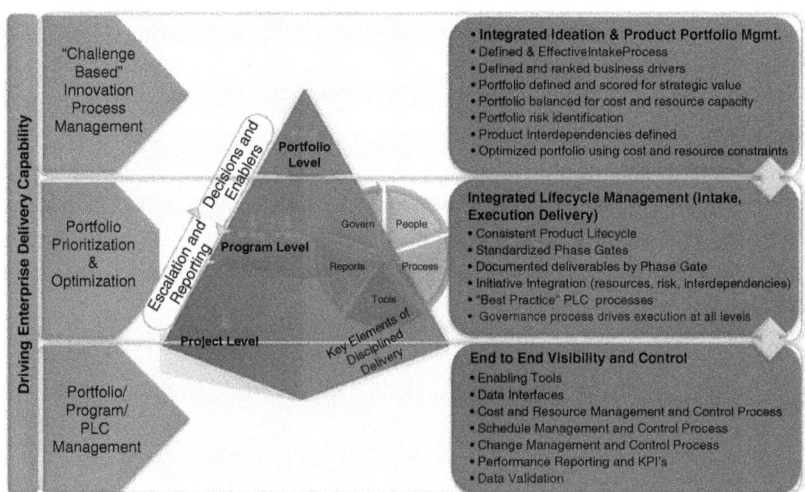

Figure 10.1 Accelerating innovation time to market with integration of strategy, portfolio, and benefits framework

(as discussed in Chapter 7) helps to largely manage and govern this innovation portfolio management.

The SP&B framework enables companies to enhance PPM decision-making by encouraging creativity, methodology, strategic thinking as well as driving execution. Thus, innovation-based PPM takes as input a variety of opportunities and ideas, the product or business objectives of the organization, well-vetted opportunities where current or new resources could be applied, current business conditions, and the resource constraints of the organization. Its output is a balanced portfolio with resources allocated across a strategic mix of development initiatives. The governance of a portfolio is strongly supported by the innovation strategy, since the business objectives are clearly understood, prioritized, and made easy to manage. There are tools to enable the governance of the portfolio, through enhanced portfolio reporting, supported decision-making, monitoring, and control, and these are discussed further in the following sections of this chapter.

Set-up of a portfolio management office and assurance for reporting to C-level executives

A Portfolio Management Office (PfMO) is a dedicated function that can play a vital role in guiding, enabling, and supporting effective portfolio management to facilitate the achievement of business objectives. This includes building organizational capabilities to manage portfolios.

The subject is based on real practical experience gained from working with a wide range of organizations differing in size and from both private and public sectors. It has also been prepared with reference to a number of relevant methodologies, notably OGC P3O (portfolio, program, and project offices). This chapter does not include details of the SP&B management processes as they are covered in the other chapters.

What is a PfMO?

A PfMO is a dedicated center of expertise responsible for guiding, enabling, and supporting an organization (or sometimes a group of organizations) to determine, drive, and deliver a portfolio of programs and/or projects to deliver change, achieve business benefits, and thereby meet strategic objectives. As indicated in previous chapters, this involves ensuring that the organization is both "doing the right things" and "doing things right". The focus is on driving optimum returns on portfolio investments as well as ensuring that the portfolio is aligned with and contributes fully to strategic objectives.

The overall objectives and scope assigned to the PfMO vary considerably depending on the organizational context, PPM maturity, and particular requirements of the organization(s). Typically, this includes providing decision-making information, insight, and support as well as methodologies, controls, oversight, and assurance. They can include building organizational capabilities to manage portfolios as well as providing operational services. They will aim to provide excellent value for money and have the capability to flex in line with evolving requirements.

A PfMO should have a brief vision statement outlining its overall aims, and how it will add value in the eyes of its stakeholders. This will be specific to the individual team and reflect organizational requirements.

Benefits of having a PfMO?

A PfMO can enable the organization to deliver change faster, better, and cheaper, while improving management decision-making and the alignment of programs and projects with business strategy. Specific benefits can include the following:

- *Increased ROI*, via facilitating selecting and driving the right projects while killing others early, improving benefits realization, and reducing delivery costs.
- *Increased organizational flexibility*, via improved opportunity capture, regular portfolio refreshes, and more rapid assured delivery.
- *Reduced risks*, via improved risk analysis at portfolio level and effective aggregation of lower-level program and project risks.
- *Improved resource and capacity management*, facilitating improved resource planning and prioritization, allocation, conflict resolution, and utilization.
- *Reduced costs*, through more effective portfolio management and disciplined delivery based on appropriate standard ways of working and enhanced RM.
- *Improved governance and controls*, providing greater visibility and control, enabling empowered executives and management to take more effective timely fact-based decisions.
- *Enhanced confidence in delivery*, via more robust planning, improved management of operational impacts, more effective controls, and timely reporting.
- *Strengthened capabilities*, notably in-house, thus increasing flexibility, reducing dependency on more costly external contractor resource, and raising employee engagement.
- *Improved integration,* between portfolio, program, and project management processes and tools. This includes improved flow of information.
- *Improved benefits realization*, via facilitating more robust identification, profiling, ownership, realization planning, delivery, and tracking.
- *Enhanced stakeholder engagement*, underpinning effective collaboration, decision making, and delivery.
- *Increased PPM maturity,* optimizing and harmonizing ways of working, with more disciplined delivery and greater process compliance facilitating the achievement of business objectives.

Types of PfMO available

There are a number of types of PfMO, driven by the wider organization and governance structures they serve. They tend to operate either at the organization ("enterprise") level or be contained within specific parts of the organization, for example, within specific business units or functional departments. Table 10.1 shows the type of PfMO.

Table 10.1 Type of portfolio management office

Intervention	Purpose/function	Scope	Focus
Enterprise Portfolio Management Office (permanent)	Support selection, delivery, and benefits realization of the organization/enterprise-wide portfolio of programs and projects. May also contain CoE (see below)	Organization/enterprise wide	Portfolio delivery (plus process execution and capability build and assurance if CoE applicable)
Portfolio/ Program Management Office (permanent)	Support selection, delivery, and benefits realization of portfolio of programs and projects for a business unit/department/ regional unit. May also contain CoE (see below)	Business unit, department, division, regional unit	Portfolio delivery/ program and project definition and delivery (plus process execution and capability build and assurance if CoE applicable)
Center Of Excellence (permanent)	Define, support deployment of, and assure adherence to organization PM processes. May also provide independent assurance function.	Organization/ enterprise wide or specific business unit, department, division, regional unit	Process definition and execution, capability building, assurance
Program Office (temporary)	Support delivery of and benefits realization for a specific program	Program	Program delivery
Project Office (temporary)	Support delivery of a specific project	Project	Project delivery

The optimal PfMO solution in specific situations will depend on a number of factors:

- Position in organization, that is, at enterprise level or at lower business unit, regional, or divisional level.
- Ownership and organizational positioning of programs and projects within the organization.
- Organization governance and decision-making structures; PfMO is designed to support executive decision-making.
- The concentration of change initiatives within the organization; for example, they may be concentrated within the IT function.

- The size of the organization. A large organization with a number of business units may be more likely to have a hub and spoke arrangement with a separate CoE.
- How closely strategy and delivery are owned within the organization. If not different PfMO functions may be owned by and cover different parts.

Depending on the needs and maturity of the organization, the PfMO can operate in a number of ways, varying between the following types:

- Supportive – focus on provision of accurate timely fact-based information to support decision-making by senior executives and management.
- Directive – provide not only information but also proactive forward looking insight, analysis, and challenge to support senior executives and management decision-making, that is, help drive the portfolio and its constituent programs and projects.

PfMO functions and services

PfMO services are centered on the following principal functions, portfolio management support, program and project management control, center of excellence (CoE), and program and project assurance. Each contains a number of elements relating to the portfolio management themes and is carried out through a series of lower-level processes and supporting tools.

The functions and supporting services are outlined below.

Portfolio management support

One of the key PfMO function is providing portfolio management coordination and support for portfolio activities like pipeline demand management, portfolio optimization, delivery management, and benefits management. This includes definition, deployment, and use of portfolio level planning and controls, including costs, risk, change, and benefits management.

- *Executive support*: Provide an "Executive PA", information, analysis, and insight to support executive decision-making and portfolio management activities.
- *Governance support*: Help define, set up, and operate portfolio governance bodies to aid effective decision-making and control over portfolio

to achieve strategic objectives. Governance meetings can include portfolio planning, regular portfolio reviews and refreshes as well as resolving issues, risks, and changes arising.

- *Strategic driver prioritization:* Coordinate and provide meaningful insights into the prioritization process, including identifying, validating, and prioritizing drivers.
- *Demand pipeline management:* Coordinate and provide meaningful insights into management of the demand pipeline, identifying opportunities, developing, and evaluating them. This can include the preparation and review of business cases.
- *Portfolio optimization*: Coordinate and provide meaningful insights into optimization to ensure that the portfolio is aligned and is contributing fully to achievement of organizational objectives. This includes investment risk analysis as well as constraints analysis.
- *Portfolio delivery planning*: Prepare and control robust integrated portfolio-level delivery plans that drive and are informed by lower-level program and project plans. The plans are baselined so that progress can be assessed and changes considered.
- *Portfolio delivery controls*: Define, deploy, and operate portfolio-level controls that are aligned with wider organizational control guidelines and driven/supported by program level and project level controls.

The controls include the management of dependencies, resources, costs, stakeholders, risks, issues, and changes. The PfMO maintains an aggregate "big picture" view and facilitates management at portfolio level, that is, cross-program and project level.

It can also include the coordination of program and project gateways, key decision points to review progress and provide greater assurance in delivery and spend.

The PfMO will provide information, analysis, and insights to help ensure that executives and governance boards have visibility and control over delivery of overall portfolio to achieve business objectives.

- *Benefits management*: Define, deploy, and operate benefits management across the portfolio. It includes supporting programs and projects through end-to-end benefit management process, including identifying, mapping, planning, tracking, and reviewing benefit realization.
- *Information hub*: Ensure the accessibility, integrity, and security of portfolio information as well as ensure effective communications with stakeholders. This includes documentation management, configuration

management, communication and stakeholder management, knowledge base management, and reporting.

- *Portfolio reporting*: Provide timely, reliable portfolio-level reports to ensure executives and governance boards have visibility of and insights into portfolio status, highlighting trends, significant variances, and problems requiring attention. The reports will facilitate effective timely decision-making.

Program and project support

Provide guidance, coaching, mentoring, and support with deployment and use of PPM planning and controls, including cost, risk, and change management. Also provide PPM resources, notably support for program/project set-up and recovery.

- *Program and project planning support*: Provide guidance and support to programs/projects to ensure they have robust plans in place that are driven by and inform the overall portfolio plan. The plans provide baselines against which progress can be assessed and changes considered.
- *Program and project controls support*: Provide guidance and support for programs and projects to deploy and operate controls that are aligned with wider organizational control guidelines and portfolio-level controls. The controls include the management of dependencies, resources, costs, stakeholders, risks, issues, changes, and gateways. This includes the escalation of matters to portfolio level for resolution. The aggregate "big picture" views maintained by the PfMO can be useful and facilitates management at portfolio level, that is, cross-program and project level.
- *Program and project reporting support*: Provide guidance and support for programs and projects by preparing reports. The PfMO can act as a critical friend, analyzing and challenging and assuring reporting information on status, trends, variances, and problems requiring attention and/or escalation.
- *Resource capacity management*: Maintain portfolio-level resource forecasts and schedules, showing demand and capacity and highlighting resource surpluses and shortfalls. Use "big picture" view to optimize utilization and resolve resource bottlenecks and conflicts.
- *Resource management*: Manage resource pool of internal PPM resources, including coordinating their allocations, performance

management, and releases. This also includes coordinating the sourcing and management of external consultant and contract resources.

- *Program/project start-up and recovery resources and support*: Provide a range of dedicated/specialist PPM resources to start-up programs and projects; similarly supply resources to recover programs and projects in difficulty.

Center of excellence

Develop organizational PPM capability and maturity through providing a "center of excellence" for defining, supporting deployment, and use of best practice portfolio, program, and project management processes and tools. This also includes training, coaching, professional development, and knowledge management.

- *PPM processes*: Provide "center of excellence" for defining, deploying, and supporting best practice portfolio, program and project management processes that align with the organizations' operating model and culture, industry standards, and relevant external methodologies, for example, OGC standards, PMI.
- *PPM tools*: Provide a "center of excellence" for defining, deploying, and supporting appropriate portfolio, program, and project management tools.
- *PPM maturity management*: The PfMO can play a lead role in assessing PPM maturity and driving action plans to increase it across the organization and portfolio.
- *PPM role profiles and competency framework*: Includes coordinating definition and supporting use of standard role profiles, performance management processes and tools, competency frameworks, and personal development planning activities.
- *PPM capability building*: Involves arranging and/or providing training, coaching, and mentoring, helps to develop peoples' capabilities, undertake their roles, and improve organizational PM maturity. It can also involve supporting capability and resource planning.
- *PPM professional development*: Determines, coordinates, and supports the selection and use of professional courses and accreditations to drive up PPM skills and knowledge.
- *Knowledge management*: Promotes knowledge sharing and a collaborative culture through facilitation of a PPM Community of Practice and capturing/sharing of lessons learned.

Program and project assurance

The objective of this is to provide independent assurance on program and project plans and progress via program/project monitoring and reporting, oversight of gateways, reviews, health-checks and use of external audits and reviews.

> *Process compliance*: The PfMO can monitor program and project adherence to agreed controls. This is important to enable consistent and effective management across the portfolio, supporting effective decision making, and improving project delivery. The PfMO can have authority to enforce minimum standards required.
>
> *Program and/or project assurance*: This concerns involvement in product quality reviews, monitoring process compliance, scrutiny of program/project information, oversight of gateways, undertaking program/project reviews and health-checks, arranging and supporting external audits and gateways.

Control

The PfMO can undertake this function via a number of activities, including the following:

- *Portfolio Information Hub* – Coordinate and undertake the deployment and use of processes and tools to manage portfolio information, ensuring its accessibility, integrity, and protection.
- *Compliance* – Monitor adherence to agreed portfolio, program and project control processes, including the use of quality management tools and techniques. This helps to ensure a sufficiently disciplined approach to delivery and enables the aggregation of program and project information to allow effective management at the portfolio level.
- *Scrutiny* – Monitor and challenge the consistency, completeness, and accuracy of program and project information, including that supplied to senior executives. The PfMO can act as a "critical friend" and help to identify early warning of issues with client satisfaction, deliverable quality, and planned or unplanned schedule and cost variances.
- *Gateways* – Oversee the use and completion of program and project gateway reviews (stage-end reviews), key decision points in the lifecycles.

- *Benefits management* – Coordinate deployment and support use of benefits management to ensure benefits are identified, owned, profiled, planned, and realized. This will include maintaining an aggregate view to ensure strategic objectives are achieved.

In some cases, certain process controls may be owned by other functions, for example, finance and procurement. Here, the relevant functions may supply resources to PfMOs to deploy and use the processes.

Assurance

Assurance aims to help stakeholders understand the health of programs and projects:

- Confirm achievability and assure that sufficient management systems are in place to monitor, manage, and deliver outlined business objectives.
- Provides confidence in delivery and in spend, confirming that investments are strategically aligned and delivering the required outcomes and benefits.
- Promotes transparency, accountability, and control.

The assurance should be carried out on a systematic basis throughout the program and project lifecycles. It ensures adherence to the right project processes and that the right people are involved at the right time to perform the necessary checks to ensure successful project delivery. The outputs of this process provide an early indication to project stakeholders of potential deviation in time, cost, or quality and help to target remedial actions.

The PfMO can undertake this function via a number of activities, including the following:

- *Product reviews* – Review program and project products, both management products (e.g., plans, control logs) and specialist products (e.g., design products, implementation products).
- *Compliance* – Monitor adherence to agreed program and project management and control processes, including the use of quality management tools and techniques.
- *Scrutiny* – Monitor and challenge the consistency, completeness, and accuracy of program and project information, including that supplied to senior executives.

- *Monitoring* – Monitoring of scope, cost, and schedule changes and issues and periodic review gates.
- *Health-checks* – Conduct internal project health-checks/reviews to identify early warning for client satisfaction issues, deliverable quality, and planned or unplanned schedule and cost variances.
- *Gateways* – Oversee the use and completion of program and project gateway reviews (stage-end reviews), key decision points in the lifecycles.
- *External audits* – Arrange and support external audits and/or gateways to help identify potential problem areas and improve performance.
- *Knowledge management* – Support knowledge management processes, ensuring that lessons learned are captured and used to improve future performance.

As part of the governance process, the program office is responsible for ensuring that delivery assurance and quality management are tightly integrated throughout the program lifecycle. The Program Office monitors this process through a set of integrated tasks. The Program Office performs delivery assurance by monitoring key checkpoints and control processes.

Having an "eye" on the strategic investment and their benefits

PfMO positioning in the organization

We have discussed different types of PfMO earlier in the chapter, and it is very important that a PfMO is positioned correctly within an organization in order to operate effectively. There is no single answer as it will depend on the wider organizational structure, the type and functions of the PfMO itself, and the nature of the change portfolio. However, it does need to report to a senior executive with sufficient influence over the organization.

An organization/enterprise-level PfMO will typically report into a chief operating officer (COO)/chief financial officer (CFO) or perhaps a direct report of a COO/CFO. Reporting into a neutral function can help the PfMO to be seen as a provider of "honest" accurate information. There are occasions when the PfMO may better report to say a chief information officer (CIO), where portfolios are dominated by IT change, or other functions such as finance. Should the PfMO be focused on demand management and portfolio optimum it may be positioned under a function such as strategy, with PfMOs focused on delivery under a change or delivery function.

Similar principles apply with PfMOs operating at a lower level, such as a business unit or geographic region. Again the PfMO may typically report into a COO or alternatively another function director, for example, CFO/Finance Director, Risk Director, CIO.

Structuring the PfMO organization

This includes overall chosen place of PfMO within the organization, covering structure; people, which includes roles, capability, and team size; processes; and tool.

Structure

The portfolio office can be structured in a number of ways depending on its type and the organization's requirements. A typical structure of a full organization-level PfMO is illustrated in Figures 10.2, 10.3, 10.4, and 10.5.

The PfMO may be further broken down as shown in Figure 10.3.

There are a number of variants, as illustrated below: separate strategic portfolio office and delivery offices. This is common where accountability for portfolio pipeline and selection is separated from that for delivery.

Separate CoE: This is a common option in decentralized PfMOs, where a number of lower-level PfMOs are supported by a central organization level CoE.

Roles

Table 10.2 lists a number of typical roles used in PfMOs. Those used will depend on the functions/services provided. The roles do not necessarily correspond to full-time jobs and can be combined or, in some cases, split to meet specific requirements.

Team size

There are a number of factors affecting the size of the PfMO, including:

- the level within the organization at which the PfMO operates, for example, enterprise, business unit

- the functions of the PfMO, that is, portfolio management support, program and program support, CoE, assurance
- the number, scale, and complexity of the programs and projects within the portfolio(s), recognizing potential economies of scale
- the P3M3 maturity of the organization, for example, degree to which PPM processes are standardized and optimized at portfolio, program, and project levels
- the need to align with and support wider business strategy and planning cycles and allied activities
- portfolio demand and stability
- the PPM tools available, including the presence of collaboration and automated reporting tools
- the governance structure that the PfMO supports

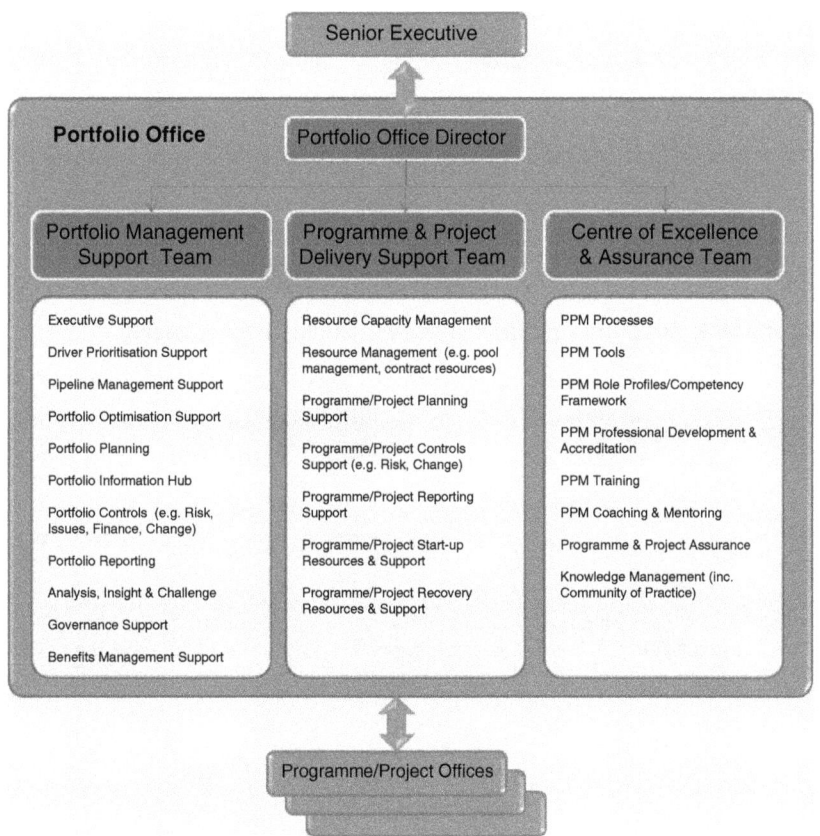

Figure 10.2 Structure – traditional

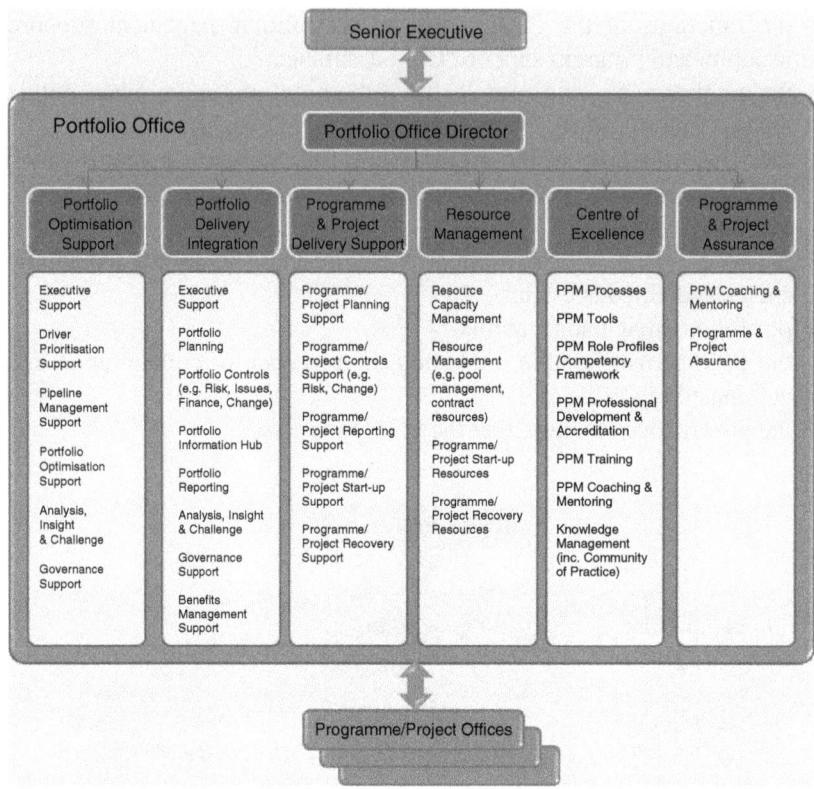

Figure 10.3 Structure – portfolio office with multiple functionality

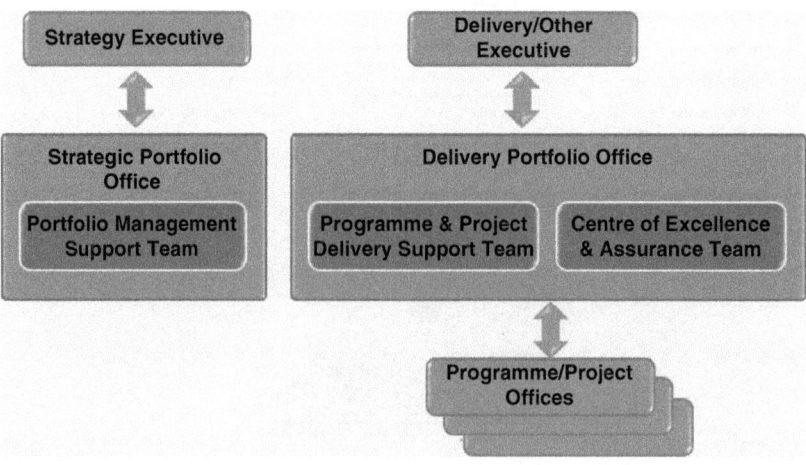

Figure 10.4 Structure – strategic portfolio office and delivery portfolio office

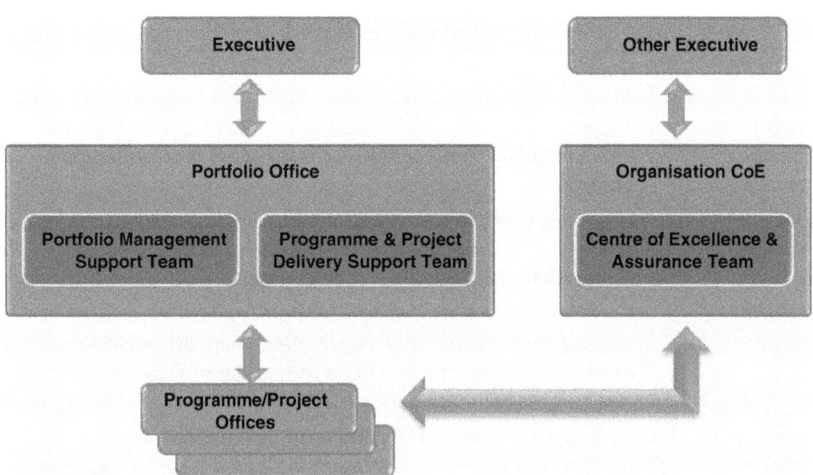

Figure 10.5 Structure – integrated PfMO and center of excellence

- the degree to which other functions own processes and resources, for example, finance, procurement, HR
- number, nature, and diversity of stakeholders involved
- the skills and experience of available staff, including their ability to multi-skill
- opportunities to combine roles and the need to cover for holidays, sickness, training, and so on
- the duration of the functions and activities, noting some may vary considerably over time, for example, the need for deployment and training of processes and tools.

PMOs are typically sized in three main ways, viewing costs as a percentage of overall program or project costs, viewing headcount as a percentage of overall program or project headcount, or using activity-based resourcing, establishing workloads of the team, and the number of people required. With a PfMO specifically, the third method is usually the most robust. A typical approach could include the following:

- establishing the functions the PfMO will undertake
- determining the services and activities required for each function, at least key activities in outline
- estimating workloads of each activity and aggregating the workloads
- assigning the work needs to roles, recognizing opportunities or the need to combine or share functions/activities where the workload does not equate to a whole number of people
- making allowance for absence cover and other pertinent factors.

Table 10.2 Typical roles in portfolio management office

Role	Role purpose
PfMO sponsor	Champions and directs the establishment and operation of the PfMO, ensuring that it supports achievement of organization's objectives.
PfMO manager	Leads and manages the establishment and operation of the PfMO, ensuring that it is a high-performing team, adding value to achievement of organization's objectives.
Portfolio analyst(s)	Coordinates portfolio management processes, that is, driver prioritization, demand pipeline management, optimization, delivery management, and benefits realization. Provides analysis and insights to inform decision making.
Planning manager	Manages planning process and ensures the preparation, baselining, and control of integrated aligned plans at portfolio, program, and project levels. Actsas custodian of portfolio-level plans.
Resource capacity manager	Manages portfolio resource demand and capacity forecasts and schedules, instigates action to ensure that programs and projects have required resources, resolve bottlenecks/contentions, and optimizes utilization.
Resource manager	Manages resource pool and provision of contract resources. Provides PPM resources programs and projects in start-up or recovery. Drives PPM role profiles, competency framework and professional accreditation.
Finance manager	Manages financial management processes, both revenue and costs, preparing and managing portfolio budgets. Guides and supports programs and projects estimate, budget, control, and report costs, providing analysis and insight.
Risk manager	Manages risk and issue management process controls, driving activity at the right level to ensure the identification, evaluation, and mitigation/resolution of risks and issues that threaten achievement of objectives.
Change manager	Manages change control processes within the portfolio to ensure that changes are identified, assessed, authorized, and implemented effectively at the right level.
Quality assurance manager	Coordinates effective quality management process controls. Provides program and project assurance via quality reviews, monitoring, scrutiny, reviews, gateway oversight, reviews, health-checks, and external audits.
Information manager	Ensures documentation is accessible, stored and protected, using reports and communications to share information. Promotes knowledge sharing by facilitation of a PPM Community of Practice and coordination of lessons learned process.

Communications manager	Facilitates effective stakeholder management and communication. Establishes a stakeholder management framework and supports stakeholder engagement and communications to encourage collaboration and support.
Reporting manager	Manages reporting process controls at portfolio, program, and project levels, producing executive dashboards/reports at portfolio level, to facilitate visibility of status and effective timely fact-based decision making.
Benefits manager	Coordinates benefits management process across portfolio of programs and projects. Includes identifying, mapping, and profiling benefits as well as planning, tracking and reviewing benefit realization.
Secretariat	Supports definition, deployment and operation of the governance arrangements to facilitate effective visibility, decision making, and oversight over the portfolio. This includes providing a secretarial function for the governance boards.
Tools manager	Responsible for definition, support, maintenance, and continuous improvement of PPM systems and tools required. It can include acting as a systems administrator, including providing first-line user support.
PPM consultant	Responsible for guiding and supporting definition, deployment, use, and continuous improvement of PPM processes and tools. Can provide independent assurance functions.
Training manager	Arranges and/or provides training for portfolio, program, and project staff to help develop their capabilities and undertake their roles effectively.

Processes used in the PfMO

The PfMO will, depending on its type, functions, and services, use a wide range of PPM processes as shown below:

- benefits management
- business change management
- change control
- configuration management
- demand pipeline management
- dependency management
- document management
- financial(cost) management
- gateway management
- governance management

- integration management
- issue management
- lessons learned (knowledge management)
- planning
- optimization
- procurement (supplier management)
- quality and assurance management
- risk management
- reporting
- resource capacity management
- resource management
- scope management
- strategic driver prioritization
- stakeholder management and communication.

The PfMO can use them or be involved with them in a number of ways, potentially as follows:

- drive development and continuous improvement of processes and tools
- drive deployment and usage of processes and tools, providing training, coaching, and support
- provide ongoing guidance and support for program and project management
- coordinating activities such as workshops and reviews, for example, risk workshops, gateway meetings
- create and maintain portfolio level data, providing an integrated view of program and project data (e.g., plans, dependencies, risks, issues, change) to support decision making
- providing analysis and insight to inform decision making
- monitor and report on program and project data (e.g., metrics/profiles/trend analyses)
- monitor and report on compliance with agreed processes.

Tools used in PfMO

The PfMO will use a wide range of tools to support the processes it coordinates. It is important to ensure that the right tools are selected and used according to the scale, maturity, complexity, and other needs of the organization.

Aligning PfMO with governance structure

As indicated above, the PfMO can play a key role in helping to define, set up, and operate the governance structure for the portfolio. This structure effectively sets out the decision-making authorities for both the various boards and individual roles accountable and responsible for the portfolio and its constituent programs, projects, and allied business change activities. This drives the reporting and other information requirements. Clearly defined structure and levels of responsibility ensure that the right level of senior sponsorship and participation happens and this is essential forgovernance activities.

The PfMO is primarily concerned with supporting the boards and roles operating at or above the portfolio level, providing them with reports, other information, analysis, and insights. This is dependent on information flows with programs and projects. This is illustrated in Figure 10.6.

Key stakeholders – PfMO interaction

The PfMO needs to interact with a broad range of stakeholders, including senior executives, governance boards, other portfolio offices, program/projects (including their PMOs), and functions (e.g., finance, risk, HR). This includes defining, deploying, coordinating, and supporting a range of processes. It also has a key role to play in ensuring the effective and efficient flow of accurate timely information across an organization.

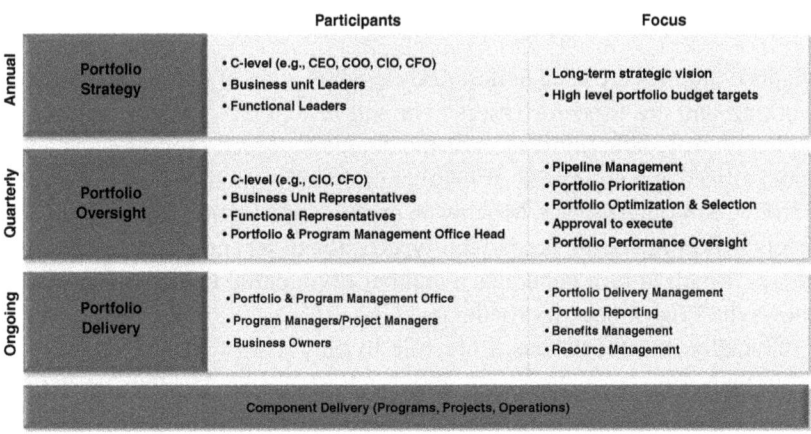

Figure 10.6 Governance structure

Measuring PfMO performance

It is important to measure the performance of the PfMO and the added value it provides. Outcomes and benefits metrics use the performance of the portfolio as a whole to assess the performance of a PfMO, for example, an effective PfMO should enable a reduction in time to market or increased resource utilization to be achieved. Care needs to be taken with the measurements in that there are a number of factors other than PfMO performance that can affect the outcomes and benefits.

More direct measurements of PfMO outputs can also be used, such as the following:

- Product delivery – Delivery of PfMO products to required quality and timescales, for example, production of reports, achievement of optimization process milestones or delivery of training sessions.
- Stakeholder satisfaction – 360-degree reviews conducted with key senior customers of PfMO services, potentially covering timeliness, quality of deliverables, responsiveness, and advice.
- Process controls and assurance – assessment to ensure that key controls are up to date, comply with standards and, are fit for purpose.
- PfMO maturity – assessment of PfMO maturity (see below).

Again, there is no single optimum set of measures. This will depend on wider organizational requirements and priorities as well as the type and functions of the specific PfMO.

PfMO maturity and benefits of knowing it

Maturity models are used to describe elements of an organization's way of working and are used for assessment and benchmarking purposes. They typically provide an indication of the degree to which processes used are standardized and optimized. A number of maturity models exist, including P3M3, CMM, and OPM3. Moving an organization up through the maturity levels will improve the predictability, effectiveness, and control of its processes, which in turn generates a number of potential benefits. Table 10.3 shows the PfMO maturity roadmap.

Crucially, the PfMO has a big role to play in raising the maturity of an organization as a whole by coordinating and supporting the definition, implementation, use, and continual improvement of the organization's governance, processes, and tools as well as the development of

Table 10.3 PfMO maturity roadmap

PM Maturity Roadmap: PfMO

Level	Level 1	Level 2	Level 3	Level 4	Level 5
	Initial/ *ad hoc*	Planned/ repeatable	Defined/ organized	Integrated/ managed	Optimize/ sustain
Potential PfMO evolution	No effective PfMO model, often due to past failure(s) with a project office.	PfMO focuses mainly on strategic projects and/or PPM best practices	PfMO provides effective mentoring, training, and oversight for program/ project managers, and teams.	An enterprise PfMO provides proactive support for programs and related projects.	Enterprise PfMO has evolved to a true decision support office for executives.

people capabilities. This will normally lead to improved performance and ultimately facilitate achievement of strategic objectives.

Setting-up or transforming a PfMO

Overall approach

This section outlines a generic best practice approach for PfMO set-up or transformation. It provides a menu of activities and products which can be selected and adapted to best fit the needs of the situation.

The approach proposes that the change be managed as a program or project, depending on scale and timescales, using best practice program and project management disciplines as required. It recognizes that people and organizational elements are fundamental to successful change and driving out the business benefits, for example, winning the "hearts and minds". As such, it includes the use of change management disciplines.

Transformation follows a similar path to PfMO set-up, albeit the start position clearly will differ and hence the action required to achieve the desired target state will differ. Work is likely to focus on identifying, prioritizing, and addressing gaps or shortcomings in capabilities, services, and performance.

The generic approach has seven phases to define and implement the PfMO to reach a steady state. This is outlined in Figure 10.7:

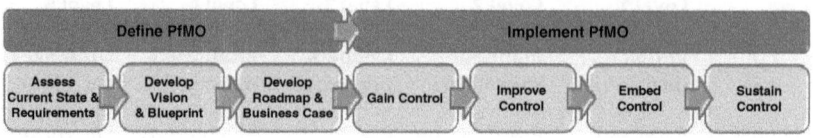

Figure 10.7 Seven phases to define and implement a PfMO

The timings shown are typical durations, albeit these can vary considerably depending on the particular situation and requirements. Experience of delivering value and creating momentum suggests that timeboxing the phases would be helpful.

The phases can also be merged where appropriate. Work in early phases would drive down into as much detail as is possible within the agreed timeframe and would highlight any areas to be developed more thoroughly in subsequent phases.

Each of the steps is described in more detail below, with the key activities, inputs and outputs. Some of the actions within each step may happen in parallel rather than in sequence.

Defining PfMO

Define PfMO involves three steps as shown in Figure 10.8: Assess current state and requirements, develop vision and blueprint, and develop roadmap and business case.

- *Assess current state and requirements* –The objective of the assess requirements phase is to gather and analyze information to understand the objectives, drivers, and requirements of the organization that will drive the design of the PfMO. This will include the current "as is" environment in terms of capabilities, processes, and tools as well as the complexity and status of the portfolio, program, or project (as appropriate). It will also include the objectives, requirements, and priorities of key stakeholders, identifying gaps that are expected to be closed through implementation of a PfMO.
- *Develop vision and blueprint* – Define the PMO vision and blueprint to guide, enable, and support the organization to achieve its objectives. This includes the PfMO aims and objectives as well as its service

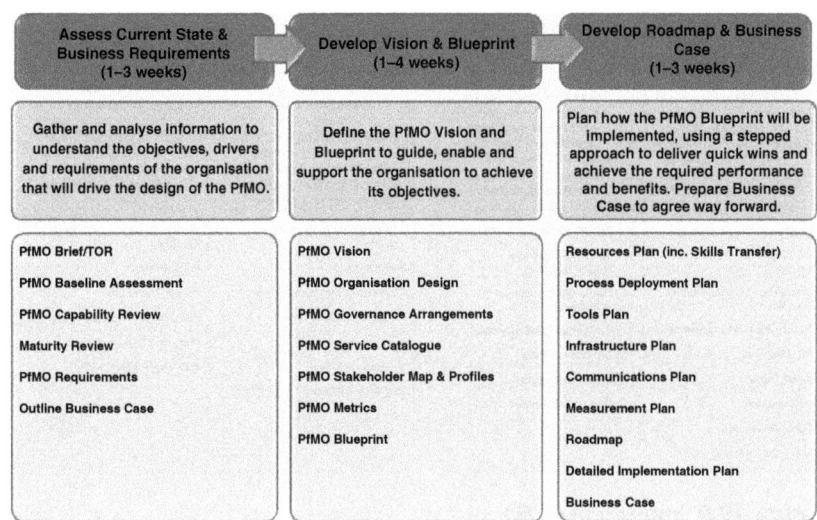

Assess Current State & Business Requirements (1–3 weeks)	Develop Vision & Blueprint (1–4 weeks)	Develop Roadmap & Business Case (1–3 weeks)
Gather and analyse information to understand the objectives, drivers and requirements of the organisation that will drive the design of the PfMO.	Define the PfMO Vision and Blueprint to guide, enable and support the organisation to achieve its objectives.	Plan how the PfMO Blueprint will be implemented, using a stepped approach to deliver quick wins and achieve the required performance and benefits. Prepare Business Case to agree way forward.
PfMO Brief/TOR	PfMO Vision	Resources Plan (inc. Skills Transfer)
PfMO Baseline Assessment	PfMO Organisation Design	Process Deployment Plan
PfMO Capability Review	PfMO Governance Arrangements	Tools Plan
Maturity Review	PfMO Service Catalogue	Infrastructure Plan
PfMO Requirements	PfMO Stakeholder Map & Profiles	Communications Plan
Outline Business Case	PfMO Metrics	Measurement Plan
	PfMO Blueprint	Roadmap
		Detailed Implementation Plan
		Business Case

Figure 10.8 Define PfMO

catalog, governance, organizational structure, processes, tools, and performance measures. It is important to recognize that a PfMO will change over time as processes and behaviors become embedded into the standard way of working. It is rarely possible to jump straight to a high level of maturity as some areas, such as project management skills, take time to develop through either training or recruitment. As such, it may be necessary to define an initial design for the PfMO, the desired end state, and perhaps one or more intermediate states.

- *Develop roadmap and business case* – Plan how the PfMO vision and blueprint will be implemented, using a stepped approach that best fits the organization's priorities, capacity, and ability to implement controls; it will deliver both quick wins and achieve the required level of performance and benefits. The stage can also involve preparation of the business case to provide a formal justification to proceed. The roadmap is split typically into a number of coordinated workstreams covering people (resources), processes, tools, and infrastructure. It will also incorporate communications to ensure that all affected stakeholders are engaged. Each workstream is assigned an owner, responsible for its delivery; review and sign-off arrangements need to be clearly stated.

Implementing PfMO is shown in Figure 10.9:

- *Set up/gain control* –The purpose of this phase is to set up the initial PfMO design rapidly, ensuring that it provides the organization

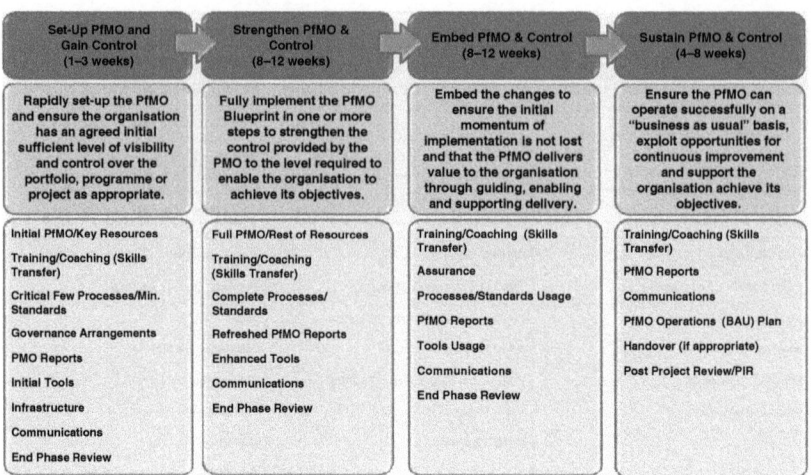

Set-Up PfMO and Gain Control (1–3 weeks)	Strengthen PfMO & Control (8–12 weeks)	Embed PfMO & Control (8–12 weeks)	Sustain PfMO & Control (4–8 weeks)
Rapidly set-up the PfMO and ensure the organisation has an agreed initial sufficient level of visibility and control over the portfolio, programme or project as appropriate.	Fully implement the PfMO Blueprint in one or more steps to strengthen the control provided by the PfMO to the level required to enable the organisation to achieve its objectives.	Embed the changes to ensure the initial momentum of implementation is not lost and that the PfMO delivers value to the organisation through guiding, enabling and supporting delivery.	Ensure the PfMO can operate successfully on a "business as usual" basis, exploit opportunities for continuous improvement and support the organisation achieve its objectives.
Initial PfMO/Key Resources	Full PfMO/Rest of Resources	Training/Coaching (Skills Transfer)	Training/Coaching (Skills Transfer)
Training/Coaching (Skills Transfer)	Training/Coaching (Skills Transfer)	Assurance	PfMO Reports
Critical Few Processes/Min. Standards	Complete Processes/ Standards	Processes/Standards Usage	Communications
Governance Arrangements	Refreshed PfMO Reports	PfMO Reports	PfMO Operations (BAU) Plan
PMO Reports	Enhanced Tools	Tools Usage	Handover (if appropriate)
Initial Tools	Communications	Communications	Post Project Review/PIR
Infrastructure	End Phase Review	End Phase Review	
Communications			
End Phase Review			

Figure 10.9 Implement PfMO

with an agreed initial sufficient level of visibility and control over the portfolio, program, or project as appropriate. This needs to be done rapidly, with focus on consistent implementation of a "critical few" processes/"minimum sufficient" standards to enable the demonstrable delivery of quick wins. As indicated above, the plan will be split typically into a number of coordinated workstreams, each assigned an owner and having defined review and sign-off arrangements.

- *Improve control* – The purpose of this phase is to fully implement the PfMO blueprint to strengthen the control provided by the PfMO to the level required to enable the organization to achieve its objectives. This may involve one or more steps, depending on the organization's requirements and capacity to implement change. As stated above, the plan will be split typically into a number of coordinated workstreams, each assigned an owner and having defined review and sign-off arrangements.

- *Embed control* –The purpose of the embed phase is to embed the changes to ensure that the initial momentum of implementation is not lost and that the PfMO delivers value to the organization through guiding, enabling, and supporting delivery. The phase should be run over a set number of reporting cycles or a set period of time with a clear focus on ensuring that the PfMO is delivering its objectives. Any issues of adoption should be addressed with the support of key stakeholders.

- *Sustain PfMO*–The purpose of the final phase is to ensure that the PfMO can continue to operate successfully on a business as usual basis, identifying and exploiting opportunities for continuous improvement. It checks if the PfMO is achieving its aims in terms of supporting the organization to achieve its wider objectives.

Ensuring key success for PfMOs

Critical success factors for setting up and operating PfMOs successfully are listed below. They will of course vary with the specific case; however, "people" factors are typically of utmost importance.

- *Focus on organizational objectives* – The PfMO objectives, service catalog, deployment approach, and operation will be focused to fit the organization's objectives, requirements, and position. Similarly the governance and controls will be aligned with corporate governance arrangements as and where appropriate.
- *Executive sponsorship and positioning* – The PfMO will be positioned within the organization and actively sponsored at the executive level to enable it to operate effectively.
- *Leadership* – Strong visible leadership is critical to PfMO success. The leader must have excellent leadership and collaborating skills, communicating and influencing skills as well as PPM technical skills, an ability to see the "big picture" and practical experience of program and project delivery. It is important that the leader has credibility in the eyes of senior stakeholders.
- *Tailored approach* – "A PfMO for every situation". It is imperative to ensure that the PfMO is set up and operated to meet the objectives and requirements of the organization, that is, not one size fits all.
- *Holistic integrated approach* – The approach needs to recognize that setting up and running PfMOs successfully depends on having the right scope, structure, processes and tools, organizational maturity, and people skills, that is, it is not just a case of designing and deploying a set of processes.
- *Maturity based* – There is a need to recognize the importance of ensuring that a PfMO is aligned to an organization's evolving culture/ways of working. There is no point in jumping to level 4 if the organization is not ready for it, that is, "don't try to run before you can walk".
- *Roadmap with quick wins* – This approach allows rapid set-up, the delivery of quick wins to meet client needs and a clear roadmap to broaden and deepen capabilities and performance.
- Proactive value add – The PfMO proactively adds value in the eyes of stakeholders, helping the organization to achieve its objectives,

that is, PfMO is not seen as an administrative burden. This includes proactively providing forward-looking insight, advice, and constructive challenge.

- Integrity of PPM data and analysis –PfMOs need to provide accurate and timely PPM data as well as proactive analysis and insight to provide real visibility and facilitate effective fact-based decision making.
- Lean approach – PfMOs are based on a small flexible team of dedicated personnel that employ "just enough" processes (i.e., keep it simple, not overly bureaucratic) and appropriate tools to increase effectiveness and lower operating costs.
- Skilled resources – It is imperative to have people with the capabilities and experience required, particularly in setting up/transforming PfMOs and wider organizational capabilities.
- Pragmatic processes and tools – Processes and tools are based on repeatable best practice, must work, and must be appropriate for the needs and capabilities of the organization involved, that is, "what matters is that it works, not what the text book says".
- Stakeholder communications – The PfMO will place great emphasis on facilitating stakeholder involvement to support effective delivery, manage stakeholder expectations, and ensure that stakeholder needs are met. that is, "communicate, communicate, communicate".

In addition, innovation-based portfolio management brings in the following benefits:

- captures and maintains industry leadership
- cuts investment for major innovation investment by 25–30 per cent +
- increases revenues by a factor of two to three
- increased profitability: higher margin innovation return yield
- accelerates adoption of systematic approach to new business creation and commercialization
- product and business improvement program investments aligned to corporate strategy with enterprise visibility/control
- simultaneous implementation: business improvement programs (BIP) and innovation product programs
- work of interdependent teams streamlined and accelerated
- increased efficiency and throughput across the organization

Key points

This chapter has provided an outline of the PfMO and how it can play a major role in helping organizations to define and deliver portfolios of change to achieve their strategic objectives. It has also outlined how to set up or transform a PfMO, and the keys to ensuring it really adds value for the organization it serves.

In a nutshell, the PfMO is the organizational enabler underpinning the SP&B management process as it plays a central role in determining, deploying, coordinating, and supporting all the processes used to define the portfolio, control delivery, and ensure benefits are realized.

Excellent portfolio management requires high caliber people operating within an effective organizational environment enabled and supported by pragmatic best practice processes and tools, that is, a holistic integrated approach, that is, "the right people", *using the right processes and tools in the right organizational environment. The PfMO will help to ensure all these elements are in place and working effectively.*

Concluding remarks for Part II

In Part II of this book, we covered SP&B investment decision where we defined portfolio management, its trend, and benefits for the organization. This was followed by an in-depth review of the SP&B framework where we evaluated the approach to convert strategy and innovative demand into actionable plans. We demonstrated the use of business/strategic drivers and benefits impact statements to prioritize, optimize, and select the portfolio of investment taking into account the organizational constraints and risks.

Next we went into the underlying objective of RM where we identified that it was not simply to balance current project requirements with company capability and capacity, but rather to create a systematic and comprehensive approach to recording, prioritizing, and reporting on all current and future needs to enable better forecasting – projecting out how many and what type resources will be needed over the coming period. Increasingly, revenues are derived from harnessing and selling talent. Whether you have a product or services business, organizations have to manage and prioritize resources meticulously.

This was followed by benefits management where we came to terms with tracking and measuring business benefits obtained as a result of investment decision made by the management. However, we have to ensure that these investments are realized according to plan, and the innovative project ideas included as part of the portfolio are successfully implemented as projects with realizable business value.

To make all this happen, we went into the practical details of "how to" set up PfMO to support governance and assure the successful delivery of the SP&B management framework.

The practical knowledge in Part II of this book strips away false values and makes you realize what you really want. If you want to change and gain the competitive advantage or ascertain the strategic leverage in the market as an organization, then stop chasing butterflies and get to work digging the gold in portfolio management.

PART III

Leadership and Governance for Execution Strategy

In this final Part III of the book, I highlight the importance of the innovation decision based on the pipeline of ideas and how your strategy, portfolio, and benefits framework help to select the project or initiative that needs to be executed.

The development of the project execution plan was a natural part of my program training for setting projects off on their complex road. However, understanding where you want to go is very different from appreciating how you intend to get there. This is not peculiar to the world of projects as every commercial venture needs a business plan and an execution strategy. The complexity of execution varies a great deal but the principles are the same.

An execution strategy is a discipline and delivery mechanism which involves both art and science to ensure that the stated benefits in the business case for an initiative are realized to improve the business's competitive advantage.

An execution strategy to be excellent in its delivery requires clear leadership style and governance from senior executives. Excellent leaders who can convert the "right" strategy into desired business results (operations) through effective execution (implementation) of projects have a definitive personal style, attitude, and personality that make strategy execution successful.

Researches have shown that successful leaders are driven by, firstly, their urge to shape their organization's future. This involves a consistent and coherent view of the future for the business, for example, allocating resources and building trust and commitment from below. For this an intimate knowledge of the overall market is necessary. Where this is not the case, problems can arise, especially when differences of vision emerge among members of the leadership team. It is the combination of market and organizational knowledge and a personal view about future direction that provides the stimulus and motivation to shape the future. Secondly, they are driven by the fundamental views each executive holds about how an organization should be managed, how people should be handled, and in what way and with which other executives the individual more easily identifies.

Here I like to investigate how excellence in execution strategy can contribute to an organization's road to success. This will be followed by the role of leadership and governance in facilitating successful execution. I will then discuss on the need for collaborative decision approach and how significant it is to build the team for execution success. As such the following describes the chapter outline:

In Chapter 11, we explain a framework and perspective to establish the link between increasing shareholder value and successful implementation of projects through a delivery capability vehicle (the program management office or PMO) enhanced by a culture of execution excellence. Regardless of the size, shape, style, or organizational authority, the ultimate measure of a PMO is the degree of influence on and contribution to improving shareholder value.

In Chapter 12, we examine, firstly, the important characteristics that leaders will increasingly need in ensuring that an execution strategy is implemented successfully. Secondly, we examine how leaders will need to spend their time in mentoring and coaching their teams to achieve the vision set out for them in the program.

In Chapter 13, we investigate the ability to make decisions as a core leadership skill. Some decisions can be made quickly by one person, while others require the whole project team to convene. Sometimes decision-makers have the luxury of time to carefully analyze all the issues involved, while some decisions must be made with lightning speed, lest the business forfeit a market advantage or allow a deal to slip away.

In Chapter 14, we examine the nature of building teams, specifically in program and project initiatives. We also propose a leadership model useful in managing project team dynamics. Last, we address the special challenges posed by "virtual" project teams.

CHAPTER 11

What Is Excellence in Execution Strategy and Its Influence in Organizational Success?

Excellence in execution strategy is a discipline and delivery mechanism which involves both art and science to ensure that stated benefits in the business case for an initiative are realized to improve the business's competitive advantage. In this chapter, we will also explore the role of programme management office (PMO) and how it helps to embed a culture of execution excellence in organizations.

This chapter explains a framework and perspective to establish the link between increasing shareholder value and successful implementation of projects through a delivery capability vehicle (the PMO) enhanced by a culture of execution excellence. Regardless of the size, shape, style, or organizational authority, the ultimate measure of a PMO is the degree of influence on and contribution to improving shareholder value.

In addition, I try to prove that the job of a chief financial officer (CFO) needs to be redefined to support excellence in execution strategy. Over the last decade the CFO's job has evolved dramatically. The person who was once seen as merely the chief accounting officer and technical expert, narrowly focused on the firm's financial statements and capital structure, now needs to operate more as a business partner with the chief executive officer (CEO). He/she has a much larger mandate for ensuring that the organization's strategy is oriented toward building shareholder value – and is ultimately responsible for the success of his/her organization's projects.

The changing landscape: execution is a discipline

A brilliant strategy, blockbuster product, or breakthrough technology can put you on the competitive map, but only solid execution can keep you there. You have to deliver on your intent. The executives of various companies we have spoken to think of execution as the tactical side of business. "That's the first big mistake" claim Larry Bossidy and Ram Charan in their book *Execution: The Discipline of Getting Things Done*. Tactics are central to execution, but execution isn't tactics. The authors further define execution as:

> . . . a systematic process of rigorously discussing hows and whats, questioning, tenaciously following through, and ensuring accountability. It includes making assumptions about the business environment, assessing the organization's capabilities, linking strategy to operations and the people who are going to implement the strategy, synchronizing those people and their various disciplines, and linking rewards to outcomes. It also includes mechanisms for changing assumptions as the environment changes and upgrading the company's capabilities to meet the challenges of an ambitious strategy.

Research of a thousand companies in 50 countries by Gary Neilson, Karla Martin, and Elizabeth Powers as reported in "The Secrets to Successful Strategy Execution" in the June 2008 issue of *Harvard Business Review* indicates that majority of companies aren't very good by their own admission in translating important strategic and operational decisions quickly into actions. Execution is the result of thousands of decisions made every day by employees acting according to the information they have and their own self-interests. Changing customer expectations and complexity of demands mandate that execution excellence capability becomes an embedded and core element of your organization's performance culture.

Studies by KPMG and Standish Group have shown that in many large companies more than 60 per cent of projects go grossly over budget and far behind schedule and are beset with technology that is nonperforming. When we have shared the figures with some executives, they have responded as if this state is "normal". They consider these numbers neither surprising nor troubling!

Over the years we have often seen companies that are considered progressive and have team-based projects in place struggling to meet time to market. Their projects are late; their team members are spread too thin, with teams "lurching" from one milestone to another; and management schedules expect unrealistic goals that almost demand burnout among participants.

Knowledge advantage holds little meaning without action advantage

Jeffrey Pfeffer and Robert Sutton in their book, *The Knowing-Doing Gap*, highlight five key reasons companies have a gap between knowing and doing:

- Talk substitutes for action
- Memory substitutes for thinking
- Fear prevents acting on knowledge
- Measurement obstructs good judgment
- Internal competition turns friends into enemies.

The main point of their research indicates that it is not enough for the people in the organization to know what to do and how to do things. If they are not able to change their work habits, knowing doesn't help. However, doing something different requires some additional skill. It is important to know *what to ignore* and *what to pay attention to*.

In the article, "Linking Execution with Strategy in Support Functions", in the March/April 2008 issue of Ivey Business Journal, Robert Angel shares research showing that many CFOs, chief information officers (CIOs), chief marketing officers (CMOs), and human resource (HR) executives believe that they are already involved in strategy and execution, both in respect to their own functions and the overall organization. However, it seems that the involvement can often be somewhat superficial. His performance research indicates that 23 per cent of CFOs only provided strategic planning input when asked. Even when the CFO was involved, often performance-related practices in execution were reported to be quite basic.

According to a September 2006 *Economist Intelligence Study*, while almost all CFOs aspire to play a more strategic role, many say they "struggle in practice".

A company cannot deliver on its commitments or adapt well to change unless all leaders practice the discipline of execution at all levels. Few businesses need to spend more than a tenth of their time on strategy; execution is all – and never more so than in today's post-recessionary world, where the ability to do more with less depends on engaged and enabled employees (as expressed in "Bosses Caught in the Middle", by Jane Simms in the May 2010 issue of *Director Magazine*).

Execution has to be part of a company's strategy and its goals. It is the missing link between aspirations and results. As such it is a major – indeed, the major – job of a business leader. Robert Kaplan and David Norton in *The Execution Premium: Linking Strategy to Operations for Competitive Advantage* highlight that the ability for a company to translate its strategies into action and deliver to their customers provides a significant advantage for organizations. If you don't know how to execute, the whole of your impact as a leader will always be less than the sum of its parts.

Developing an execution performance-based culture using the PMO

Business change is legitimized in the organization by the senior management leaders, typically, the CEO and CFO. They alone possess the authority and accountability over the political and economic resources to initiate and sustain investments in business. In turn they charge the PMO with the stewardship over these investments. Their expectation in this is simple: realize increased performance or economic value from business change investments that exceed the total cost of the investment, including the cost of capital required to fund the investment. Figure 11.1 reflects the major focal points for developing execution excellence in a company as a performance-based culture.

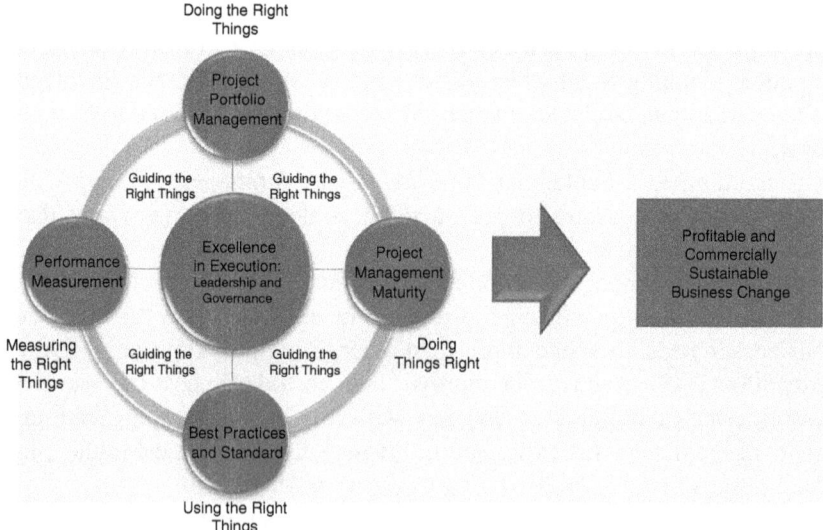

Figure 11.1 Major focal points for execution excellence

Doing the right things is about managing a balanced and profitable mix of project investments aligned with business strategies designed to maximize profitability. This can be accomplished through implementation of project portfolio management processes.

Doing things right means achieving and sustaining the appropriate level of business and project management maturity. This involves getting the right people on the project to implement the processes most appropriate for the culture and performance of the organization. Within the context of these processes, proper education, mentoring, and coaching assure that the associated capabilities are adequately developed and maintained. The objective is to sustain the discipline required to realize the expected or desired return on project investments.

Using the right things is about implementing a PMO that is built to last using proven project management industry standards and emerging best practices.

Measuring the right things are executed is about evaluating and measuring all three focal points to give us confidence that our final execution and original intent are aligned.

Guiding the right things is about governance and project leadership. There are four components in governance that focus on the effectiveness and efficiency of project management: portfolio direction, project sponsorship, project management, and disclosure and reporting. The "Guiding the right things" goes across all the four focal points as described above.

Demands on ultimate shareholder value

A study by Booz Allen Hamilton showed that more shareholder value has been destroyed in the past five years as a result of strategic mismanagement and poor execution than was lost in all of the compliance scandals combined. The research analyzed 1200 firms with market capitalizations over $1 billion for the six-year period from 1998 through 2004 and identified the poorest performers – the 360 companies that trailed the lowest-performing index for that period, the S&P 500. They found that only 13 per cent of the value destroyed by these companies resulted from compliance failures; the other 87 per cent was attributable to strategic and operational blunders involving poor project delivery, misplaced product innovation with disruptive technologies, inadequate brand management, meagre customer relationship management, misalignment of employee incentives and strategy, derisory handling of supplier relationships, and broken distribution channels, among others problems.

To enhance and to protect shareholder value, CEO, CFOs, and board directors need to look beyond traditional categories of share value and anticipate the much larger menu of project delivery and risks to the enterprise's earnings drivers and culture. Of course, taking this more expansive view is difficult, even at the most well-managed companies.

The ultimate concern of the ultimate boss goes beyond profit and loss analysis. Shareholders are not only concerned with short-term results today but also fretful about tomorrow and the company's ability to have consistent performance. The need for reliable knowledge about valuation has never been greater. In recent years increasing pressure has been applied to CEOs, CFOs, and boards to implement shareholder-value-based management systems.

The investment community increasingly recognizes the importance of intangibles in the shareholder value equation. Leadership, strategy execution, brand, human capital, and EHS (environment, health, and safety) performance are all currencies in today's marketplace. A report by Clark Eustace on "The Intangible Economy" for the European Commission noted: "Intangibles such as R&D, proprietary know-how, intellectual property, and workforce skills, world-class supply networks, and brands are now the key drivers of wealth production while physical and financial assets are increasingly regarded as commodities."

The International Accounting Standards Board defines an intangible as an "identifiable, nonmonetary asset without physical substance held for use in the production of goods or services, for rental to others or for administrative purposes". We adopt a broader view. "Intangibles" describes the human, intellectual, social, and structural capital of an organization. Thus, intangibles include people, relationships, skills, and ideas that add value but are not traditionally accounted for on the balance sheet.

The growing importance of intangible assets was emphasized by John Kotter and James Heskett in *Corporate Culture and Performance*, a book that showed that 60–95 per cent of stock market valuations are made up of intangible assets such as cultural, intellectual, and structural capital. Hard assets such as property, plants, and equipment can account for as little as 5 per cent of the stock market valuation.

Now companies are including organizational mastery of project management as a core competency next to other forms of cultural and intellectual capital. This particular organizational capability is the "language of work" or the "discipline of execution". It translates strategy into actions to achieve an organization's desired objectives and is thus treated as an asset. In his book, *EVA: The Real Key to Creating Wealth*, Al Ehrbar writes: "The practice of constantly trying to please Wall Street with the 'right' earnings number causes corporations to do all manner of dumb things. In the stock market, the real question isn't, 'What have you done for me lately?' it's 'What are you going to do for me tomorrow?' "

So what do shareholders really want? As Richard Wittington of Wittington Advisors responds, "The execution by [the executive] team is very important. Have they made product transitions, and made them when they say? Many companies don't really get much revenue from a new product for several years. Others introduce a product with a backlog of orders, and those orders ship on time. That's a big difference." Figure 11.2 summarizes the execution premium as an essence of intangible assets giving rise to shareholder value.

Kotter and Heskett, previously cited, learned some interesting things when they compared those firms with a strong, adaptive culture against those with rigid or weak cultures. In the former:

- The revenue grew more than four times faster.
- The rate of job creation was seven times higher.
- The stock price grew 12 times faster.
- The profit performance was 750 per cent higher.

Other real-world studies show substantial gains from having mastery of project management as a core competence processes. The Gartner Group reported that the average savings from using a project management process

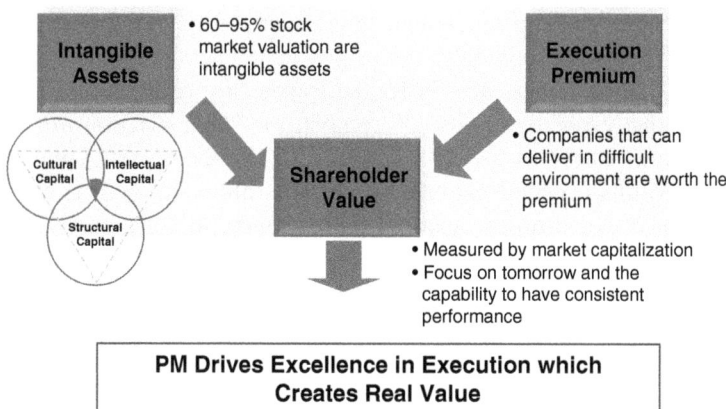

Figure 11.2 Effective project management drives execution excellence, which creates real value

is 30 per cent. Likewise, the Software Engineering Institute concluded that using project management processes reduces project costs by 35 per cent.

These figures suggest that a project costing $70,000 and using sound project management processes would cost about $100,000 or more if project management processes hadn't been used.

A recent survey of 303 representatives from companies with a PMO uncovered high levels of satisfaction. Results showed that companies that have successfully rolled out project management initiatives rarely find them to be a waste of money. Sixty-nine per cent ranked project management "very valuable" or "valuable". Twenty-eight per cent rated them as moderately valuable. Only 3 per cent found them of little value. None responded "no value".

A Standish study found that when a PMO directly links the strategic planning process with project management across the organization through portfolio management and reporting, the organization could expect to reduce delivery costs of the overall project portfolio by at least a tenth.

We don't mean to bog you down with statistics, but we do want to communicate one vital take-away: "Companies that can deliver in a difficult environment are worth the premium for their performance".

The contribution of implementation excellence to shareholder value

Figure 11.3 depicts a framework linking excellent execution performance to increasing share price. The five routes depicted in the figure show the impact of a successful project management capability within an organization. The five distinct outcomes converge to increase shareholder value.

Route 1 shows results of a PMO that repeatedly delivers on promises at a pace that exceeds the rate of competition. This success propagates project management as a core competency. This competency cultivates an agile, results-oriented culture. In addition, although there is a period of imbalance and drop in business performance, this ultimately fosters operational excellence across the organization. Processes and technology are also affected, giving rise to changes that are required to accommodate the higher project management maturity and execution performance. The ensuing organizational productivity then increases performance and lowers operational costs, increasing the value of the organization.

We observed this phenomenon with regard to product development at a large financial services organization. Significant functional and business process modifications were required in the product development area

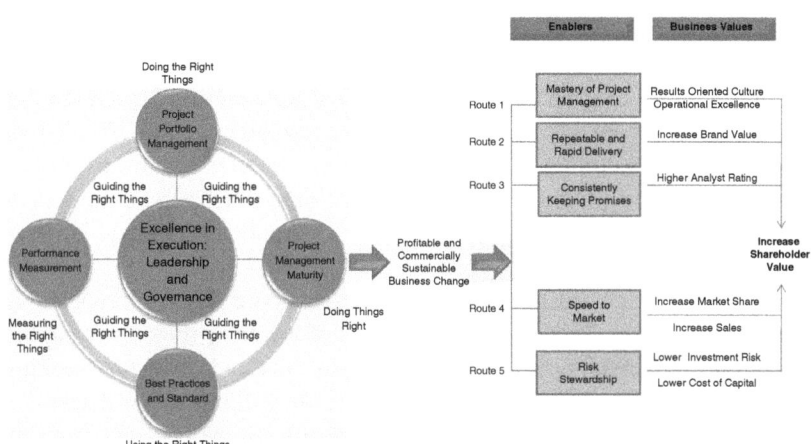

Figure 11.3 Contribution of execution excellence to shareholder value

because of improved project execution. This exposed upstream product development process inconsistencies, lack of discipline, and inadequate rigor and capabilities needed to produce timely competitive products. New processes were designed and a formal product development lifecycle was implemented. Project management processes were also integrated into the product lifecycle. The outcome was that the product delivery timeframe shrank from 18–24 months to 3 months. Sales increased significantly from an abysmal 67 per cent of target in 2004 to over 210 per cent of target by the middle of 2006.

Repeatable and rapid delivery with effective execution, *Route 2*, increases your delivery with customers. The recognition of your brand and capability actually increases your brand value. When investors seek out organizations with strong brand value, their interest increases the share value.

Consistency in execution on *Route 3* results in keeping promises to sponsors and customers. This produces greater confidence in Wall Street analysts by mitigating one of their top concerns – the effective and efficient utilization of an organization's resources. Increasing market share and higher sales are the result of delivering the right products and services when and where necessary. A recent example of this phenomenon in reverse: Nokia CEO Olli-PekkaKallasvuo is being replaced to soothe frustrated shareholders/investors because, as some articles explain, "the CEO can't seem to deliver on his promises to enter the smartphone market and build the company's US presence".

Speed to market, on *Route 4*, energizes the sales force, increasing their confidence and credibility on the street. Sales increase when the sales force achieves and can sustain advantages over competitors. "In some companies, speed-to-market is the difference between a huge profit and a marginal profit or even a loss", write Gerald Kendall and Steven Rollins in their book *Advanced Project Portfolio Management and the PMO*. Our experience with a computer company that implemented a rigorous project management process shows that the average time to respond to new marketing requests improved by a factor of four and the average time to develop a pilot improved five-fold.

Route 5, risk stewardship, shows lower investment risk from repeatable effective execution. This can have the effect of lowering the cost of capital coupled with increasing returns on the capital invested. Investors seeking to find organizations that are increasing in value will buy more shares.

Companies with project management as a core competence and a strong PMO have significant influence and material effect on shareholder value. It is possible to construct a credible framework with a balanced scorecard that clearly illustrates and aligns business strategies and objectives to seemingly unrelated or obscure connections between project performance and shareholder value. Kaplan and Norton in *The Execution Premium: Linking Strategy to Operations for Competitive Advantage* show managers how to weave organizational principles into a more effective management system that respects the differences between strategy and operations yet integrates them in a powerful way using the Balanced Scorecard, a performance measurement system.

Redefining the role of the CFO

CFOs have come a long way from the days when they were regarded as narrowly focused, box-checking specialists in finance and controls. The CFO is actively engaged in devising and executing strategy and overseeing operations in partnership with the CEO. The rise of strategic delivery and risk management as a board-level concern offers them an opening to drive the strategic agenda and make sure that it contributes to the overall imperative of increasing shareholder value. The above framework aligning business strategies with projects supported by clear key performance indicators (KPIs) and a balanced scorecard forces the CFO to redefine his/her role. Leading CFOs – what we call "strategic activist CFOs" – are embracing this opportunity; those who ignore it will be circumscribing their future roles in the leadership of the company.

The CFO has a view of the organization from 30,000 feet, providing an enterprise-wide perspective. The strategic activist CFO has an innate ability to understand what makes each business in the portfolio tick and where the risks lie. In addition, the CFO's traditional responsibilities bring a tremendous amount of independence and objectivity to the project and risk management process. The ability to create transparency and dialog between functional and business unit leadership will become crucial in this new era. How can CFOs best adapt? Our experience shows that CFOs need to ask these basic questions:

- Are strategic and tactical planning dynamically linked and real time?
- Is performance personality based or embedded in the culture?
- Is the budget activity based?
- Is performance rewarded?
- Are resources/capital reassigned dynamically? Strategically? With changes in ROI and NPV?
- Are all projects tracked for performance?

With this strategic approach the CFO becomes the enterprise-wide project portfolio manager, a position from which to oversee and ensure strategic spend and track strategic impacts.

We believe the CFO is well positioned to drive the company's execution agenda, orient it toward increasing shareholder value, and engage with the board of directors. Risk, result, and value are, after all, completely interconnected concepts. The CFO already manages result and value at many companies – why not project performance and risk as well? The traditional tasks given to the CFO – accounting and compliance – will continue to be essential, of course. But they provide a unique vantage point for addressing the new challenges of ensuring strategic spends and tracking strategic impacts to the organization.

CHAPTER 12

What Is the Role of Leadership in Successful Delivery Execution?

Since the evolution of man, it is an instinct in our nature to follow the tract pointed out by a few leaders; we are gregarious animals in a moral as well as physical sense, and we are addicted to routine, because it is always easier to follow the opinion of others than to reason and judge for ourselves. As such the subject of leadership has been in existence since man started to follow. During the writing of our book on "Sun Tzu and the Project Battleground" (2005) both David and I realized how much of thinking and work on leading and leadership existed in China 2500 years ago. If you Google on leadership you will get literarily millions of hits within ten seconds.

We do not want in this chapter to cover in detail about leadership, but what we want to do is to identify the role of leadership and governance in today's and tomorrow's businesses in "making things happen", as we believe that the actions of business leaders today will change the destiny of their organization tomorrow. Tomorrow's business will look very different internally from those with us today. This will be the consequence of new corporate values that will underpin the importance of the workforce to company success. In their turn, the values will be based on a new culture that eschews closed communities at work and recognizes the benefits of sharing information, localizing decision making, training constantly, communicating fully and opening up the company to make it more transparent and accountable to its stakeholders.

The brave new world of tomorrow's organization

Looking to this brave new world of tomorrow's organization, the question one must ask is "What will be the role of leaders capable of taking us to the new world?" To answer this question I need to paint a picture of what tomorrow's businesses will look like. Over the three decades my personal observation on the trends in businesses is that they are becoming more "open book", internally and externally accountable, egalitarian, and employee-centered.

These trends will continue to occur in companies and as Tom Peter (1994) said: "Welcome to the new economy where most of the world's work will be done in semi-permanent networks of small project oriented teams."

The organizations are becoming more flatter where whole layers which once provided stages in career progress and promotion are stripped out, task enrichment, multi-skilling, job rotation/job sharing, and giving the responsibility to employees for their own development as means of maintaining motivation, morale, and loyalty are changes we are seeing now and will continue to see in the future.

As power and authority are disseminated, employees will need to feel that senior management has sufficient confidence in them – and, importantly, in themselves – to give them the freedom, or empowerment, to work with minimal managerial supervision. Management by exception will characterize this hands-off approach, and as managers step back from day-to-day operational detail – leaving this to team leaders while they fulfil their strategic management responsibilities – performance monitoring, appraising, and disciplining procedures will become peer owned and operated, frequently becoming two-way, in which "interviewer" and "interviewee" participate in 360-degree review simultaneously.

Looking at these trends and observations, it is clear that a leader's role will become one that increasingly encapsulates the responsibility of *"entrusting empowerment and enablement to teams"*.

Perspectives on leadership and their role in tomorrow's organization

I find that management and leadership are often confused, and while to many this may seem like a play on words, in my mind the two are clearly different. Management is about providing direction and administrative control while leadership is about empowerment. Others will certainly argue with me over this, but I don't think the debate is that important. What is clear is that the future business environment will require a new breed of leadership to be successful.

When you consider in the background of the changes from caves to computers, the current younger generation certainly has the edge on most of us with gray hair. They see the computer and its connectivity as being the new business environment. I certainly would not challenge its impact, but I would, as I hope is already apparent, promote the idea that this is just a medium. For while the IT age has enabled us to achieve much more than was physically possible when I started my career it is the application that is important. Computers can take out the drudge, but I doubt I will see one in my lifetime with an artificial imagination.

We must not only address the skills of using computers but we must also focus on the need to address the relationships that these bits and bytes will connect. I often comment in seminars that when Alexander Graham Bell invented the telephone he had to wait to find someone to ring. Such was the case of the Dot.com boom, some great ideas with no capacity to deliver most of them.

Certainly the younger generation has an advantage that they have never known a time without being part of a wired world. Now we should also focus on how to give them the capacity to build the new virtual environments that harness both the technology and the futurist thinking that can exploit the technology.

Jake Jacobs (2008) recently joined the Pcubed Board of Directors whose notions about leadership have been forged by a long history of action and achievement in multiple fields – the military, business, television, and publishing. In an interview with him in the Pcubed Insight magazine (2012), he highlighted:

> What leaders are supposed to be doing is, among other things, hanging around the people who work for them and mentoring them. So if you're sitting in an office, you're mentoring absolutely nobody. If you're involved in a company that actually makes something, everybody on the production line has to see you all the time. And if you can't get your paperwork done because you're down there finding out what's going on and mentoring the younger leaders, that's tough. You do it when everybody has gone to sleep. That's why you get paid more money.

Lee Iacocca (1984) in his autobiography said, "During the first couple of weeks in a new job, you look for tell-tale signs. You want to know what kind of fraternity you have joined." He went on to say of his early days at Chrysler Motor Corporation, "Everyone worked independently .... All of Chrysler's problems really boiled down to the same thing. Nobody knew who was on first. There was no team, only a collection of independent players, many of whom hadn't yet mastered their positions." Iacocca reformed all Chrysler's work teams, balancing them to ensure intra-team efficiency, with himself at the center as the orchestrator or principal linker. In this position, Iacocca exercised team management skills of an effective team leader to redefine culture, values, order of conduct, relationships, and corporate goals.

In Stephen Covey's (2005) book the eighth Habit, I was touched by his inspiring opening statement where he said "To the humble, courageous, 'great' ones among us who exemplify how leadership is a choice not a position".

In his book we find a combination of knowledge, skill, and attitude for leaders. Stephen Covey's leadership emphasizes people's guidance becoming better. Path finding is the toughest of all since we have to deal with several personalities, issues, agendas, and levels of trust. Focusing tools that enhance path finding are creating a mission statement and a strategic plan.

Better execution incorporates aligning goals and systems and empowering others, which helps organizations to find their voices and to achieve greatness. Utilizing structures and systems is needed in organizations for reinforcement purposes. Empowerment on the other hand is a model of trustworthy behavior. Empowered people do not need supervision, which inspires trust. When people are empowered, they find their voice by doing the things they want. Their individual voices blend with the voices of the organization. This type of directed autonomy shifts the manager from a controller to an enabler. Empowered mission statements are produced when enough people are fully informed and interact freely and trustfully.

In answering what will be the role of a leader in today's and tomorrow's organization, the words of Narayana Murthy (2009) comes to my mind. To the question of what is leadership, he mentioned that "A leader is first and last a change agent. Progress is his agenda . . . His responsibility is to raise the aspiration of his people, to make them more confident, energetic, enthusiastic, hopeful, and determined to seek a glorious future for the community and for themselves."

Finally, like Sir Graham Day, ex-Chairman of Powergen, Plc, I am drawn to the words of Professor Abraham Zaleznik (a tutor at Harvard's Graduate School of Business): "Leadership is made of substance, humanity and morality . . . ". In an item Sir Graham contributed to The Lust of Leadership (Simon Caulkins 1993), he wrote:

> Leadership is the ability to change compelled performer into willing participants. If you only have a mandatory leadership, you have the three negatives: pressure without motivation; process without substance; organization without improvement. True leadership addresses those negatives. The attributes which ultimately matter most are the abilities to communicate and inspire.

A very long time ago my grandfather introduced me to a great entrepreneur in India who said *"trust with accountability and teamwork with actions"* will be the stepping stone for success. Over the years I realized how true it was as these words encapsulate my own sentiments on leadership for today and tomorrow.

Project leadership in the global execution: changing rules of engagement

In our world of projects, it was always the project manager that held sway over every action and reaction. You will note I have taken the step of choosing the term project leader. Historically the role was one of strictly management and many that I work for and with, in later years, often struggled to appreciate the difference between focus and fascism. This approach worked in the traditional hierarchical single-point environment, but the future project team may be dispersed across geographic and national boundaries, and such an edict style management is unlikely to prosper.

We look for many attributes in project leadership, from mentor to street fighter and clearly every project needs a slightly different emphasis to be effective. As projects globalized and virtual teams are formed, we see as a distinct possibility that there will be more of a holistic structure. To effectively lead such a venture will mean greater deployment of authority and thus more focus on communication as opposed to edict. Often many of the players will be from external organizations with second-tier responsibility to their own management, probably from multicultural backgrounds where a single style of leadership would fail to draw their proactive support.

As we see the financial marketplace is starting to recognize the potential for different business models and shareholders already place great store by the charisma and profile of business leaders. It is therefore reasonable to assume that if virtual organization is to be accepted then the standing of business leaders must also reflect confidence to the market. In any event, we are here looking at projects and these need strong and effective leadership.

Therefore, we must develop the new breed that can deliver on the promise. Project management has never been an easy ride but now we are talking of raising the stakes and alongside this traditional style of relationship management by dictate will fall short. Leadership skills starting with vision and strategic thinking will need to be merged with inspiration and communication as never before as project teams may need to function without daily or hourly direction but must share and support the project goals from afar.

It is interesting that the army has a very strict command and control structure but promotes leadership through its officers on the setting of "what" and leaving the lower ranks to establish the "how". So the nature of leadership is both command and inspire, which many will see as a contradiction. I have no problem with this idea since leadership must be positive at all times and give approvals when necessary, the art is perhaps understanding when approval is really necessary.

An old adage I learnt was that he who wants to lead the orchestra must sometimes turn his back on the crowd, or to put it another way a good leader can step on your toes without messing up the shine.

Thus in this new era of virtual integration, the leadership needs to focus on maintaining a balance between control and innovation. The global complexity of projects is already in my view beyond traditional structures and in time must become more complex as the boundaries between organizations get grayer.

We must also consider those that are to be led in this quest to understand the nature of the new leaders we need. What is now emerging as a potential business model is outside the reference of most of the working population. The concept of being part of virtual organization is tearing at the fabric of their comfort zones. They need to understand and appreciate the drivers in order to function and yet we seldom challenge ourselves in terms of understanding our own perspective of the world.

Good leaders must take due note of the background against which each organization or individual player is assessing the direction they see being taken or which they are being asked to follow. The drivers can be very diverse and often conflicting and leaders need to adjust their style and communicate differently in each case. Individuals must rationalize their position as well.

The primary job of the leader is to create the environment in which people can be successful. The role of the leader is to provide the vision, let people know how their role fits into the vision, and help them understand how to implement it. The conductor owns the culture. If you change the conductor, you change the choir.

There are and will continue to be doubters who see only change to their position and crave the status quo, but we have already seen that volatility of the global marketplace is fired by influences which are outside our control. The more we adapt to promote flexibility of response, the greater the challenge for the individual to be proactive.

It is difficult to measure leadership except through results. The connection between leadership and performance is an indirect one, but intuitively we believe that leadership is a major contributing factor. Management development does not directly impact behavior, it is seen through a sequence of changes from theory to awareness, skill enhancement, and then to behavior. Leadership training will influence management capability, which will affect implementation skills and thus performance. In this virtual world we are looking to stretch the envelop of business relationships, so the leadership has to be futurist.

I have often seen leadership categorized in the above manner, which I feel sets the nature of what I believe will be the cornerstones of dynamic virtual operations. This skills profile is what we should be encouraging for the future leaders in this changing landscape we are trying to exploit. The challenge for most organizations is where do you find these hybrid beings or can you develop them from existing management pools.

I don't profess to have the answer or that it is possible to develop such a beast, but the further we progress into the millennium the greater the urgency, in my view, to try. Many wiser than me have spent their lifetime dissecting the essence of leadership.

For those leading the charge, they must consider the nature of leadership power and assess where they are versus what may be necessary to meet the upcoming challenges. Resource power is a common trait within organizations since authority is derived from command and thus fails to use persuasion, whereas professional power comes from knowledge and experience but is often very traditional and works by collective assessment. Position power is based on authority and seldom uses any form of consultative perspective. Expert power is derived from experience and knowledge. These four subsets will be easily recognized, but when reflecting on the virtual proposition perhaps none directly fits the required profile.

Effective leadership is about more than applying checklists of tactics. It is the difference between theory and being straightforward in one's dealings with the team. Good leaders believe in what they are doing and constantly cross-check events against these ideas and involve their teams on a regular basis. This may be more difficult as we progress more toward following the sun working. There has to be some degree of entrepreneurship if one is to take full advantage of the new thinking and exploit the virtual network, since entrepreneurs think the unthinkable and then do it. At the same time leaders must be adaptable to change and focus on pulling the best from their team.

To many they may see this as somewhat philosophical and perhaps even fluffy. In response I would suggest they have yet to understand the changes that are taking place in the market and that have still to emerge. If meeting these demands and trials is a focus for the sustainable business in a global environment, then in my view we need special leaders to take us there.

The most exciting question is "Who will be the leaders to take us into tomorrow's world?" To this interesting question, there are a number of answers, any of which could be right or wrong! It depends on whose view of tomorrow are we subscribing to. Given that the picture of the future is changing rapidly, I might argue that the only sensible answer is that suggested by Darwin – those who will be leaders are those who through adaptation become the most fitted for the job.

Certainly in my career I have debated this question with leaders internationally, and although few have arrived at exactly the same interpretation of the signs, most agree on three points: firstly, a colossal paradigm shift from current practices is inevitable; secondly, the human resources is central to survival, and development investment in it will become increasingly important; and thirdly, there is no "single malt" model that at this time represents an ideal model for the tomorrow. Rather, they say, "a blend of practices (American, European, Indian, Chinese and Japanese) is likely to prove the most robust and palatable 'beverage' ".

Finally, as we look to harness a whole new facet of leaders, Charles Handy (1994) aptly pointed out in the Age of Paradox "what got you where you are won't keep you where you are". The rules of engagement are changing and so must the leadership that takes us forward.

The next chapter will investigate the ability to make decisions as a core leadership skill. Some decisions can be made quickly by one person, while others require the whole project team to convene. Sometimes decision makers have the luxury of time to carefully analyze all the issues involved, while some decisions must be made with lightning speed, lest the business forfeit a market advantage or allow a deal to slip away.

CHAPTER 13

How to Build Consensus Group Decisions for Projects and Portfolio Success?

Leaders of initiatives and project teams must make decisions constantly. In fact, the ability to make decisions is a core leadership skill. Some decisions can be made quickly by one person, while others require the whole project team to convene. Sometimes decision makers have the luxury of time to carefully analyze all the issues involved, while some decisions must be made with lightning speed, lest the business forfeit a market advantage or allow a deal to slip away.

The effective project leader systematically builds decisions upon a solid foundation of knowledge of project goals, objectives, and relevant information. Those decisions may be made under conditions of tremendous stress and uncertainty, or they may be made in a rigorous, controlled process with data. Some decisions are most appropriately made using "automatic" thinking (intuition), while others benefit from structured analytic or statistical techniques. Nevertheless, the way in which decision makers think about the decision-making process itself should remain consistent.

This chapter describes a collaborative method to build effective project decisions that can be applied across the whole organization. The approach has been effective in both government and commercial arenas on issues ranging from deciding multi-million dollar procurements to allocating project resources. By thinking about the decision as a three-step process – framing the decision to be made, generating alternatives, and deciding the course of action – decision makers can better understand how best to achieve the goal of creating and implementing decisions that endure.

Decision context

How should we define the concept of a "decision"? Decision expert Kenneth Hammond in his book *Judgments under Stress* defines a decision as a response to a situation in which (a) there is more than one possible course of action; (b) the decision maker can form expectations about the outcomes following each possible course of action; and (c) each outcome has an associated consequence that can be evaluated.

The collaborative decision method in Figure 13.1 shows a simple yet powerful way for systematically approaching project decisions. There are three common characteristics of tough project decisions. First, there is usually a degree of conflict or disagreement among stakeholders. Second, these decisions are usually made with incomplete or inaccurate information that leads to uncertainty about the outcome of the decision. Third, there may be some level of ambiguity in key decision elements (such as the lack of a clear objective). Yet, we have to ask, why do some decision makers appear to thrive under conditions of conflict, uncertainty, and ambiguity while others seem paralyzed by indecision?

Decision theory

John Von Neumann and Oskar Morgenstern are generally credited with developing modern decision theory in their 1947 classic *Theory of Games and Economic Behavior*. This book presented a mathematical treatment of utility theory, relative to optimal economic decision making. Many subsequent works on decision theory tend to focus on this normative (*how it should be*) approach, which is rooted in probability theory that was developed in the sixteenth century. Actual human decision

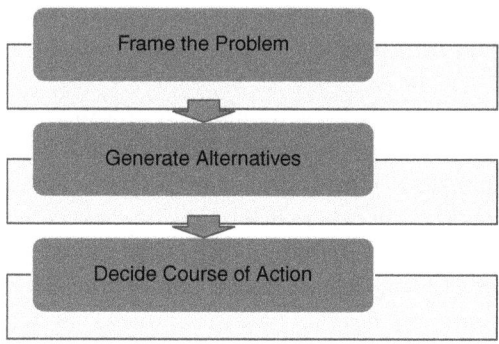

Figure 13.1 The three steps of a collaborative decision method

making, however, is often far more complex, especially under real-life pressures of time constraints, dynamic conditions, uncertainty, and high stakes.

Humans employ both automatic and controlled thinking processes, according to research by Reid Hastie and Robyn Dawes, as explained in their book *Rational Choice in an Uncertain World: The Psychology of Judgment and Decision Making*. Automatic thinking – intuition – is often defined in terms of pattern recognition without evident conscious thought. By contrast, controlled thinking processes employ obvious logic (such as *if...then* analysis). An extensive body of research indicates that humans tend to alternate between automatic and controlled thinking when making decisions. Researchers have studied professionals from all walks of life to attempt to describe their decision-making processes. A key conclusion is that the human mind has a remarkable ability to create patterns from facts and experiences, which are then stored in long-term memory and form the basis for subsequent decisions. Experienced professionals rapidly, and often unconsciously, assess developing situations on the basis of these stored memories to choose alternative options. This rapid pattern recognition and option selection based on stored memories is the essence of intuitive decision making.

In contrast to intuitive decision making, decision analysis can be defined as the use of probability theory to structure and quantify the process of making choices among alternatives. Decision analysts tend to approach a decision problem by structuring and decomposing issues into component parts that are presumably easier to decide, then aggregating those smaller decisions into a composite. Thus, the expectation is that "good" component decisions will aggregate into a "good" macro decision. Stated another way, decision analysis involves putting the facts in order and deciding based on the importance of each fact.

Intuition versus analysis

Many decision analysts belittle intuition as a valid method for making decisions, but both analysis and intuition are useful techniques. An intuitive approach is most useful in high-speed, high-risk, and high-uncertainty situations with experienced decision makers; while an analytic approach is often better in nontime critical situations where the decision maker must explain, defend, and/or justify a decision, or where the decision maker may not have as much experience. In addition, decision analysis can help guard against the biases to which humans are susceptible when relying on intuition.

In my book, *Sun Tzu and the Project Battleground: Creating Project Strategy from the Art of War*, David Hawkins and I demonstrated how one of the best-known generals in history considered war an art rather than science, which meant that there is no absolutely right answer to any problem. A friend of mine who is a commander and veteran of the Ministry of Defence, UK, once commented: "Intuitive decision-making works on the belief that, due to the judgment gained by experience, training, and reflection, the commander will generate a workable first solution . . . Intuitive decision-making is generally much faster than analytical decision making . . . The intuitive approach is more appropriate for the vast majority of typical tactical or operational decisions."

The collaborative decision method

The collaboration of the project team can be an effective insurance policy against the individual biases that often interfere with good judgment when relying on intuition. People are unique; each one of us perceives the world differently. Our brains filter incoming information based on what we are "ready" to see, thereby exposing us to the risk of overlooking key dangers and opportunities. Perhaps the overriding advantage of having more than one person involved in the decision process is the diversity of perspectives gained, which in turn provides additional insight into possible opportunities or risks. Moreover, people tend to support best that which they helped create. If you need the commitment of a group of people to execute a decision (remembering that an unimplemented decision is an academic exercise at best), get them involved in the decision process!

Nothing in life is free, and the price of additional perspectives and enhanced "buy-in" is time and effort. Collaborative decisions generally take longer than independent ones because you must allow for open dialog and a free exchange of ideas. In addition, you must manage the group's dynamics for useful decisions to result. Most of us have had the experience of sitting through long, boring meetings where nothing substantive gets decided.

Collaborative decision meetings must be carefully planned and facilitated. Ideas must be allowed to diverge sufficiently to ensure consideration of fresh perspectives and to encourage creativity. The second part of the meeting is where the group begins to drive to closure to select an alternative. Another way to express this idea is divergent thinking (opening up the realm of the possible), followed by convergent thinking (making a choice). This is an approach described by Sam Kaner and his co-authors in *Facilitator's Guide to Participatory Decision-Making*.

A few cautions about collaborative decision making are in order. First, individual self-interest can overcome the drive to make a choice for the common good. For example, how many meetings have you attended where a department manager announced that he/she didn't need all of the budget allocated for the department that quarter, and therefore it would be returned to the corporate coffers for reallocation? Second, if the "arrows are flying", it is probably not a good time to convene a decision meeting. Finally, if the decision makers aren't directly affected by the outcome of their decision, there's a danger that they won't take the process seriously enough to really take a critical look at all of the ideas before making a selection.

Step 1: the proper frame

The single most important step in the decision method is establishing a proper frame for the decision. How the problem or decision is defined also determines the available alternatives from which a selection can be made. The frame is the overall context for the decision. What is the ultimate objective of the decision? What is the root cause of the issue or problem? Decision makers sometimes lock onto a particular decision frame without critically examining the overall objectives of the decision itself.

Let's imagine that we are choosing among alternative houses built by a general contractor, and we frame our decision problem as creating decision criteria that will yield a technical score for each alternative house. We could build a technical score by using decision factors such as presence of a front door, windows, and so on, but how useful would that score be? However, if we frame our decision problem as coming up with selection discriminators, it changes the way we think about the decision problem and should result in more appropriate decision criteria. For example, once the target audience is identified, you'll better know where would their focus be so that decision criteria could evaluate the need for a conservatory, a study room, or open space area, or in another example a bungalow versus townhouse.

Our recommended framing technique is rather simple: Keep asking the question "why?" until it doesn't make sense anymore. Popular in the quality management profession for years, this technique is sometimes referred to as the *Five Why's* tool because you can generally ask the question "Why?" five times or fewer before you get to the root cause of a problem or issue.

The proper decision frame opens up the spectrum of possible solutions, allowing truly creative possibilities to emerge. The typical decision maker tends to focus on point solutions (*the way we've always done things*)

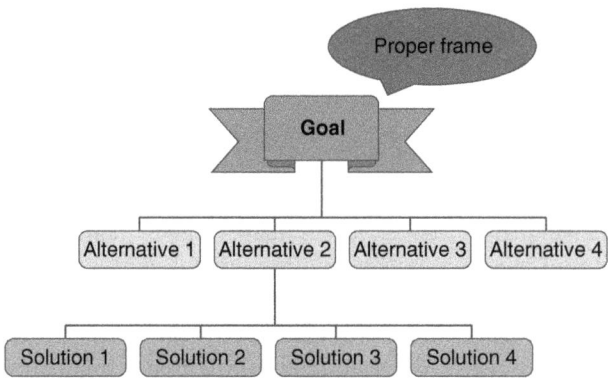

Figure 13.2 The decision hierarchy

instead of taking the time to step back to examine the underlying goals of the decision. As shown in Figure 13.2, by asking the fundamental question "Why", a decision maker can see alternatives and options that are not readily apparent if the chosen frame is constrained to answering the question "What's wrong?" Think of it this way: You must take the journey up the decision ladder from symptom to cause before you can travel back down to find a true remedy.

Step 2: generating alternatives

The second step of the decision method is to generate alternatives. This is where decision makers can leverage creativity for good decision making. The most important rule to remember at this step is *size counts*. The more options and alternatives generated by the decision team, the greater the likelihood the team will encounter an innovative solution or alternative. Decision expert Robin Hogarth sums it up succinctly in *Judgment and Choice*:

> Imagination and creativity play key roles in judgment and choice ... Predictive judgment requires the ability to imagine possible outcomes ... In many choice situations alternatives are not given but must be created ... Indeed, it can be said that a person who exhibits neither creativity nor imagination is incapable of expressing "free" judgement or choice.

The single most important rule to remember in the alternative generation phase is to keep idea creation separate and distinct from idea evaluation. In other words, don't criticize or judge ideas as they are being created.

Numerous studies have shown that far more ideas are generated when the group defers judgment to a subsequent phase of the decision meeting. The group must open up the spectrum of the possible (divergent thinking) before coming to closure on a set of alternatives.

There are various creativity techniques available to the project team. Many of us are familiar with classic brainstorming, where the meeting participants shout out ideas as a facilitator records them on large sheets of paper. There are also techniques that use the power of analogy as a way to stimulate creativity. Forced analogy is a very useful and fun-filled method of generating ideas. The idea is to compare the problem with something else that has little or nothing in common and gain new insights as a result. You can force a relationship between almost anything, and get new insights: companies and whales, management systems and telephone networks, or your relationship and a pencil. Forcing relationships is one of the most powerful methods to develop ways, to develop new insights and new solutions. Another very powerful creativity technique that is easy to facilitate in a group setting is to leverage the power of wishes. Ask the participants to suspend disbelief for a few moments and think about what they would do if they were omnipotent and all things were possible. The resulting ideas can be creative *and* usually seem impossible to implement.

The project leader's job is to help the group find ways to overcome the obstacles of the "impossible" ideas in order to make them feasible options. Indeed, it can be said that nearly all truly innovative ideas look infeasible to many people when they are first created. For example, according to the creativity consulting firm Synecticsworld, Alastair Pilkington was washing dishes one evening when he observed grease forming on the dishwater. He connected this to his work and the particularly difficult problem at the time of how to make plate glass smooth. Wishing he could make plate glass by pouring it on water so that it would be perfectly flat, he conceived the idea of pouring molten glass onto liquid tin. Pilkington's idea revolutionized the glass industry and the process is now used worldwide.

A project leader encounters many different kinds of decision meetings; but perhaps nowhere is creativity more important than in developing a project portfolio. A creativity technique that we have used with excellent success is to ask the group to sit back for a moment and imagine what success would look like five years hence if all their wishes came true. Then we ask each person to write down his/her description of that ideal future state. The next step is to share the scenarios with the entire group. Next, by facilitating the group through a process of dialog and debate, we help the group forge a shared vision of the future and the necessary project portfolio to help achieve that future. This technique is a wonderful way to leverage the power of intuition in the context of a defensible decision process.

Step 3: deciding the course of action

Once the group has properly framed the decision problem and generated a sufficient number of alternatives, it is time to begin the process of convergence – getting to a solution. This third step of the decision method is where decision analysis tools are generally the most useful. The decision facilitator's task at this stage is to help the group evaluate the alternatives and choose a solution. This can be achieved through a combination of intuitive and analytical approaches. In situations where speed and uncertainty are key factors, the intuitive approach requires that the decision makers look at the options and choose a workable solution, then continually refine that solution as new information becomes available.

Simple group ranking tools such as multi-voting and nominal group technique directly tap into the intuition of the members of a decision team and quickly summarize group results. We even ask intuitive questions directly when examining the results of these activities: "*Does this look right to you?*" Intuitive decision making is improved through experience, either actual or simulated, so a careful project leader doesn't rely on purely intuitive approaches with inexperienced decision teams.

A key challenge for the decision team is to find a way to systematically analyze how the alternatives stack up in order to choose the "best", or most preferred alternative. This can generally be accomplished in one of the two ways: comparing the alternatives to one another or scoring the alternatives against some set of objective-rating criteria. Comparing more than two alternatives can be a bit confusing, so it can be helpful to establish a simple 2×2 matrix with the alternatives arrayed across the top and along the vertical axis, as shown in Table 13.1. The decision maker can compare each option to every other option and derive a set of weights by which they can order the alternatives from most to least preferred: "*Do you prefer a or b? Do you prefer b or c? Do you prefer . . .* ". (The same technique can also be used to weight criteria for a ratings model, described next.)

The second basic method for ranking alternatives is to score each alternative against an objective set of ratings. This is a preferred technique when there are more than a handful of alternatives, because metrics can become unwieldy with large numbers of alternatives. To use rating scales, the decision maker must create and weight a set of decision criteria by which the alternatives are judged. These decision criteria should be few

Table 13.1　A decision matrix can help groups sort through alternatives to get at the most preferred one

	A	B	C	D	Row Totals	Weight
A		0.20	0.33	1.00	1.53	8%
B	5.00		2.00	4.00	11.00	56%
C	3.00	0.50		2.00	5.50	28%
D	1.00	0.25	0.50		1.75	9%
Column Total	9.00	0.95	2.83	7.00	19.78	
					Grand Total	

in number, reasonably independent of one another, and be clearly and unambiguously defined.

Groups often run into trouble when the decision criteria (and/or associated rating scales) are defined in the same way by all decision makers. If the decision criteria lack a common definition for all members of the decision team, the team results should be called into question, since various team members may have evaluated the alternatives differently. For example, let's return to our general contractor example. Assume we are evaluating the quality of the house a general contractor has built, and our chosen rating scale is one through five. If we don't all agree on the underlying meaning of a "one", "two", and so on, a consensus score lacks precision at best and, at worst, is no better than a random number.

During an analytical decision process, a good rule of thumb is to follow Albert Einstein's famous advice to keep things as simple as possible, but no simpler. The less complex the decision model, the more likely the group will actually understand the evaluation process, and the better the odds of the group coming to consensus on a result. There are two basic ways to simplify a decision model: by eliminating decision criteria and by eliminating alternatives. Starting the process with the critical few decision discriminators is the key. In our construction example, would you bother verifying whether each alternative house had doors and windows? Local building codes demand that all houses have doors and windows, so unless you defined it in some unique way, such a criterion is not a decision discriminator.

Once the decision team has settled on the decision criteria that are truly needed and no more, the next place to look to simplify the decision problem is to eliminate alternatives. A word of caution is appropriate here. The decision team should only attempt to eliminate those alternatives that have no chance of being selected as the best. In other words, if an alternative is clearly inferior to at least one other alternative for every decision criteria, why consider it any further? Source selection teams refer to this as "narrowing the competitive range". Decision analysts call this the "decision dominance principle".

Project management decision-making in action

We recently helped one customer team prioritize a project portfolio using our three-step method. The customer had an internally generated project list that exceeded the corporation's available resources. While people in different functional areas had generated the project list, many of the projects were cross-functional in nature. In addition, project resources needed to be allocated and de-conflicted from a corporate perspective. The leadership team assembled in a conference room for a two-day process of creating decision criteria and rating the projects against the criteria.

The customer team spent most of the first day choosing the correct frame for the overall corporate objective. While one might imagine that this would be obvious, getting people from different functional perspectives to agree on a succinct statement of the overall corporate goal was not a trivial task. Using successive waves of brainstorming and evaluation, the team established a frame to which they were all committed.

Once they had a consensus decision frame, the customer team had to craft a set of decision criteria by which they could measure the value of the projects' contributions toward the corporate goal. This also required significant discussion and successive waves of voting in order to ensure that the team had a good set of well-defined criteria. Finally, the team evaluated the project list against the criteria and established a numerical score for each of the projects.

The fourth step of this process will be for the customer team to examine how the projects relate to one another and the available resources in a project management tool. Once they understand the project relationships and identify the resource conflicts, they'll be able to use the project rating score to prioritize which projects will be implemented and which will be deferred or eliminated.

The decision method is a structured approach to decision making with wide applicability. Whether you are struggling with an important engineering decision or trying to decide a policy matter, you must be careful not to let conflict, uncertainty, and ambiguity slow you down. While certainly not a panacea, the decision method can help project teams spend their time more effectively and efficiently while they seek solutions to difficult decision problems.

In the next chapter we will review why some teams and team leaders appear to thrive under those conditions of conflict, uncertainty, and ambiguity, while others seem paralyzed by indecision. So building a team for project execution success is as much art as science. Many team-building efforts fail because teamwork essentials aren't fully understood. In the coming chapter we examine the nature of building teams, specifically in program and project initiatives, and also propose a leadership model useful in managing project team dynamics.

CHAPTER 14

How to Build Teams for Execution Success?

Project teams can sometimes resemble children's soccer. Anyone watching a swarm of five-year-old children kicking at the soccer ball knows that each child is usually focused on his/her own performance, oblivious to the overall aim of scoring goals while learning soccer skills. The road to project success is often littered with conflict resulting from disagreement among stakeholders. Program leaders must function with incomplete or inaccurate information. And there is often ambiguity or a lack of a clear definition of success in key program elements. Some teams and team leaders appear to thrive under those conditions of conflict, uncertainty, and ambiguity, while others seem paralyzed by indecision.

So building a team for project success is as much art as science. Many team-building efforts fail because teamwork essentials aren't fully understood. In this chapter, I examine the nature of building teams specifically in program and project initiatives. I also propose a leadership model useful in managing project team dynamics. Lastly, I address the special challenges posed by "virtual" project teams.

I believe that effective project teams share four common characteristics. *First*, they can articulate the common goals they are committed to achieve. *Second*, they acknowledge a mutual dependency on and demonstrate trust for one another. To accomplish this, there must be an understanding of and respect for team roles and responsibilities. *Third*, the team must accept a common set of behavioral norms – a common code of conduct. *Fourth*, they must accept the reward system that they will share.

Conflict, uncertainty, and ambiguity in team building

As projects grow increasingly complex, project leaders are forced to rely on teams composed of highly skilled "knowledge workers". Since knowledge workers often resist close management, the centralized, command and control project management models have given way to loose, networked models where experts leverage their intellectual capital in support of primary project goals. Of course, these loose networks aren't without challenges.

Technically challenging environments nearly always foster conflict among team members. By itself, conflict is not unhealthy. Quite the contrary, conflict – frequently manifesting itself as disagreement – is often a necessary precondition for group progress. Conflict can be an indication that the group is comfortable with open debate. However, conflict must be managed effectively so it is a source of power and not a demotivating element. Nothing can derail a project faster than a breakdown in teamwork resulting from unmanaged conflict.

By their very nature, complex projects almost always involve a high degree of uncertainty. Project leaders and team members must function with incomplete, inaccurate, or unknown information. This uncertainty can result in "second guessing" within the project team and other project stakeholders. So uncertainty must be acknowledged and accepted as an unavoidable condition.

Our crystal balls aren't perfect. Consequently, frequent and open communication is essential to keep the team – and stakeholders – focused on the project objective. Weekly status reports, flash reports, frequent emails, and simply talking to one another on a regular basis can help keep uncertainty under control and mitigate its damaging effects on teamwork.

Ambiguity is another characteristic of complex projects that must be addressed by the team. More often than not, confusion surrounds key project elements or objectives. Even worse, ambiguity sometimes results from conflicting definitions of words. We recently worked with a large project team in a multi-national corporation where the team members kept arguing about the project "scope". Interestingly enough, when we pressed for their definition of "scope", we found that they were arguing over eight very different definitions!

The project team can mitigate ambiguity by taking the time to establish – and publish – a common set of terminology to serve as a team reference. A pre-written systems management dictionary can serve the same purpose. Other tools that can reduce ambiguity include a highly visible status board containing project goals, the plan, and progress relative to the plan, frequent communications meetings, and frequent, informal dialog among the project team members.

Forging a common goal

The objective of project leadership is to inspire and motivate the team to achieve project goals. How the leader accomplishes this objective can vary widely as a function of the skills and style of the leader and according to the situation. Some useful project leadership techniques are as follows:

- defining and broadcasting the project vision
- creating the desired work environment
- understanding how the group will respond to various leadership techniques
- understanding interpersonal traits within the team
- reinforcing desired team behavior
- setting the example
- rewarding achievement
- establishing and radiating the project leader's credibility.

Given the complexity of most project environments, the project leader doesn't necessarily have to be the leading technical expert. Nor does he/she need to have the most tenure in the organization. The project leader needs to exude *credibility*, which is a result of acting with integrity, demonstrating concern for others, and following through with actions that match spoken words.

A popular metaphor for a traditional project team is an orchestra. The orchestra conductor interprets the score and tightly controls the rhythm, pace, and melody for the players. Each player knows precisely the part he/she plays in the output, since it has been predefined by the score and can only be adjusted by the conductor. Of course, this puts tremendous pressure on the conductor, who must not only be attuned to every nuance and detail of the performance but must have intimate knowledge of each performer's part. There are some projects that are most appropriately conducted like an orchestra. Many aerospace projects – especially those concerned with human safety – are best run in this fashion.

By contrast, when the project is comprised of high-technology knowledge workers engaged in innovative technical work in a virtual work environment, perhaps another metaphor is more relevant – a jazz combo. A jazz combo is a tightly focused, smoothly functioning team of musicians. Like the jazz combo leader, the enlightened project leader provides the overall context and structure (melody) for the group, while each of the individual contributors is free to creatively employ his/her talent within that structure for the benefit of the program. Moreover, as in the jazz combo, leadership for a given project phase or activity may seamlessly shift to someone other than the designated project leader. The ability to foster a collaborative environment, both within the core team and among the team and other groups of stakeholders, is a core leadership skill for running a project.

Understanding individual goals in team building

While project leaders often focus on establishing a common goal, truly successful leaders look beyond the primary project goals and examine each team member's individual goals, many of which can be sources of considerable conflict. The project manager must continually probe below the surface to understand how the team members' and other stakeholders' individual goals and concerns will affect overall team performance.

While it may appear obvious that project team members agree on a set of common primary goals (such as completing the project on time and under budget), team members will usually act in concert with their individual goals – regardless of whether they match the team's goals. These individual goals, sometimes referred to as "hidden agendas", often remain invisible to the rest of the group. For example, we worked with an organization where the common team goal was increased profits, while the individual goals were very different and drove some interesting behavior. One team member's individual goal was to build an enduring legacy – not always a profitable activity. Another team member wanted to build a stream of fun and engaging work for himself, despite the fact that the fun and engaging work came at the expense of more profitable but less interesting work. Thus, while both men easily agreed on the common goal of enhanced profitability, their actions, driven by individual goals, resulted in behavior that had the opposite effect.

It's incumbent upon the project leader to surface all individual goals. As long as those individual goals stay submerged, they can have the same effect as an iceberg lurking beneath the ocean waves – they can destroy teamwork before you even realize what has happened.

Mutual dependency and trust among team members

Some months ago, we worked with a project team that was embarking on a new project. During a group intervention, we asked the team members to write their job roles on sticky notes, along with the inputs they required to do that role and the outputs they produced. Once the team finished writing, we posted the notes on a blank wall and asked each member to tape a piece of yarn from their output to at least one other project team member who needed that output to do his/her job.

Once the taping was done, the project leader had a surprising revelation. Not only did he agree with the roles that the team members had written for themselves but also all the pieces of yarn went directly to his card! In other words, the project team members were thoroughly confused about their roles, and they did not recognize any interdependencies with their peers.

When the project leader and the team members are unclear about roles and responsibilities, conflict and frustration is the result. Moreover, each team member must clearly see how his/her role supports overall team goals. It's incumbent upon the project leader to discuss team roles and clearly describe how the roles support overall project success.

Further, each team member must earn trust by consistently shouldering his/her share of the work and performing duties appropriately. When a team member is perceived to be shirking responsibilities, mutual dependency is lost, trust is damaged, and teamwork breaks down rapidly. The leader must accept responsibility for fostering mutual dependency and trust by:

- clearly defining and documenting roles and responsibilities
- developing a clear organizational structure and diagram team interdependencies
- defining the scope of authority of each member
- insisting on absolute integrity.

A common code of conduct for team members

One useful technique to manage conflict in project teams is to establish a team "Code of Conduct". Sometimes referred to as "operating norms", a code of conduct establishes explicit expectations of acceptable group behavior. Managers often incorrectly assume that a code of conduct is implied and understood. Unfortunately, implicit expectations are rarely understood and much less accepted by all team members. This mismatch between expectations and reality can lead to frustration and anger, which may result in a breakdown in teamwork.

The code of conduct may address acceptable ways group members should communicate among themselves (such as "attack ideas, not people"); it may describe forbidden behavior ("no gambling on company property"), or it may attempt to clarify norms intended to improve productivity ("mobile phones must be set to 'silent' in the team room"). The project team should discuss and agree on an explicit code of conduct early, before interpersonal conflicts fester and team productivity grinds to a halt.

To be effective, a common code of conduct needs to:

- Cover areas that aren't explicitly covered by other standards, such as contracts or memoranda of agreement.

- Clear up gray areas.
- Resolve potential sources of conflict.

The value of shared rewards

Most project team members want to do a good job. People generally like to take pride in their work, and they want to feel appreciated for their efforts. We know of one company that took tremendous pride in the great number of high-achievers on their staff. Unfortunately, the top company executive resisted expressing his appreciation for individual efforts that were often recognized – in writing – by customers. While it's tempting to speculate on his misguided motives, the result of his neglect was obvious: Key staff left and those that remained felt unappreciated by management.

Shared rewards can reinforce teamwork and instill pride in collective accomplishment. These rewards can take many forms: cash, certificates, pizza parties, dinner on the company and so on. One of the most effective rewards we've used is a simple printed certificate presented to deserving team members during weekly team meetings. We called it the "GRUNT Award". GRUNT is an acronym that stands for "Greatness is Rarely Understood or Noticed at the Top". At the end of the meeting, the project leader would single out an act of significant achievement (such as volunteering to work extra hours to meet a deadline) and announce, "... While greatness is rarely understood or noticed at the top, somebody noticed and we appreciate your efforts." That simple act is all it took to reinforce positive behavior and foster team spirit.

Building a virtual team

A virtual team is one that operates without the physical limitations of distance, time, or organizational boundaries. When you're based in London and you're working on a project with people in Seattle, Hamburg, and Beijing, that's a virtual team. As project teams become more networked, collaboration across geographic and cultural boundaries becomes more prevalent. Moreover, with companies trying to minimize expenses, travel is much less likely than in past years. For better or worse, virtual teams are here to stay and project leaders must learn to deal with them.

Researchers have studied the top reasons why some virtual teams fail:

- They don't have a compelling shared vision.
- They don't clearly identify network participants and their respective roles.

- Team goals are incompatible with individual goals.
- The team doesn't communicate clearly and sufficiently.

These reasons should appear familiar since they're identical to the top reasons traditional project teams fail! Virtual teams have some unique challenges, however. The inability to physically see and verify progress on a drop-in basis ("management by walking around") can be especially challenging for some leaders. One virtual team that we work with on a regular basis uses periodic face-to-face meetings, along with a regularly scheduled teleconferenced staff meeting to foster a sense of teamwork. Interestingly enough, the breakdown in teamwork appears to follow a predictable cycle that's almost directly proportional to the length of time between face-to-face meetings. When communications become sporadic and emails become rancorous, the team knows that it's time for a physical meeting to strengthen their bonds.

Psychologists claim that 80 per cent or more of human communications is nonverbal. This presents special challenges to project leaders of virtual teams. Communications are the lifeblood of any project team, and virtual teams are often forced to forgo this 80 per cent of the delivery channel by their lack of physical presence. How often is email to be misinterpreted simply because the recipient can't rely on visual cues from the sender's face to help interpret the written words? Relying on teleconferences and emails is a poor substitute for face-to-face communications and, as in the example described in the previous paragraph, can lead to mistrust and a breakdown in teamwork. Some virtual teams use videoconferences, but bandwidth and technology limitations can make videoconferences more distracting than helpful.

The distributed nature of work isn't likely to change. In fact, given the rise in popularity of telecommuting, virtual teamwork will become even more of a factor in project teams. There are some techniques that have proven effective in managing virtual teams:

- use a face-to-face team kick-off meeting
- develop and implement a solid communications plan that leverages electronic as well as telephonic communications
- establish a virtual project information center on the web
- establish and publish a clear code of conduct, including acceptable email etiquette
- continuously monitor effectiveness of communications.

We view effective teamwork as an essential element of project success. Our experience shows that successful project teams share a common goal, acknowledge interdependency and trust among themselves, accept an explicit common code of conduct, and share rewards. While these four attributes alone won't guarantee project success, the absence of one or more attributes certainly increases the risk of project failure.

Concluding remarks for Part III

In Part III of the book we deep dive into the ability to execute the initiatives that were selected from the integration of the innovation ideas and investment decisions made through the strategy, portfolio, and benefits framework. We discussed in detail the contribution of your excellence in execution strategy to shareholder wealth and the significance of setting up a vehicle of delivery capability within your organization so as to underpin the principles in executing well. We further evaluated the role of leadership in successful delivery as being the ability to entrust, empower, and enable high performance teams.

Next we evaluated and investigated the ability to make decisions and a core leadership skill, as some decisions can be made quickly by one person, while others require the whole project team to be convened. Sometimes decision makers have the luxury of time to carefully analyze all the issues involved, while some decisions must be made with lightning speed, lest the business forfeit a market advantage or allow a deal to slip away. The final area we covered was to examine the nature of building teams specifically in program and project initiatives for we believe that for execution to be successful we need high-disciplined teams with innovative leadership who can deliver what is promised!

As in my opening page of the book, I stated "The actions of today becomes the destiny of tomorrow, a company can change its destiny not by wishing for it but by working for it – through its leader's decisions and actions" – the essence of this statement is that as leaders and individuals we must "Align what we think to what we say and do what we think and say" both in private and public, as the quality of work and outcome will depend upon the quality of intention, the quality of the mind, and the intellect behind.

Epilogue

It is customary to complete any writing with the writer's perspective on the future of this approach to business. In the past this has been relatively easy since in most cases the projection goes well beyond the time when the writer will have to justify his or her projections. In this case there is already much that has been proven and with the speed of technology and globalization any prediction probably only has a few years to make its mark. In this case I feel confident that forward-thinking and progressive organizations will have out stripped my ideas in a very few years and have their companies ensure the good innovative ideas bubble to the top, so that they can make better investment decisions and can manage implementation with less wasted resources and time as part of the normal everyday business vocabulary. And by aligning and enabling innovation, investment, and implementation, the companies will gain their competitive advantage in the marketplace that they operate.

Defying traditional business logic, significant developments have appeared on the business landscape over the past decade, creating new value propositions and together redefining the possible. Improved communications and the emergence of digital technology and the Internet are changing all our lives. Despite the dot.com collapse, the rules of commerce are being re-written. Not every idea or innovation results from a sudden isolated flash of inspiration. Often events trigger the emergence of something concrete from an accumulation of ideas, experience, and knowledge. The circumstances bring together disparate thoughts and suddenly make a linkage. Innovations may just be the re-alignment of old and forgotten practices, like a twist of a kaleidoscope, revealing a new pattern. However to enable innovation, organizations must recognize that imaginations from their employees are their greatest strength; it goes beyond reason and it is the only light that can take the company anywhere. As Swami Vivekananda quoted, "Imagination properly employed is our greatest strength, it goes beyond reason, and it is the only light that can take us everywhere."

Those readers who have enjoyed many years in business will remember the many fads that have been heralded as the new business thinking of the future. The better of these often embody traditional values and common sense, albeit with new buzzwords. These revalidations may be valuable nonetheless, by challenging the *status quo* and providing a benchmark for the next few years.

We all need to take time once in a while to review where we are and where we think we should be going. This book integrates many established ideas on innovation, portfolio investments, and execution, but recent advances in communications and technology give an added dimension.

The interconnectivity of people and their ideas have made businesses re-evaluate their business profile on how to harness the most important asset of their organization: people. Here lies the most important issue of all. The future purpose of all companies and all organizations must be allied to a better understanding of all people's potentials and needs, which to date seem often to have been cursory. Their future success depends on this. It is only in developing this most precious and least understood resource that companies can hope to survive into the future. In an increasing competitive environment, unless the nature of competition itself undergoes a radical change, only two courses of action are possible: be better than the competition in terms of current practice or change the rules of the game. Both way people's originality and capacity to produce and be committed hold the key. This need not be nominal. It can be in the form of a major "paradigm shift". Few people seem yet to realize, perhaps wish for, the extraordinary extent to which they have the ability to transform themselves, their environments, and their companies.

My final words are decisions and actions can be good if organizations can empower their employees to a great purpose or goal so that they are highly motivated to do this great work. Greatness for an institute comes from its people who having visualized that goal concentrate all their education – whether it is political or economic ideal, an ideal that has appealed to their heart; then a new enthusiasm comes to them, and when there is enthusiasm, sincerity and ardour a consistency of purpose automatically follow. When there is no enthusiasm or inspiration, consistency of purpose can never be.

When people are inspired by a great purpose, then something higher than themselves moves forward, they discover within themselves a new source of energy, and if this energy is not dissipated with past memories, or future anxieties or present excitement, if these three holes through which all the mental energy is leaking are blocked properly, the entire energy that they discover within themselves is available for focusing on the various activities that they are doing in the world. Their mind transcends limitations, the consciousness expands in every direction, and one finds oneself in a new great and wonderful world. Dormant forces, faculties, and talents become alive, and one discovers oneself to be a greater person by far than one ever dreamed to be (The Yoga Sutras of Patanjali). Then our decisions and actions are artistically done and as such they change our destiny.

Appendix: Failure Is Not An Option: Portfolio Management in UK Government

Shan Rajegopal and Tim Brett

> Pcubed's research indicates that a tremendous amount of effort and money is being invested in trying to achieve the benefits of portfolio management in the public sector. Yet success appears restricted to a small minority. Departments struggle with the practicalities of effective implementation and fail to realize the benefits of their project investments.

In association with Intellect, the trade body for the UK technology industry, Pcubed undertook a study across multiple central government departments in the United Kingdom to explore what the obstacles to success are and how they might be overcome. Based on the evidence, we've developed *ten keys to success as recommendations* – not only for public sector executives but anyone looking to implement portfolio management.

Based on a review of Pcubed's recommendations, MPA Executive Director David Pitchford noted: "These findings closely mirror MPA's experience of the application of portfolio management of public projects. We look forward to supporting important improvements in this area alongside the ICT supplier community and other stakeholders."

In conclusion, this report suggests how the UK government can benefit from portfolio management and recommends approaches that will give departments a strong chance of success.

The context for this study

When the Coalition government took over from the Labour government in May 2010, arguably its greatest challenge was to cut budgets in a sensible and defensible way such that the allocation of investments and program funds would continue to be spent in alignment with the government's vision. To support this strategy, the government announced that it was not cutting pensions, benefits, or frontline provision but would meet budget reductions through the vehicle of the "Operational Efficiency Programme", a national effort to seek ever greater efficiencies in operations. Through that work, the government would be seeking savings of £14.7 billion per year from changes to and reform of accountability, back office and IT, procurement, assets, property, local incentives, and empowerment.

This drove some unpredictable but understandable behaviors. Due to a sense of fear and uncertainty about the future, some senior executives tended to reinforce the perceived importance of their project portfolio, leading to a growth in some areas of the number of projects and programs. Many programs within the government had inadvertently evolved into "little enterprises", which posed real challenges for organizations needing to change. These programs would often sit outside existing hierarchies and accountabilities and develop their own "ways of working", which were opaque to the rest of the organization. Many such programs resided deep within silos. In addition, these organizations would habitually seek to implement many programs in parallel with significant dependencies or interdependencies. Severe weaknesses emerged in terms of:

- organizational capability to deliver many programs simultaneously;
- impact of change on front-line staff and their customers;
- time needed from senior management to fulfill their responsibilities.

As such there has been pressure for the government to deliver against its policy promises in a difficult environment and time. The government needs to understand and coordinate the impact of change initiatives and investment programs on staff and organizations and needs to consider its organizational ability to deliver. This requires methodical prioritization and selection of the right projects or initiatives to be implemented. It needs to have evidence that every penny is being spent wisely and will secure the expected benefits from change initiatives and investment programs.

Recent research shows that more and more organizations are implementing portfolio management as part of their long-term business capability. Pcubed sees four reasons for this uptake:

- Government sectors have raised the bar for financial accountability for programs and projects, and in some cases this accountability is mandated. This has given a new level of urgency for portfolio management within government agencies.
- Senior executives are now demanding greater visibility of and accountability for their portfolio of projects. That calls for the availability of reliable reports and metrics that can lay out what's happening right now

and what's coming next. As these managers move to other positions, they take their knowledge of the portfolio tools and techniques with them because they understand the impact on the organization. As a result, the expectation for portfolio management is going up.

- Now that portfolio management has been around for 10–12 years, a lot of research has gone on, best practices have surfaced, and implementations are becoming more mature and achievable.
- The technology offerings have matured and become adept at helping organizations to create the kind of visibility and accountability those executives want. Those systems have become a key driver in making portfolio management achievable.

Pcubed is asserting through this study that with such challenges, central government can tap into a proven method for ensuring investment is made in the right areas. That method is increasingly being recognized as project portfolio management (PPM).

How the study was conducted

Over the past year, Pcubed held a series of interviews with civil servants across several central government departments, including:

- Crown Prosecution Service
- National Audit Office
- Her Majesty's (HM) Revenue & Customs
- Department for Education
- Department for Work and Pensions
- Department for Business, Innovation and Skills
- UK Border Agency
- Ministry of Justice
- Cabinet Office.

The interviewees represented corporate project management offices (PMOs) or those responsible for the implementation of corporate portfolio management processes. Pcubed also met several senior executives who play a central role in the portfolio management of a typical large departmental or IT portfolio. This included business leads (chief executives and director generals), IT department heads (chief information officers), and the key suppliers of IT infrastructure.

It was our intention to establish these practitioners' success in laying the foundations of portfolio management in their respective departments and to examine how they had, if at all, built a disciplined portfolio management culture and structure.

The interviews were structured around standard questions and were undertaken by members of Pcubed's public sector team. Pcubed provided interviewees with the questions in advance and briefed each on the main themes and intentions for this report.

The questions covered five key themes:

- Organizational adoption
- Capability
- Perceived benefits
- Constraints
- Improvements.

Since public sector budgets have been cut over the last two years, the importance has increased for central government departments to adopt a disciplined approach to portfolio management. The expectations have remained the same for achieving the same project outcomes and business benefits, with the "mantra" being to deliver the same (or more!) for less.

What we have found through this study is that even an immature portfolio management environment can help a chief executive ensure that he or she isn't throwing good money after bad. Also, in terms of opportunity, the leaders of public sector agencies can seize this time to establish portfolio management discipline and feel more confident that they'll receive top–down endorsement for stopping poorly performing projects.

What is project portfolio management?

PPM is a disciplined approach to overseeing the collection of projects and programs in which an organization invests. These initiatives are intended to realize the organization's strategy in order to maximize business benefits, and each is undertaken with a certain level of risks and constraints. A PPM process and governance framework uses various techniques to provide tangible results for businesses, ensuring that project investments contribute directly to realizing corporate goals.

The ultimate outcome of portfolio management efforts depends on the type of organization. Experts who have studied the use of portfolio management within companies have identified several elements that influence the portfolio environment:

- *Cultural*, particularly with respect to the readiness of the organization to work in a more structured, disciplined, and transparent way.
- *Environmental,* including political, legal, and mandatory conditions.
- *Maturity level,* to manage expectations for outcomes and understand the appropriate place to begin in the portfolio management process.
- *Executive buy-in,* the collective will of the leadership to adopt a more systematic and accountable way for managing project selection.

Many organizations "flirt" with PPM. They try out formal numerical or measured assessments for project prioritization and selection and then quickly reject it as being inflexible, time-consuming, or providing faulty results. This outcome often comes out of a failed first attempt to develop and use a prioritization tool. While many of these first attempts do fail, and many of the instruments that are designed to support them produce incorrect and meaningless results, the approach itself shouldn't be rejected out of hand. The "Operational Efficiency Programme: final report (PDF)", issued by HM Treasury in 2009, recommends that public sector organizations "implement portfolio management processes to prioritise projects and resources and to reduce overlap and duplication in IT-enabled change projects".

For an organization to create a viable solution for effectively prioritizing and selecting projects, it must first define a framework within which it will operate. For many organizations, this framework is created within an umbrella concept of PPM – simply put, the concept of dealing with all of an organization's projects as a single portfolio. While the projects within the portfolio are still managed as individual initiatives, from a senior management perspective they are viewed in the aggregate as a collective means of establishing the organization's goals.

We encounter one of the biggest challenges of portfolio management right up front: Which projects should be included and which ones shouldn't? Given that a portfolio management approach should encompass all the initiatives an organization is undertaking, this really becomes the question: Which projects are we going to do and which ones should we reject? More than any other question about a portfolio of projects, this is the hardest to answer but also the most meaningful.

The act of prioritizing and selecting projects is hard, not necessarily because of the mechanics of the process, but because it demands that we make choices. For every project that we do take on, there may be five, ten, or a hundred that never see the light of day. We must make choices with imperfect information. We can never be quite sure whether the results of one project will better serve the organization than those of another or whether the estimates of cost and benefits provide a truly accurate picture of organizational return. Choosing the right project is what allows an organization to succeed and thrive. The wrong projects can take a successful, high-flying organization into a death spiral from which it may never recover.

It was with these challenges in mind that Pcubed, in association with Intellect, embarked on its research with representatives of central government departments.

Based on Pcubed's considerable experience of portfolio management in central government and on feedback from various government representatives, Pcubed believes that there's a set of common issues preventing the effective adoption of portfolio management within the public sector.

The practice of implementing portfolio management processes to ensure the project portfolio is strategically well balanced and provides "value for investment" is now well recognized and accepted. Pcubed conducted research to understand why – despite their best efforts – many central government departments and other organizations have failed to implement portfolio management effectively against a backdrop of increasingly frenetic and cost-constrained business change initiatives.

The research didn't seek to challenge the inherent value of applying portfolio management processes to organizations, but rather it sought to investigate why it was proving so difficult to implement and sustain. The study analyzed and highlighted key constraints and blockers to successful implementation. We also explored options to either remove constraints or tailor the generic portfolio management practices into something more fit for supporting a typical central government environment.

The ten inhibitors to portfolio success – and how to remove them

Today's central government leaders are facing emergencies. They need to react swiftly and with clear thinking to the dynamics of the situation. But what often happens, Pcubed has found, is that many managers take defensive actions that impede their ability to respond to a crisis. They often propose across-the-board spending cuts, coupled with a reduction in headcount. They take a position of aversion to risk and resistance to change. They lose focus, straying from the organization's mission and adopting a short-termist mentality. Given that the Coalition government's crisis is broadly couched in financial terms, this is understandable.

Change should never be new to managers, especially those managing portfolios. Change is part of the project environment, and successful businesses learn to deal with its presence. What is unique is both the speed and range of the dynamics, which elevate ordinary challenges to crisis level.

Pcubed's study reveals that there is a fundamental preparedness that is required by managers to deal with uncertainty and emergencies. The most insightful executives exploit these periods to find the new opportunities they present. However, the majority of executives in the public and private sector would benefit from PPM and the way that its data and methods can provide them with the wherewithal to deliver their portfolio of projects successfully in the current environment.

Our research showed ten key themes that Pcubed believes act as key inhibitors to successful portfolio management implementation:

- Marking your own homework: the lack of independent assurance
- Myopic delivery: over-emotional accountability
- Portfolio of key projects: the portfolio isn't holistic
- Absorb and adapt: the impact of ministerial imperatives
- Unwilling to fail: the unwillingness to work corporately
- Unclear benefits: the limited measurement of benefits
- Interdependency and risk stewardship: the unwillingness to manage interdependencies and risk corporately
- Horse-trading: the pervasive effects of emotional, unstructured, inconsistent decisions
- "Suppliers Can Do Anything" mentality: ignorance of suppliers' resource capacity
- Deliver more, for less: the impact of unpalatable challenges.

The sections below discuss each of these themes and the evidence collected by Pcubed that has warranted their inclusion.

Marking your own homework

One of the departments interviewed has established a clear gating process that captures early initiatives and subjects them to appraisal by a central assurance body that isn't answerable to the delivery organization or "senior responsible owners" (SROs). Consequently, because this assurance body openly publishes clear quality parameters by which a preliminary business case will be appraised, SROs can operate on a level playing field and be advised by this objective body as to the likelihood of their initiative moving forward into "portfolio optimization" territory.

This raises three key areas of guidance for public sector bodies. First, establish a portfolio office (or similar) that answers to the C-level individual who has overall accountability for the portfolio. Some readers will recognize this as a principle of management of portfolios (MoP). Second, establish firm guidelines and corporate behaviors to encourage a shared belief in what accountability means for SROs. Third, as much as possible remove the stigma that accompanies the stopping of failing projects or projects that are unlikely to achieve their purported benefits. Pcubed endorses the mantra: Kill early, kill often.

Myopic delivery

Interviewees cited examples of their organizations having a "silo" mentality – internal divisions keenly focused on the delivery of their own work and reluctant to enter into the corporate delivery mentality, which portfolio management requires. As with program management, portfolio management calls for interdependencies to be tightly managed and the competing demands of "business-as-usual" activities and project activities to be balanced. The silo mentality is closely allied to an over-enthusiasm for personal accountability – that is, "I must deliver my initiative at all costs", even at the expense of ignoring the project's place in the wider portfolio.

The silo mentality spills over into an assumption that there's a wide gap between work registered under business-as-usual and that which is delivered by project teams. Portfolio management helps to balance the commitment of resources to maintaining standard business operations while still supporting an organization's need to deliver change.

This does not mean, however, that investment decisions are made separately for the two types of work. This isn't done for two reasons. First, the people who deliver organizational change come from both project and non-project-focused parts of the organization. Second, there's usually a mixture of business-as-usual and project-type work in all parts of the organization.

Portfolio management discipline ought to be such that the delivery of true business-as-usual is resourced, wherever that work resides in the organization. This will establish what capacity remains in the overall workforce to support change. At this point, senior executives can prioritize all change initiatives based on standard prioritization methods.

Portfolio of key projects

This may sound benign but it isn't. Interviewees said that some change initiatives aren't considered as being part of the official change portfolio and the impact of business-as-usual is insufficiently integrated into the overall portfolio management approach. This is a complex problem.

According to some sources that Pcubed interviewed, for logical reasons the Cabinet Office's Efficiency and Reform Group has focused senior civil servants keenly on the delivery of major projects. In some organizations the formal portfolio only includes projects above a certain value while the business-as-usual processes deal with everything else.

Ironically, the cost of delivering these business-as-usual projects could be higher than the cost of delivering major projects. Yet that difference is invisible to management due to poor baseline tracking, minimal resource management, and a perception that delivery of change initiatives under business-as-usual is "free" because an organization's workforce is paid for by operational costs rather than project costs.

Pcubed firmly believes that all change initiatives ought to reside in the official portfolio and be subjected to standard project management and portfolio management discipline. A quick win to achieve this is to ensure that the definition of a change initiative and business-as-usual is widely communicated across the organization.

Absorb and adapt

Pcubed heard from most interviewees that "ministerial imperatives" were consistently a cause for portfolios to become imbalanced. They tended to promote the importance of initiatives that would not necessarily be more attractive or more achievable than other proposed initiatives. However, there is (understandably) a limited appetite for staff strongly to challenge initiatives to which senior government officials have committed.

Once a public sector organization such as a ministry has established itself as working under mature portfolio management lines, it gives the senior civil servants a strong grounding to challenge both running and new "ministerial imperatives" because their position and relative "strength" in a portfolio can clearly be articulated.

A mature portfolio management organization has weighted strategic drivers – endorsed up to ministerial level – that provide clear parameters for the attractiveness of individual initiatives. A senior civil servant in such circumstances can therefore provide evidence to a minister as to the anticipated benefits of other proposed initiatives that may be greater and even more effective in terms of agency reputation.

Unwilling to fail

The stigmatic "fear of failure" is a primary cause cited by Pcubed's interviewees for why projects that are overspending, overdue, and unlikely to deliver the expected benefits continue to be delivered. The interviewees said that public sector bodies need to embrace a "willingness to fail" culture and the ability to move onto the next project with project and program managers' performance being based on their actions and not necessarily just the outcome of their projects.

Pcubed has frequently been engaged by public sector bodies needing specialist support to deliver particularly complex projects, only to have them shut down within months because the benefits aren't going to be achieved. This displays a strong adherence to good practice and would be endorsed by Office of Government Commerce methodologies (OGC). (OGC is now part of the Efficiency and Reform Group.) A willingness-to-fail culture must be tied to the repeated review of business cases and project initiation documents to ensure a project will deliver the benefits identified at the start.

To help this, the Efficiency and Reform Group has made it clear that its review of major projects will continue. This in itself may help promote the change to a willingness-to-fail culture. Departments can mirror this by establishing their own assurance bodies to provide this service. To some extent it exists already through gateway reviews; but these are applied inconsistently across the public sector, and departments may struggle to apply the right level of rigor due to reduced staffing to perform the reviews.

Unclear benefits

Perhaps the most frequently repeated point made by interviewees was that benefits management wasn't implemented in their organizations. A portfolio can't be optimized unless the performance of current projects is understood (is the project on schedule? is it on budget?) and the anticipated benefits analysis is current and robust.

At the basic level, a portfolio can be optimized purely on the strength of business cases presented during the early project stages. As we mentioned earlier, these business cases can be appraised by an independent in-house body and can be scored against an organization's strategic drivers. Central government bodies generally follow HM Treasury rules for the production of business cases for medium to large projects, and this is a strong start. The target should be an expectation for basic business cases to be produced for all change initiatives defined as projects.

The maintenance of benefits management data is the next step of maturity toward improved portfolio management in central government departments – and this step seems some way off. Assuming that business cases are now being produced for all change initiatives, a move in the right direction could be enforcement of basic PRINCE2 expectations that business cases are reviewed at each stage gate, thereby also triggering a review against the portfolio. MoP proposes that staged release of funding is an effective mechanism to bring improved control and meaning to these gates.

Evidence from the interviews points to a simple tenet: Portfolio management can only thrive in an environment where the project management "basics" are followed and where meaningful, unambiguous management information can flow between project and portfolio teams. These include the need for:

- regular schedule updates against a stable baseline
- managing resource estimates and measuring forecasting capacity
- cost to be controlled
- reporting to be frequent, analytical, and insightful
- risk management to be applied consistently
- meaningful reviews to be performed at each stage gate.

The absence of any one of these processes may mean that significant decisions are made at a portfolio level without the confidence that the data is current and holistic.

Interdependency and risk stewardship

The interviews delivered a clear message: Interdependency and risk management need to be taken more seriously at an enterprise or corporate level and driven as an effective process down through the organization. A basic requirement for effective portfolio management is the ability to balance risk at a corporate level and to prioritize initiatives based on their achievability, while also considering other non-project specific enterprise risks that can affect project outcomes. For example, the announcement by a minister of a likely future policy change could be a driver for the delay to initiating any new projects or programs aligned to the current policy.

The Efficiency and Reform Group has indicated that it will need to address some inconsistencies between management of risk and its key project management methods, particularly the recently published "MoP" guidance. The escalation of the right risks to the right level of the organization's governance is a tough structure to establish, and in Pcubed's experience this can best be managed by a disciplined portfolio office. In particular, that office can drive consistency and discipline around *what can be* escalated to the appropriate level and likewise have the authority to push less important risks back down to the projects and programs for resolution. A central portfolio office would also manage the portfolio interdependencies.

Horse-trading

It's vital to remove the emotion from the appraisal of initiatives that are being proposed for entry into the portfolio. Pcubed was given examples of SROs taking strong accountability for the success of initiatives, a practice that the public sector has been at pains to make a success. However that accountability has led to a behavior pattern whereby SROs perceive that they have failed if their initiative is excluded from the portfolio or is stopped in favor of another. While objectively the decision may be right, organizations have tended to find that strength of personality can push unsuitable initiatives into the portfolio, with examples offered of "horse-trading" taking place to arrive at a mutually satisfactory answer. Portfolio management, with its fact-driven composition, is a reliable antidote to this when allied with strong leadership.

"Suppliers can do anything" mentality

Alongside a controlled and disciplined approach to risk, resource capacity data is vital for supporting portfolio optimization. In Pcubed's experience, the majority of large public and private sector organizations are some distance from the resource management maturity required to make high-quality portfolio optimization decisions. This is in part – but not entirely – due to the size of the organizations. It's also due to the fact that the people and work effort required to deliver an IT project aren't visible to those making portfolio optimization decisions. For these large organizations, the last 20 years have seen IT services shifted out to specialist suppliers, with in-house project teams being only a small part of the cost and work effort needed to deliver IT projects. Hence, a target portfolio management model for these organizations should see suppliers playing a major role in the provision of information relating to resource capacity and project performance.

Deliver more, for less

A senior executive from the Cabinet Office has challenged the view that ministerial imperatives are justifiable reasons to blow the budget or fail to deliver elsewhere. In this executive's view, a ministerial prerogative shouldn't be a great barrier. While the proposed projects will be aligned to generally legitimate priorities, they need to be exposed if they're not in line with investment criteria already agreed at a departmental level and responsibility clearly allocated for any decision to proceed.

Maturity shifting

The underlying obstacles to implementing a successful and objective approach to portfolio management are organizational in nature. For many agencies the art of "getting things done" means political influence and lobbying. In this environment, project prioritization falls into the realm of backroom dealing and horse-trading. The projects that are initiated are those that receive the greatest political favor, not necessarily the ones that have the greatest organizational impact.

In organizations that are overly driven by politics, the concept of a formalized project initiation process is viewed as a threat to the political status quo, not as a useful enabler to manage strategic priorities. Any effort to formalize the definition, prioritization, and initiation of projects is perceived as an effort to undermine existing power bases in the organization. Succeeding with portfolio management in these environments is not simply a matter of effectively implementing a prioritization framework; it requires wholesale cultural change in how the organization initiates and manages its projects. It also poses a leadership challenge for the C-level executives who need to take their management teams on this journey.

The figure below shows the spectrum of cultural change required through behavioral reform. It represents Pcubed's estimate of the general maturity of the organizations interviewed in moving from bad to good portfolio management behaviors. Pcubed recommends that executives evaluate where they are and change their approach to a more positive way of working to implement portfolio management practices.

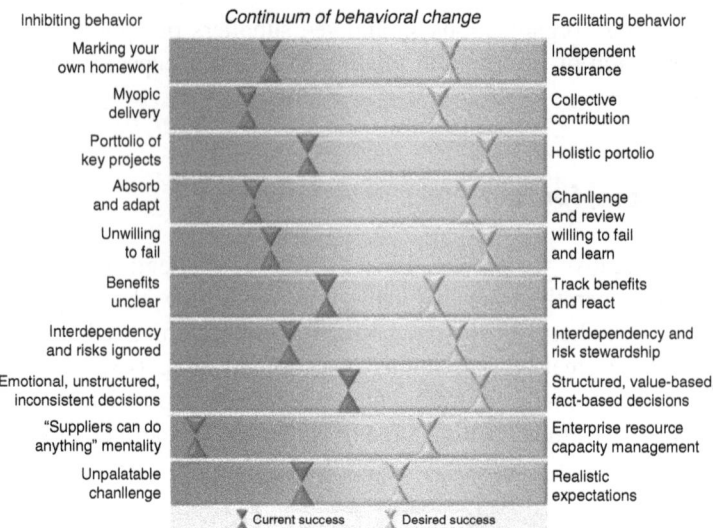

Inhibiting behavior	Continuum of behavioral change	Facilitating behavior
Marking your own homework		Independent assurance
Myopic delivery		Collective contribution
Portfolio of key projects		Holistic portolio
Absorb and adapt		Chanllenge and review
Unwilling to fail		willing to fail and learn
Benefits unclear		Track benefits and react
Interdependency and risks ignored		Interdependency and risk stewardship
Emotional, unstructured, inconsistent decisions		Structured, value-based, fact-based decisions
"Suppliers can do anything" mentality		Enterprise resource capacity management
Unpalatable chanllenge		Realistic expectations

Current success   Desired success

Adopting and implementing good portfolio management practice is challenging. The portfolio management practice can easily be susceptible to vulnerabilities. However, Pcubed recommends a few guidelines for increasing the chance for portfolio management success in a politically sensitive environment. We haven't listed these in any particular order; the sooner each is taken, the better the potential for success.

The keys to portfolio management success

Key inhibitors	Key to success
Marking your own homework	• Establish portfolio office (or similar) that has overall responsibility for assurance of the portfolio • Establish firm guidelines and corporate behaviors to encourage a shared belief in what accountability means • Remove the stigma that accompanies the stopping of failing projects or projects that are unlikely to achieve their purported benefits
Myopic delivery	• Tightly manage portfolio interdependencies • Prioritize all change initiatives based on standard optimization methods • Balance business-as-usual and project activities • Balance commitment of resources to maintaining standard business operations while supporting organizational need to deliver change
Portfolio of key projects	• Ensure that all change initiatives reside in the official portfolio and be subjected to standard project management and portfolio management discipline

	• Ensure that the definition of a change project and business-as-usual is widely communicated across the organization
Absorb and adapt	• Challenge ministers and provide evidence as to the anticipated benefits of other proposed initiatives that may be greater and even more effective in terms of agency reputation
Unwilling to fail	• Inculcate a "willingness-to-fail" culture that is tied to the repeated review of business cases and project initiation documents to ensure that a project will deliver the benefits identified at the start
Benefits unclear	• Maintain benefits management data • Enforce basic project management expectations that business cases are reviewed at each stage gate, thereby also triggering a review against the portfolio • Perform rigorous project management tracking
Interdependency and risk stewardship	• Portfolio management office to drive consistency and discipline around what can be escalated to the appropriate level and likewise have the authority to push less important risks back down to the projects and programs for resolution
Horse-trading	• Use fact-driven decisions versus emotional judgment for project selection
"Suppliers can do anything" mentality	• Visibility of resource capacity data is vital for supporting portfolio optimization
Deliver more for less	• Expose projects that are not in line with investment criteria already agreed at a departmental level and responsibility clearly allocated for any decision to proceed • Require cultural change in how the organization thinks about and manages its projects

Establishing a culture of portfolio prioritization

Overcoming the key inhibitors we list above requires an organization to establish a culture that can allow meaningful portfolio prioritization to occur. The critical success factor isn't defining the mechanism by which prioritization can be achieved, but by gaining agreement that real and objective prioritization is essential. This is the point at which many implementations of PPM fail. While lip service is paid to the concept of prioritization, this is often tempered with a belief that political influence and organizational stature serve as proxies for real prioritization.

While any mechanism can support the culture of portfolio prioritization, in order to be effective, that mechanism must be objective, consistently applied, and aligned with the strategies of the organization and business units that it supports. While a framework that depends upon consensus agreement among senior managers can be perfectly effective – and has worked successfully – the focus must be on the strategic value of individual projects, not on organizational politics or individual agendas.

The change to a culture of portfolio prioritization must be led by the most senior executive in the department and based upon a commitment to manage for the success of the organization as a whole. To be maintained, it must be based upon concrete and tangible measures of accountability and portfolio outcomes.

The organization needs to select a portfolio of initiatives that will have the greatest impact in achieving the organization's goals and needs to define the portfolio based upon its ability to deliver those goals. To date, this isn't commonly achieved in central government. Based upon this research and Pcubed's collective experience with organizational project management practices, we can assert that only a minority of organizations today have a formal method of project portfolio prioritization that is part of its operational DNA.

How to respond to organizational size and complexity

Even in the most sizable and complex of departments focusing on a few crucial practices can make the difference between success and failure of a portfolio management initiative:

- Only review and prioritize when it's necessary
- Avoid detailed resource management
- Use your hierarchies effectively
- Get the basics right.

Let's examine each.

Only review and prioritize when it's necessary

Does a portfolio management process need to be rigid? Does every project need to be reviewed by the senior management team? A common early mistake is to mandate that all projects throughout the organization be reviewed and prioritized together as a single ordered list. This quickly becomes overwhelming when the five to ten projects that senior managers thought they had turn into 500 or more projects.

Can we adapt or tailor the process to the environment in which we are operating? Definitely, yes. PPM practices, at their core, focus on strategic fit, return, and risk across the portfolio. Resources are a factor in the analysis, but good portfolio analysis doesn't really concern itself with details such as "named resources". At the highest level the goal is to look at what projects should be undertaken and why. If a project list that achieves all the company's goals can't be accomplished because of lack of resources, then and only then should the company decide whether to add more resources or scale back the list of approved projects.

Avoid detailed resource management

While resource capacity information is crucial to effective prioritization, some software vendors Pcubed has worked with claim that PPM can be more efficiently undertaken if highly detailed resource information is available to executive decision makers; from Pcubed's perspective that simply wastes time asking executives to make decisions that are better made at lower levels. It's for this reason that Pcubed advocates a concept of the "scalable project portfolio management framework". There are different things that need to be done at each level. The correct view of PPM is that it works best when the focus is simultaneously on both the top–down process and the bottom–up process.

Use your hierarchies effectively

The reason we have organizational hierarchies is to ensure that decision making happens at the appropriate level. So, too, should it be for portfolio prioritization. For most organizations, project portfolio prioritization should be defined and managed at three key levels: strategic, business units/tactical, and department/functional. Beginning with the top–down process, executive management needs to take responsibility for the following activities:

- evaluating the list of projects
- grouping projects by line of business, product or function
- confirming alignment
- prioritizing projects
- determining level of acceptable risk
- defining value threshold
- confirming high-level resource capacity
- confirming timing
- eliminating the bottom tier (cutting, killing, and cancelling projects).

Once a review has been completed, the prioritized lists, segmented by line of business, product, or function, can be given to the next level of management for its review.

Segmenting the portfolio by function or line-of-business has a number of advantages. Most companies segment their IT resources by one of these categories, so that even if resources appeared to be available at a high level, they might not at the detailed level. It also ensures that the responsibility for successful implementation rests with the people who are on the front line.

Get the basics right

Finally, a good PPM process does require a structure; but from Pcubed's perspective that structure isn't generally dependent on software tools or fully deployed project management processes. By taking a scalable approach to PPM, each level of the organization can concentrate on making decisions and setting up the management structures that will encourage the visibility and flexibility an organization needs in order to obtain results.

After all, the most expensive PPM software in the world coupled with the best project management processes still won't help if the organization continues to approve too many new projects and fails to focus on those already underway.

By adopting an effective PPM process that empowers people to solve the problems in front of them, the right PPM information can be provided to the right parts of the organization at the right time. And in so doing, Pcubed believes many of the portfolio prioritization and optimization problems that organizations are currently experiencing can be solved.

Greater opportunities to exploit PPM

As the uptake in PPM increases, the appropriate central government bodies can benefit from embracing aspects of PPM on behalf of the Coalition government. Is it so crazy to suggest that a central portfolio office could focus on delivering the initiatives needed to turn the economy around and meet other specific government targets? A chief portfolio officer could be charged with finding ways to expedite delivery and improve the effectiveness of critical indicators of success for all major programs.

"Previously Government projects have had a poor delivery record", said Francis Maude, Minister for the Cabinet Office and Paymaster General, in announcing tough controls for major government projects, specifically to improve performance in delivering on time and in budget. "There was no cross-governmental understanding of the size and cost of the Government's Major Project portfolio, and projects often began with no agreed budget, no business case and unrealistic delivery timetables. This Government will not allow that costly failure to continue ... "

Chief Secretary to the Treasury Danny Alexander added: "It is essential that we bring the public finances back under control. Unless the deficit is tackled, there won't be the economic confidence to support jobs, investment or growth. To do this we need to improve the way the Treasury controls public spending. Government's largest projects must receive maximum scrutiny, so that we can avoid the huge cost overruns seen in the past."

In 2011 the Prime Minister confirmed the mandate for the Major Projects Authority (MPA) within the Efficiency and Reform Group in the Cabinet Office. The MPA has oversight of central government's major projects at both an individual and a portfolio level. It aims to address the findings from the National Audit Office report, "Assurance for High Risk Projects", published in June 2010, and from the "Major Project approval and assurance guideline (PDF)" undertaken as a new partnership between the Cabinet Office and HM Treasury with the fundamental aim of significantly improving the delivery success rate of major projects across central government.

For the MPA to be successful, the behavior of portfolio owners needs to change from lack of accountability to delivering the promised value. In life, promises are expected to be kept, yet we may forget to check to see whether the promise was delivered. In the case of portfolio management that promise is manifested in a clear, visible benefits case that is reviewed constantly.

PPM as a life saver

The current economic and political crisis is putting stress on well-planned portfolios. Even in the best of times, we can benefit greatly from a well-defined and scalable PPM process and a robust PPM support system.

In these times, PPM can be life-saving for an organization. It can help to reduce the damage from the current economic upheaval. And it can help to plot a course for recovery and to use the various stimulus programs to full advantage.

CASE STUDIES

Case Study 1: Petroleum products company, capital expenditure portfolio optimization, global refining

The challenge

The optimal allocation of capital to proposed projects in a multi-billion dollar capital expenditure portfolio is key to the long-term health of the refining business and to achieving an acceptable return on capital employed for the enterprise. Projects were previously assessed primarily on the basis of financial measures, with decisions regarding other selection criteria made in a disjointed and unstructured fashion. Senior management could not assess the strategic value of a particular mix of projects or come to terms with the fact that strategic value was even considered in selecting the projects in which to invest.

Our solution

The Global Refining management team engaged Pcubed to define a methodology for assessing the strategic value of proposed capital projects and optimize the three-year capital project portfolio for Global Refining. In addition, senior management was provided with enhanced information regarding the business case and benefits for all proposed capital projects.

The value and business benefits delivered

The optimization methodology allowed the company to subsequently reduce annual capital spending by "$400MM" while still preserving the most critical and strategic projects. At the same time, the approach allowed the company to redirect "$200MM" of capital expenditure towards growth and improvement projects to generate long-term competitive advantage.

Senior management received enhanced information on the business case and benefits of all capital projects and of the overall portfolio. Strategic business drivers and appropriate metrics were defined to assess the strategic alignment of capital projects. Rich decision support information was provided on the selected capital portfolio. A view of the strategic health of the capital project pipeline was generated and a structured approach was established for using capital planning to implement the strategy. Transparency of decision making regarding capital projects was greatly enhanced.

Case Study 2: Petroleum products company, project management, oilfield management

The challenge

The Facilities Technical team on the oil field was responsible for the project management of all technical projects and for the coordination of all asset development projects. Multiple partner companies provided resources for the projects, with resource pools being used across all projects. Projects were consistently running late, resources were under-utilized, facility engineers were unable to accurately forecast time and schedule, and project prioritization was haphazard. Faced with these challenges, management explored options for consolidation of their schedule and resource management processes.

Our solution

The company engaged Pcubed to develop project management processes in order to better manage all resources and projects. Pcubed consolidated all business partners' schedules and resource management, using Microsoft Office Project Server, to provide all parties with single-sourced information. All processes were validated for the ability to provide the data needed to support timely resource and project decision making, after which the solution was prepared for a roll-out across the rest of the organization.

The value and business benefits delivered

Based on similar engagements within the same organization an estimated improvement of 20 per cent in wrench time (resource utilization) was realized with annual cost savings/avoidance in the 3–5 million dollar range. The improved visibility into technical project schedules and timelines resulted in a reduction in cycle time, mitigating the need to add to contractor head count to maintain an acceptable level of service on technical projects, further enhancing the value generated from the improvements.

Amongst a wider array of benefits the client achieved from the implementation, the primary results were consolidated visibility of technical project schedules, accurate forecasting of project timelines, and the optimization of resource availability. Both operator and business partners were included to provide a complete resource management picture. As a result, the team was in the position to proactively manage all resource assignments to ensure highest utilization.

Case Study 3: Leading global bank

The client

The client is a leading global bank with a strong presence in both traditional retail banking and investment banking. The company employs over 80,000 people in 75 countries and generated over US $130B revenue in 2007.

The challenge

The investment banking division identified the need for a solution to better manage discretionary spend in projects and programs. The solution needed to increase visibility, control, and insight in the planning and delivery of key business initiatives. After researching several business options, Project Portfolio Management (PPM) was identified as the discipline to support the effort. Pcubed created a roadmap to pragmatically implement a PPM solution.

Our solution

Pcubed proposed a three-phased roadmap for implementing the PPM solution across the entire operations group within the investment banking division. The first phase focused on improving the annual planning process, moving away from subjective decision making employed in the past towards a metric-driven, strategic, and financial valuation framework. The second phase focused on status-reporting processes during project and program execution. Once the new portfolio management processes are fully established, the third phase will focus on improving project management and benefits management, where realized benefits will be compared with the estimated figures. In summary, the solution provided the following:

- Increased transparency during annual planning
- Decision-making support to selecting the optimal "book of work" for implementation
- Reduced effort spent on status reporting by redesigning and automating the reporting process
- Reduced financial reporting risks by using an online, single-source integrated platform
- Improved overall delivery of initiatives by using standard metrics to track performance.

The results

With a pragmatic and results-oriented approach, Pcubed designed and deployed the PPM solution within the investment banking division, meeting tight timelines imposed by the fast-paced financial services world. The success of the deployment within the division has attracted the attention of other groups within the bank, potentially leading to a roll-out of similar capabilities.

Case Study 4: Car manufacturer

The client

The client is one of the most successful and globally known premium manufacturers of sports cars remaining in the United Kingdom. In recent years much of the business has enjoyed significant investment, resulting in them becoming an industry leader in many areas, including manufacturing facilities and dealer networks.

The challenge

The business came under new ownership in 2007, giving it significant flexibility, particularly in relation to its IT systems and processes which had previously been mandated by its parent company. Due to the aggressive time constraints that were agreed for the separation, many of the fixes that were implemented to maintain business continuity were not opti-mized. Coupled with a historical lack of investment within IT many issues were beginning to surface, exposing the business to risk.

Under the new internal management a complete review of the depart-ment's strategic direction, spending plans, internal capability, and its ability to support the business was required.

Our solution

Pcubed was engaged to baseline the current situation within the IT depart-ment and support the development of a strategy and vision for IT based around Pcubed industry's best practice and internal customer feedback. Based upon this strategy it was asked to review all currently proposed work and provide a recommendation for how best to deliver it.

The deliverables for the engagement comprised four key elements:

- Baseline current department constraints by conducting a full budget and resource review
- Support the development of a departmental strategic vision and busi-ness drivers aligned with the enterprise vision, industry best practice and customer survey
- Understand delivery requirements and provide a project prioritization method using Portfolio Management lite (PfM lite) toolset
- Develop a proposal for restructuring the department based on a clear understanding of the delivery and support requirements

The benefits

By baselining the departmental constraints, any further decisions around restructuring and delivery could be accurately assessed for achievability.

By conducting a company-wide survey to obtain the current percep-tion of the IT delivery capability a baseline for measuring improvement was created, and it also provided a corporate-wide understanding of what IT needed to achieve.

An IT strategic vision and supporting business drivers were developed in conjunction with the senior management team to provide a high level of direction for all future decision making.

By conducting a full portfolio analysis of the existing business require-ments Pcubed provided a consistent mechanism for prioritizing project requests and an ability to demonstrate where projects were misaligned with the strategic drivers. This gave a recommendation on which of the projects should be stopped and also showed where nearly £1million of proposed investment could potentially be saved.

By providing an understanding of the complete portfolio, the resource requirements could be tailored to suit delivery and ongoing service requirements. This also showed clearly where specific resources were lacking or retraining was required.

Results

- A jointly developed IT vision and strategy against which all future decisions could be based
- A full Portfolio analysis based around the above strategic drivers using PfM lite toolset
- A full understanding of budget constraints and resource availability to deliver the portfolio
- A proposed organizational structure to deliver as much of the Portfolio as possible while supporting the other delivery requirements of the department based on industry best practice.

Case Study 5: Large oil and gas company

The client

The Oil and Gas company is the downstream business that employs 51,000 people in over 80 countries and focuses on supply and trading, refining, marketing, and transportation of oil and petroleum products. Information Technology & Systems (IT&S) support the Downstream's complex and changing landscape and calls for a five-year investment of $350–$400 million per annum to transform the transactional systems, deliver a simplified landscape, and recover the IT estate for improved operational integrity and to lower support costs. IT&S believes this strategy will align its project portfolio to business imperatives and Governance Board priorities and help the company achieve its strategic objectives.

The challenge

In 2011, the company's IT&S considered that their projects and programmes had a good, but not complete, coverage of the areas for strategic performance, opportunity, and benefits delivery. They had suffered in the past with an inability to articulate how well each project is aligned with the overall strategy, and how each project ranked when budget-cut decisions were being made. The requirements for the engagement were as follows:

- Realize strategy – to align the Downstream business strategy and themes to IT&S and Strategic Performance Unit's (SPU) strategies through agreed prioritized business drivers.
- Select right projects – to develop a Strategy & Portfolio Management Framework to help prioritize and optimize the Downstream investments by strategic value and refine the selection based on budgetary constraints.
- Improve processes – to link our client's Benefit Management Framework with Business Drivers through process performance indicator and financial performance indicator.
- Gain visibility – to provide a platform of multiple views on Portfolio optimization to manage effective decisions in a non-confrontational and a fact-based environment.

Our solution

Pcubed was engaged to provide an overview of the steps and efforts involved in analysing and deploying a fit for purpose Strategy & Portfolio Management Framework within Downstream IT&S, taking a pragmatic approach by leveraging Pcubed's intellectual property and best practices. The deliverables for the engagement comprised of the following key elements:

1. **Portfolio Management Process** – develop a portfolio management process that aligns and translates strategies into actionable projects through agreed business drivers
2. **Business Drivers Definition** – support the development and the ranking of business drivers to enable IT&S to prioritize objectives and align investments on key business drivers using the pairwise comparisons methodology, designed to make complex decisions easier to address when achieving consensus.
3. **Portfolio Selection Approach Adoption** – assess the attractiveness of projects and programmes by measuring their relative business value based on alignment with the business drivers, create a portfolio inventory list in the Portfolio Accelerator Tool, and identify interdependencies.

4. **Portfolio Optimization** – apply corporate constraints and capacity, based on different scenarios, against the overall portfolio performance and build prioritization views depicting the right mix of projects with reporting data for each scenario.

The benefits

Before Pcubed's involvement, the Downstream IT&S had an initial approach to portfolio optimization with no clear methodology. The main benefits of Pcubed's involvement were as follows:

- Robust Strategy & Portfolio Management Framework – influences the ability to align investments with the business strategy.
- Better visibility and understanding from the business partners on the value of their Portfolios.
- Potential savings of $60m to $80m of proposed investments.
- Jointly developed prioritized business drivers aligned with the Downstream strategy to provide a baseline for future decision making.
- Ability to assess and prioritise projects in an objective way through a consistent and transparent mechanism.
- Filtering demand that is unnecessary and non-aligned to drivers through an agreed Strategy & Portfolio Management Framework.
- Tailored Portfolio Optimization Tool paired with report data and insights – which will assist the organization in optimizing its portfolio in the future.

BIBLIOGRAPHY

Part I

Global Innovation 1000 by Barry Jaruzelski, Kevin Dehoff, and Rakesh Bordia, Booz Allen, 2006.

"Innovation 2010: Return to Prominence and the Emergence of New World Order", BCG Report, 2010.

"How the Top Innovators Keep Winning" by Barry Jaruzelski and Kevin Dehoff, Booz & Co, *Strategy + Business*, Issue 61, Winter 2010.

"Expanding the Innovation Horizon" Global CEO Study, IBM Global Business Services, 2006.

"Gartner 2010 CIO Survey: A Time of Great IT Transition" Annual Gartner Survey of CIOs, 2010.

Innovation and Entrepreneurship by Peter F. Drucker, Butterworth, and Heinemann, 1985.

The Myths of Innovation by Scott Berkun, O'Reilly, 2007.

Think and Grow Rich by Napoleon Hill, The Original Classic, Forgotten Books, 2004.

Creating Strategic Leverage: Matching Company Strengths with Market Opportunities by Milind Lele, Wiley, 1992.

Creativity Is Not Enough by Theodore Levitt, Harvard Business Review, August 2002.

Clock Speed: Winning Industry Control in the Age of Temporary Advantage by Charles Fine, Perseus Books Group, Sloan School of Management, MIT, 1998.

Where Does Innovation Come From by Steve Tobak, CBS News, 29 August 2011.

The 7 Habits of Highly Innovative People by Steve Tobak, CBS News, 27 August 2010.

Managing for Creativity by Richard Florida and Jim Goodnight, Harvard Business Review, July 2005.

Managing Corporate Culture by Stan Davis, HarperCollins Distribution Services, 1984.

Organizational Culture and Leadership by Edgar H. Schein, Wiley, 1992.

How to Build a Culture of Innovation by Jessie Scanlon, Bloomberg Business Week, 19 August 2009.

Corporate Culture and Performance by John P. Kotter and James L. Heskett, The Free Press, 1992.

7 Steps to a Culture of Innovation by Josh Linkner, Innovation Generation, August 2011.

Discipline Dreaming: A Proven System to Drive Breakthrough Creativity by Josh Linkner, Jossey-Bass, 2011.

Management Challenges for the 21st Century by Peter Drucker, Harper Collins, 1999.

Leading the Revolution: How to Thrive in Turbulent Time by Making Innovation a Way of Life by Gary Hamel, HB Press, 2000.

The Innovator's DNA: Mastering the Five Skills of Disruptive Innovators by Jeff Dyer, Hal Gregersen, and Clayton M. Christensen, Harvard Business Review Press, 2011.

Innovators Dilemma: The Revolutionary Book that Will Change the Way You Do Business by Clayton M. Christensen, HarperCollins, 1997.

Complete Works of Swami Vivekananda by Swami Vivekananda, 12 January 1863–4 July 1902, Vol. 1–9, Sri Ramakrishnan Mission.

Dare to Fail by Billi Lim, Hardknocks Factory, 1996.

9 Ways of Cultivating Creativity by Tina Su, Think Simple Now, 2007.

Part II

Project Portfolio Management: Leading the Corporate Vision by Shan Rajegopal, Philip McGuin, and James Waller, Palgrave Macmillan, 2007.

"Western European Organizations Prepare Tougher IT Budgets for 2012", According to International Data Corporation (IDC) Survey, 2011.

"Operational Efficiency Programme: Final Report" by H. M. Treasury, April 2009.

IT Portfolio Management: Unlocking the Business Value of Technology by Bryan Maizlish and Robert Handler, Wiley, 2005.

IT Investment Management: Portfolio Management Lessons Learned by META Group, White Paper, 2002.

Optimizing the IT Portfolio for Maximum Business Value by Forrester, September 2007.

"Portfolio Selection" by Harry M. Markowitz, Vol. 7, Issue 1, *Journal of Finance*, 1952.

Portfolio Selection: Efficient Diversification of Investments by H. M. Markowitz, New York: Wiley, 1959 (reprinted by Yale University Press, 1970, 2nd edition, Basil Blackwell, 1991).

"Benefits Management Definition", Office of Government Commerce (OGC), Glossary of Terms and Definitions, 2008.

The Knowing-Doing Gap by Jeffrey Pfeffer and Robert I. Sutton, Harvard Business School Press, 2000.

Portfolio Management for New Products by Robert G. Cooper, Scott J. Edgett, and Elko J. Kleinschmidt, Perseus Books, © 1998.

Project Portfolio Management – Selecting and Prioritizing Projects for Competitive Advantage by Lowell D. Dye and James S. Pennypacker (eds) Center for Business Practices – PM Solutions, © 1999.

The Balanced Scorecard – Translating Strategy into Action by Robert S. Kaplan and David P. Norton, HBS Press, © 1996.

Leading Product Development: The Senior Manager's Guide to Creating and Shaping the Enterprise by Steven C. Wheelright and Kim Clark, Free Press, © 1995.

"Best Practices for Managing R&D Portfolios" by R. G. Cooper, S. J. Edgett, and E. J. Kleinschmidt, Vol. 41, No. 4, *Journal of Industrial Research Institute*, July–August 1998, p. 20.

Do the Math by Scott Berinato, CIO Magazine, 1 October 2001.

"The 21st Century Corporation," Business Week, 28 August 2000, pp. 76–214.

Designing Organizations by Jay Galbraith, Jossey-Bass, 1995.

Strategic Organizational Diagnosis and Design – Developing Theory for Application 2nd edition by Richard M. Burton and Borge Obel, Kluwer Academic Publication, 1998.

The Rework Cycle: Why Projects Are Mismanaged by Kenneth Cooper. PMI's PMNET Work Magazine, February 1993.

The Art of Innovation: Lessons in Creativity from Ideo America's Leading Design Firm, Tom Kelley, 2001.

"The Monk and the Riddle: The Art of Creating a Life While Making a Life: The Art of Creating a Life While Making a Living", 2000.

Part III

Execution: The Discipline of Getting Things Done by Larry Bossidy and Ram Charan with Charles Burck, Random House Business Book, 2002.

Sun Tzu and the Project Battleground: Creating Project Strategy from "The Art of War" by David Hawkins and Shan Rajegopal, Palgrave Macmillan, 2005.

The Secrets to Successful Strategy Execution by Gary Neilson, Karla Martin, and Elizabeth Powers, Harvard Business Review, June 2008.

The Knowing-Doing Gap: How Smart Companies Turn Knowledge into Action by Jeffrey Pfeffer and Robert Sutton, Harvard Business School Press, 2000.

"Linking Execution with Strategy in Support Functions" by Robert Angel, *Ivey Business Journal*, March/April 2008.

Bosses Caught in the Middle by Jane Simms in the May 2010 issue of Director Magazine.

The Execution Premium: Linking Strategy to Operations for Competitive Advantage by Robert Kaplan and David Norton, Harvard Business School Press, 2008.

The Intangible Economy: Impact and Policy Issues by Clark Eustace, for the European Commission, 2000.

EVA: The Real Key to Creating Wealth by Al Ehrbar and Stern Steward, Wiley, 1998.

Advanced Project Portfolio Management and the PMO: Multiplying ROI at Warp Speed by Gerald Kendall and Steven Rollins, J. Ross Publishing, 2003.

Liberation Management: Necessary Disorganization for the Nanosecond Nineties by Tom Peters, Random Housing Publishing Group, 1994.

If Not Now, When?: Duty and Sacrifice in America's Time of Need by Col. Jake Jacobs (retired) and Douglas Century, Berkeley Publishing Group, 2008.

Iacocca – An Autobiography by Lee Iacocca with William Novak, Bantam Books, 1984.

The Lust for Leadership by Simon Caulkin, Management Today, November 1993.

The Age of Paradox by Charles Handy, Harvard Business School Press, 1994.

The Age of Unreason by Charles Handy, Arrow Books, 2002.

Kaizen Strategies for Successful Leadership by Tony Barnes, Pearson Education Ltd., 1996.

A Better India: A Better World by N. R. Narayana Murthy and Allen Lane, Penguin Books, 2009.

Judgment Under Stress by Kenneth R. Hammond, Oxford University Press, 2000.

Theory of Games and Economics Behavior by John Von Neumann and Oskar Morgenstern, Princeton University Press, 1947.

Rational Choice in an Uncertain World: The Psychology of Judgment and Decision Making by Reid Hastie and Robyn Dawes, Sage, 2001.

Facilitator's Guide to Participatory Decision-Making by Sam Kaner, Lenny Lind, Daune Berger, Catherine Toldi, and Sarah Fisk, Jossey-Bass, 2007.

Judgement and Choice: The Psychology of Decision by Robin M. Hogarth, Wiley, 1987.

The 8th Habit: From Effectiveness to Greatness by Stephen Covey, Free Press 2005.

Index

Note: Locators followed by 'f' and 't' refers to figures and tables respectively.